IN THE ROUGH
The Business Game of Golf

DAVID HUEBER

TCU Press
Fort Worth, Texas

Library of Congress Cataloging-in-Publication Data

Names: Hueber, David, author.
Title: In the rough : the business game of golf / David Hueber.
Description: Fort Worth, Texas : TCU Press, [2016] | ©2016
Identifiers: LCCN 2016001669 (print) | LCCN 2016004077 (ebook) |
ISBN
    9780875656533 (alk. paper) | ISBN 9780875654447 ()
Subjects: LCSH: Golf--Economic aspects--United States. | Golf--Environ-
mental
    aspects--United States. | Golf--History--20th century. |
    Golf--History--21st century. | Golf courses--United States. | Hueber,
    David. | Hogan, Ben, 1912-1997.
Classification: LCC GV981 .H84 2016 (print) | LCC GV981 (ebook) |
DDC
    796.3520973--dc23
LC record available at http://lccn.loc.gov/2016001669

TCU Press
TCU Box 298300
Fort Worth, Texas 76129
817.257.7822
www.prs.tcu.edu

To order books: 1.800.826.8911

Designed by Bill Brammer
www.fusion29.com

I owe a special thanks to my wife, Cindy, who has been the most important person in my life for some thirty-five-plus years.

Thanks to my parents, Opal and Bud Hueber, who convinced their seven children there wasn't anything we could not do if we set our minds to it. My mother, especially, supported us in whatever we decided to do, even if it did not make much sense. My dad was once a PGA club professional and instilled in me a love and passion for the game.

When my father died more than a decade ago, I lost my mentor and best friend. As a boy, I was teasingly called "Daddy's Shadow" because I would follow my father around whenever and wherever I could. I was not embarrassed by the nickname back then. Thinking back on it now, I cannot think of a better or more appropriate moniker.

Dad, this book is a tribute to you . . . and, that all of our dreams can come true.

CONTENTS

FOREWORD

For more than three decades, David Hueber was at the forefront of golf's greatest period of growth. He had a front-seat view and a hands-on role in four significant golf organizations from the 1980s through the turn of the century.

While at the PGA Tour, he was the point man in building the tour's new business relationship with the Professional Golf Association (PGA) of America. As the chief executive officer of the National Golf Foundation (NGF), he turned that organization into a credible and capable research company and industry advocate. And, as CEO of the Ben Hogan Company, he doubled that company's sales and initiated the sponsorship of the Ben Hogan Tour, now known as the Web.com Tour. He also served as CEO of Ben Hogan Properties, which owned and operated Pebble Beach, as well as CEO of Cosmo World Group, the Japanese conglomerate that owned and operated golf companies and high-end golf courses and resorts.

In this book are many stories and an insider's vivid view of David's time as an executive from key vantage points in the golf world; so, what you'll find here is very interesting stuff because he had the extraordinary opportunity to know and work with some of the most influential and memorable people during golf's greatest period of growth.

While at the PGA Tour, David worked on the business side to grow the game and professional golf and played a valuable role in laying the foundation for the commercial success that the PGA Tour enjoys today. Following his stint with the tour, David moved on to resurrect the NGF from near bankruptcy and give it new life as a vibrant and effective research and promotional organization to stimulate the supply and demand for the game. Back then, golf was in the doldrums and was considered by many to be a dying sport. As the NGF CEO, he founded the biennial Golf Summits—the first time the golf industry ever assembled to assess the state of the game.

The first Golf Summit was held in 1986 at Westchester Country Club and turned out to be a pivotal point for the US golf industry. David then hired the highly regarded consulting firm, McKinsey & Company, to help analyze the NGF research and to develop a *Strategic Plan for the Growth of the Game* that would be presented at the 1988 Golf Summit. The NGF research revealed that the game was stagnating as defined by the number of golfers and rounds played. However, the NGF saw an opportunity to grow the game and the golf industry because the baby boomer population segment had a large number of golfers, and it was expected that as they aged, they would have the time, money, and desire to play and spend more on the game of golf.

To meet this much-anticipated growth in the game, the NGF strategic plan put forth the notion that the golf industry needed "to build a golf course a day between 1990 and the year 2000 to keep up with the anticipated demand." That Course a Day promotional campaign was featured in PGA Tour television public service announcements and caught on with the media and the golf industry. David was responsible for it, and this idea changed the course of the game and the golf business in the 1990s.

Many sectors in the golf business benefited from that shot in the arm. Golf businesses found investors on Wall Street to fuel their growth, and both PGA Tour galleries and television ratings climbed significantly.

We did build a golf course a day during that period. The number of golfers, as predicted, increased to 30 million, and rounds played increased to over 500 million. It was a monumental achievement for the NGF to ignite the transformation of the national perception of golf as a dying game and business, and to refashion it into something cool to play and a growth industry for a broadening list of involved corporations.

From the NGF, David went on to run the Ben Hogan Company and became a close and trusted associate of Ben Hogan. The Japanese owned the company back then, and as noted, the Ben Hogan Company became the title sponsor of the Ben Hogan Tour, now known as the Web.com Tour. The Hogan Company was then at its peak with an impressive staff of PGA Tour professionals and, importantly, had a hot selling golf club called the Hogan Edge. Later, the Japanese owners of the Ben Hogan Company bought Pebble Beach Golf Links, and David became responsible for that iconic property as President of Ben Hogan Property Companies.

After working for the Japanese for nearly eighteen years and always seeking new challenges, David decided to go back to school to teach and earn a doctorate at Clemson University. Before doing so, David and his wife, Cindy, had dinner with my wife Judy and me, and he asked me what course of study I thought he should pursue. I encouraged him to focus on the environmental issues confronting the future of the game. The subject of his dissertation research became sustainable golf course development and management. That last notation tells you even more about the kind of person David is. He went back to school and earned his PhD at an age when most people are planning retirement.

So, David went back to school in 2008. His research for the PhD dissertation revealed that the golf courses built during the 1990s golf boom were more costly, longer, and more difficult to play compared to the golf courses built during the other two development boom periods in the 1920s and 1960s.

These findings are important because that paradigm change in the nature and type of golf courses built has contributed to the recent decline in the number of golfers and golf rounds played. In the final analysis, golf courses are both an environmental and economic asset. In order for golf to change its course, grow the game and the golf business, it needs to once again change its image by redefining itself as a sustainable industry, proactive in preserving nature for future generations.

David has been and will continue to be an important player in the golf world. He has moved the game forward in his own, unheralded way, and the game and business of golf is better for it. David's story, like his journey through the game, is a fascinating one. Enjoy the read.

DEANE R. BEMAN
PGA Tour Commissioner 1974-1994

INTRODUCTION

What follows is a tale that feels like a long, disorienting—at times exhilarating—journey through the inner workings of professional golf and the golf industry. Whatever the sum of these adventures, it came to a recognizable end for me with the passing of Ben Hogan in 1997. This moment marked what seemed to be the changing of the guard.

During this journey, the play of golf changed from a game of shotmaking and skill, requiring what Ben Hogan described as "course management," into clearly what has become a power game. Advances in golf equipment technology enable the pros to hit the golf ball farther and straighter. The bottom line is that the golf equipment and the Augusta National course Jack Nicklaus played to win the 1986 Masters are very different from the golf equipment and course Tiger Woods played to win the 1997 Masters. In fact, many of golf's historic and classic venues had to be "Tiger proofed" in order to preserve par as the standard of excellence.

It all changed before our eyes, but we never saw it coming.

Through my dissertation research at Clemson University, I saw a paradigm shift in the nature and type of golf courses built or renovated during the 1990s which, along with the downturn in the real estate market in 2006 and the recession in 2008, led to a decline in golf participation and a threat to the sustainability of the golf industry.

Most of the incidents described in this book are firsthand accounts from my time as an executive bouncing around the golf world. I was an insider in the business game, so what you'll find here is reliable stuff. I managed to work in almost every facet of the golf industry. I got to meet, know, and work with the most influential and memorable people of the era.

This book tells what the leading players in the game and the golf business were really like. The central characters in this book are Ben Hogan, one of the five best players of all time and a highly successful golf-equipment executive; Deane Beman, a star amateur and successful professional golfer and the inventor of the modern-day PGA Tour; and Minoru Isutani, a wealthy Japanese entrepreneur, who is probably best known for having lost $350 million on the purchase and sale of Pebble Beach. Some of the other costars include Jack Nicklaus, Karsten Solheim, Greg Norman, and Ely Callaway—all names you've seen etched on a wood, an iron, or a putter, among other places.

As an executive with the PGA Tour during the formative Beman years, I was there at the birth of its burgeoning business development and played a role in building that enterprise. My good fortune continued when I was appointed president and CEO of the National Golf Foundation (NGF), but my timing was bad. The NGF was teetering on bankruptcy, and the golf industry was struggling. The game and business were heading in the wrong direction. Undaunted, we transformed the NGF into a research resource and made it a uniting force for the industry with the hosting of something new to the golf industry—the Golf Summits.

McKinsey & Company were engaged to help develop a strategic plan for the golf industry. That plan was widely embraced and successfully implemented, leading to an unprecedented level of investment that spurred golf's growth well into the 1990s.

Then, with the recommendation of Beman I moved to Cosmo World, the new Japanese owner of the Ben Hogan Company. I was recruited to become the president and CEO of the Ben Hogan Company and later Ben Hogan Properties Company (which acquired the Pebble Beach Company).

This job was the opportunity of a lifetime. I got to work with and become a close acquaintance of Ben Hogan. Our offices were next to each other, and we had coffee together at least two or three times a week. I was very lucky to be with Hogan at a time in his life when he was willing to reminisce and share some of the wisdom he had acquired. The reality is that Hogan was part of an industry, a period of time, and an ethic that was dedicated to making a hard game more satisfying for people who were willing to work at it diligently. That's hugely different from wanting to turn a game that seems hard (unforgiving clubs like the Hogan Apex blade-shaped irons might be part of the reason) into a game that seems approachable and pleasurable, even if we're not all hitting the ball prodigious distances and shooting low scores.

I had no such ethic in me which resisted innovation. I thought golf should grow and expand—so that more people would be able to play and enjoy the game without slaving away on the practice range. In a way, I was right in my analysis that making the game easier to play for the average golfer would make it a more appealing recreational activity; however, I was wrong in my assessment that all of the technological advancements in golf would be good for the game.

My perspective was non-Hogan: you *could* buy a better game with better golf equipment, and I saw that as a good thing. It came from a point of view that all growth was good—something he would never understand. But, as I would someday learn, the real joy and satisfaction in golf comes from inside, and you have to "dig it out of the dirt," as Hogan always insisted.

What Hogan never knew about me was that, like him, I was (and still am) an inveterate golf-club designer. He was no more enthusiastic a tinkerer and doodler of new designs than I. Both of us started young at this hobby, and both of us made it into a vocation. Unlike the classic Hogan club designs, my designs are modern and loaded with features intended to make golf easier to play, such as square-shaped drivers, metal woods, and hybrid woods, along with a slew of patented products including golf shafts that increase clubhead speed, and golf clubs, putters, and balls with optical-alignment features. I may have more patents than Hogan had, but my name on a golf club has no value (and thus was never used on one), whereas his name was and is the most beautiful, enviable brand in the history of the business. Ironically, I was president of the Ben Hogan Company when it sold the Hogan Edge, the most successful game-improvement club in its history. This club reflected how the game and the golf equipment business were changing, even for a traditional clubmaker like the Hogan Company.

Our differing points of view placed Hogan and me in different philosophical wings of the golfing world. All the same, it did not make him any less a hero to me, and as it turned out, he was right, and I was wrong. This was just one of the many lessons learned in my Forrest-Gump-like odyssey in the wonderful world of golf. If I could have that office next to his and still be working with him now, I'd sign on for that in a Fort Worth minute.

I have many Hogan stories to tell that have never been told before. We were close enough that his wife Valerie asked me to be an honorary pallbearer at his funeral in August of 1997. I was the only former Hogan Company president afforded that privilege. Quite frankly, I don't know why I have been so amazingly fortunate to have had the opportunity to cross paths and work with so many of the greats in the game and business. Clearly, it is the journey, not the destination that makes it all so worthwhile.

I am now at the point where I have spent time reflecting on what I have learned and am looking for ways to share that knowledge. It is why I went back to school in 2008. In August of 2012, I earned my PhD at Clemson University, where I lectured in the business school and researched sustainable golf development and management.

These pages are the sum of all the important things that happened to me from youth through middle age in the game and business of golf—mostly the business. Fortunately, I came out of it still standing, with many great stories to tell and many lessons learned about golf and life. I am honored to share them with you.

DAVID HUEBER

P.S. Ben Hogan's Secret is revealed.

HOGAN AND I DROWN OUR SORROWS

The waiter covering Ben Hogan's corner table in the Shady Oaks Country Club grillroom was seldom hard to summon. Whoever had the assignment always seemed to keep one eye peeled for even the slightest gesture that meant the club's aging icon desired service. On this late-autumn day in 1992, the waiter was asked to bring vodkas on the rocks with a twist, one for Hogan and one for me. The two of us had been sitting there awhile drinking white wine, and white wine was not doing the trick.

All of Fort Worth, Texas, had sunk into a gloom since the announcement several months earlier that Cosmo World, the Japanese parent of the Ben Hogan Golf Company, had sold its famous subsidiary to a new owner who decided to dismiss almost the entire workforce and move the operation to Virginia. For me this meant the end of a great run.

I had one of the lead roles in the drama, having spent the previous three years as president of the Ben Hogan Company. The sale meant my ticket would be punched. Mr. Hogan—you will have to forgive me, but it is difficult to call him anything else—had started the company in 1953. Even though he sold a controlling interest in it to AMF seven years later, he was on the scene the entire time and had remained both the face and the conscience of the organization. Now, that would all end. To make matters worse, this was a distress sale of a healthy subsidiary by a cash-strapped parent company. The distress was all due to Cosmo World's disastrous acquisition of the famed Pebble Beach resort on the Monterey Peninsula. At least in name, I had been in charge of that operation, as well.

Which is why I was surprised to be sitting at Hogan's table in the first place. We were in the midst of an agonizing transition. I was tasked with carrying out the new owner's directives to downsize the company and extricate it from various long-term promotional commitments. As president of the company, my relationship with Hogan had suffered in this lame-duck period, especially after it was announced that the company would move from Fort Worth to Richmond, Virginia. Naturally, Hogan was angry with me for letting this happen. With the move came wholesale terminations—in all, some five hundred people lost their jobs.

There had been a steady stream of longtime employees stopping by Hogan's office to thank him and say good-bye.

The farewells and good wishes took their toll. Day by day, the pain of it seemed more deeply etched into his face and more evident in his halting movements. Then, one morning, I stopped by his office for a cup of coffee and our regular visit. He was seated behind his oversized desk in his customary suit—a nicely tailored, light gray suit; white shirt; and dark tie—just like any business executive might wear. He had a stern look as I sat down in front of his desk. He said he had an idea he wanted to discuss with me over lunch at Shady Oaks Country Club—his sanctuary away from work and out of the public eye. I asked him if he wanted to talk about it now while at the office, and he said no, offering no reason.

This was the first time he had ever asked me to lunch. There really wasn't anything unusual about that. The grillroom at Shady Oaks was his private retreat. People left him alone there. No one bothered him for autographs, and only friends dared approach him. It wasn't that Hogan wasn't friendly or courteous to everyone; it was more in deference to what everyone thought he wanted and the mystique that surrounded him. It protected him like an electrified chain-link fence. I was a member at Shady Oaks, and I would have liked to have thought that Hogan considered me his friend by then, but even I never wanted to cross that line uninvited. So I agreed to meet him at noon at his large corner table overlooking the 18th green. I could not imagine what he wanted to talk about.

As it turned out, the big idea he wanted to share with me was quite poignant. He told me he had found a building and some property a little north of Shady Oaks Country Club and wanted to start a new golf company called Henny Bogan, and he wanted me to run it. I was flattered and replied there would be nothing I would rather do, but given the circumstances, it was probably something that we should not do. I reminded him he had signed a noncompete agreement and was legally barred from taking any role in the golf equipment field. His name for the proposed new company I later saw as a tragicomic touch. Through youth and adolescence, Hogan had been known as "Bennie" and never "Ben." Sometime in childhood, he invented a sort of alter ego for himself, whom he called Henny Bogan. The new brand name was not thought up on the spot as a clumsy evasion of trademark rights: it harkened back to Hogan's difficult, early years, like the sled named Rosebud in the final scene of *Citizen Kane*.

Hogan and I continued to talk after lunch, but we dropped the Henny Bogan idea from any further discussion. The vodkas arrived in timely fashion—"clearies," as the executive team around Hogan called them, or "seethroughs." I had never had straight vodka on the rocks before; now they were coming one round after another. The overcast sky outside dimmed. It struck me that I was experiencing one of the coolest days of my life: here I was slowly getting plastered with Ben Hogan. His guard was down, and he felt like talking. My natural inhibitions were loosened by the confidence induced by the Smirnoff. Our conversation flowed.

He told me stories that were reruns of tales told before, but I enjoyed hearing them again. It was therapeutic for both of us. Before me was someone whom the Scots admiringly called "the Wee Ice Mon" for his imperviousness to competitive pressure. Others picked up on this general sangfroid as indicative of a dislike of people, but all I could see that day, and all I remember now about Hogan was his passionate love for the game and his golf company. And his great empathy pushed him near the point of tears as he considered employees tossed out after years of dedicated service to the Ben Hogan Company.

At this point in his life, nothing worse could have happened. Ben and Valerie had no children. The Ben Hogan Company, apart from his stellar playing career, was his legacy to the game. It was his pride and joy. He told me that he regretted selling the company to AMF back in 1960. He said he had needed AMF to run and build the business because he could not do it himself. But he lost control, and there was not anything he could do about it. The regrets he expressed brought us both to the brink of tears. I had never felt so much anguish and helplessness in my life. The sense that I had let him down was probably the worst of it.

Perhaps out of necessity our conversation turned to less serious topics. There was even a little humor as he began to reminisce about happier times. I had been mostly listening, asking a question here and there. I relished this private time with the legendary figure. As the afternoon progressed, I asked him if he ever dreamed about golf. He sat back in his chair, smiled knowingly, and said, "Yes, I remember dreaming about playing at Augusta. I had seventeen consecutive holes-in-one, and on the eighteenth hole, I hit a great drive, and the ball just lipped out [thwarting the ace and a perfect score of 18]. I have never been so goddamn pissed off in all my life," he recalled, shaking his head and laughing.

I laughed with him, but to me, that dream was somewhat of a metaphor for his life. He had done his best and had come close to perfection in so many ways, only to have it fall apart at the very end. The relocation of the Ben Hogan Company was the lip-out of his life, I thought to myself. I congratulated

myself inwardly on such a profound observation. Sitting around and philos-
ophizing about the meaning of life with Hogan was beginning to seem like a
fine way to pass the time. I formulated a provocative question and posed it to
him: "Have you ever had a bad day at the golf course?"

He gazed thoughtfully for a moment, then turned back to me with his answer. "I can honestly say that I have never had a bad day on the golf course.
Learning to play this game is all about improvement. My goal was to become
a better player every day. If I learned something that made me a better player,
it was a good day. And there was never a day that I didn't learn something,
especially if it was what you called a 'bad day.' Every day was an opportunity
to improve, and in fact, there were more opportunities on bad days. My only
regret was that there were not more hours in the day to work on my game."

We both took a few more sips of the clearies. I was lost in thought at the
power of what he had just said. Breaking the silence, he leaned over to me
and asked me if I wanted a cigarette. This was about the third or fourth time
he had offered me one that afternoon, and each time I had said, "No thank
you, I don't smoke, but please go ahead." But, this time, I thought it was kind
of funny, and feeling more familiar, I said, "Ben, I still don't smoke, but I am
willing to learn." We both laughed. Our conversation had been somewhat an
emotional roller-coaster ride, and I was beginning to wonder if either of us
should drive home, so I asked him if he was feeling okay.

Ignoring my question, he said, "Did you ever learn *the Secret*?"

"Yes," I said, "you told it to me in your office, not that long ago." In fact, he
had already spent two intense mentoring sessions with me: one on the Shady
Oaks driving range and the other at his office, trying to teach me his famous
secret to the golf swing. This secret was a *Life* magazine cover story and series
of articles in 1954, and had been a mainstay of the Hogan mystique ever since.

"No, that is not what I asked you, David," Hogan said, "What I meant was . . .
did you ever *learn* it?" I was distracted, still pondering the personal epiphany
I had previously experienced when he said he had never had a bad day on the
golf course. At this point, Hogan's lower lip began to rise over his upper lip, a
sure indication of dismay. I took that as his sign he was losing patience with
me. Perhaps he was disappointed that I was not capable of comprehending his
meaning.

After another uncomfortable pause, I felt compelled to say something:
"Mr. Hogan, I guess . . . "

And then he interrupted me, saying, "That's okay, someday you might understand. Then again, maybe you won't."

1

SIR NICK MAKES A CAMEO APPEARANCE

There was never a time in my tenure at the Ben Hogan Company when Hogan wasn't sought out by world-famous golfers. Nick Faldo,[1] who by then had established himself as a world-class player, contacted Hogan's office in November 1992. Faldo had won British Open titles in 1987, 1990, and 1992. He won the Masters in 1989 and 1990 and would win it again in 1996, coolly overcoming Norman's six-stroke lead in the final round. So it was without apologies that he sought an audience with the aged Hogan. Faldo was known as a big Hogan fan, so I took it in stride when Doxie Williams, Hogan's secretary, told me my friend Jody Vasquez (author of the book *Afternoons with Mr. Hogan*) had arranged a meeting for the following Friday between the two champions.

By this time, Hogan's memory was prone to lapses. Williams wanted me at the meeting to ease the conversation along. She knew my presence would prove helpful should there be any uncomfortable pauses—a rather likely possibility. Hogan was capable of giving short, clipped answers to very long, in-depth questions. To prevent awkward gaps in the dialogue, you had to be ready with a follow-up question or some reasonably logical transition. At times, he would just forget what he was saying and needed a little reminder to get back on track.

The bigger problem was that Hogan did not accept many visitors anymore. And now that he was getting along in years, he did not really keep up with current trends and events in golf. About a year earlier, I had brought Chip Beck over to meet Hogan after we signed him as a PGA Tour staff player (to represent the Ben Hogan Company by playing Hogan equipment on the PGA Tour). Beck had finished second and ninth on the PGA Tour money list in the prior two years, so he was one of the top ten players in the world at that time. He was also one of the nicest and most polite people I've ever met.

Beck clearly was nervous about meeting the legendary figure. I led him into Hogan's office and introduced him as the newest member of our professional staff. Hogan, in gracious tones, said, "Welcome to our company."

Beck answered, "I am very pleased to be here and to now represent the Ben Hogan Company."

We sat down in front of Hogan's oversized desk and waited for him to speak. After a moment he said, "Tell me, are you going to play *my* tour?" (meaning the Ben Hogan Tour).

Beck politely responded, "No, Mr. Hogan, I play the big tour—the PGA Tour."

"Well, I would have liked to have played for the kind of money they are playing for on the Ben Hogan Tour," continued Hogan. "It teaches you how to travel, how to win . . . it's really a good thing."

Beck responded, "Yes sir, it is. It is a tribute to you, and I am proud to be a part of your company." Nothing more was said. The meeting was over. Beck showed some class by exiting agreeably and without hesitation.

With Beck's visit in mind, I held out hope Nick Faldo would fare better. Beck's time with Hogan had lasted all of four minutes, and for Faldo's visit, we had blocked off much of the morning at our offices. We had also booked a table for lunch at Shady Oaks. I had no idea how we would pass the time. I braced myself for one long, pregnant pause after another unless Nick could carry the conversation.

Faldo arrived promptly at 10:00 a.m. with an entourage that included his agent John Simpson and our mutual friend Jody Vasquez. In his hand, Faldo carried a much-worn and dog-eared copy of *Five Lessons* that he wanted Hogan to sign. That may have been the trick that lowered Hogan's guard. He shook Faldo's hand, examined the book, and sat down willingly to talk. Hogan was engaged, and to the extent that he was capable, quite animated and forthright with his responses. Faldo, to his credit, had come prepared. He asked Hogan about the golf swing, how he felt in certain positions when he swung—questions that reflected a deep familiarity with the Hogan golf philosophy. I had never seen Hogan so engaged in conversation with a professional golfer.

As it turned out, this would be the last time anyone would be granted such an opportunity. Hogan answered all of Faldo's questions, even the obtuse ones. At one point, Nick asked, "What do I need to do to win the U.S. Open?"

Hogan paused to reflect, and then told him, "You need to shoot the lowest score."

Now, there was silence. The air seemed to leak out of the room, and no one seemed to know what to say. Sitting off to the side and influenced as I was by Hogan's acerbic, bare-bones logic, I could only think that a stupid question earns its rightful response. Another moment or two passed; Faldo and his entourage started to laugh, thinking that Hogan was kidding. I knew that he was not kidding, and neither Hogan nor I were laughing. Plainly irritated, Hogan

While Hogan did have five U.S. Open medals, the USGA did not count his 1942 win in the Hale America National Open Golf Tournament (an alternative event for the USGA's cancelled U.S. Open during WWII). That tournament was held during the same time as the U.S. Open; it had 1,500-plus entries with some sixty-nine qualifying sites and was run like a U.S. Open. Most of the top players were competing, and the Hale America National Open had the largest purse on the 1942 PGA Tour. *Courtesy of the Historical Preservation Committee, Colonial Country Club, Fort Worth, Texas.*

put an end to the laughter by saying, "I am not making a joke. If by Sunday you have posted the lowest score, they will give you the U.S. Open medal. I know, because I have *five of them.*"

Faldo, his expression now duly serious, reverted to his original script of technical questions and soon had the conversation back on track. Displaying diplomatic instinct, he chose this interlude to have Hogan sign the worn copy of *Five Lessons* on a page containing one of the classic illustrations by Anthony

Ravielli. Hogan was meticulous in everything he did. It took him a little longer than one might expect to sign something, and for Faldo, he also wished to write a short, personal inscription. He looked up from the page to say there was not enough room to sign where Nick had indicated. Faldo replied, "Sign it wherever you want."

Hogan found a suitable space and set to work. "What day is today?" he asked.

I started to say, "It's Friday the . . ."

"No," Hogan interrupted, "What year is it?"

Signing completed, the conversation continued. Faldo interviewed Hogan on a number of subjects, asking him what it was like to play professional golf in his day; what were the most important tournaments; how did he prepare for competition, etc. Hogan responded to each question with an acuity and attention to detail I had not observed in a long time. He talked about how there wasn't much in purse money in the early days, how he and his wife Valerie drove from tournament to tournament, sometimes getting by on only oranges before he could cash another check. He mentioned that the North and South Championship used to be a prestigious event, and likewise the Los Angeles Open. He was blunt in saying that, in his day, a big event was an event that paid decent money. In fact, Hogan said, "The more money the tournament paid, the more important it was, as far as I was concerned."

At this point, there was another pause in the conversation. I asked Faldo which tournament was next on his schedule. He said he was heading to South Africa to play in a big event—the Sun City Million Dollar Challenge. Hogan shook his head and said something like, "That is just too far to travel to play a tournament." Then Hogan turned to Faldo and asked, "What do they pay for first place?"

"First pays a million," Faldo said.

I thought Hogan was going to go into convulsions.

Faldo returned to business, asking an array of questions on the technical aspects of the golf swing, as well as how to best prepare mentally for a major event. I particularly remember Faldo asking how to get over jumpy nerves. Hogan's response: "Preparation. If you practice properly and have successfully hit every shot that you might need to play, then you won't be so anxious." Hogan had long been the exemplar of preparation, planning, and practice and almost always answered questions of this type the same way.

Moving on, Faldo asked Hogan what the most important club in the bag was. We all knew that Hogan would not say the putter. It was usually wise not to even mention putting around Hogan because that was a sore spot with him. Hogan always believed that a putt shouldn't count the same as a full shot. At one time, he seriously suggested the hole be made larger in diameter to deemphasize putting's importance to the final score. We never did manage to produce a decent putter at the Hogan Company, probably in unintentional deference to the low regard our company founder had for the short stick.

Hogan's answer to Faldo was succinct: "The driver, because that club determines how aggressively you can play a hole. It will make or break your round." At this point, it was getting close to lunchtime. Faldo mentioned he would hit practice balls after our lunch at Shady Oaks Country Club. Would Hogan watch him hit a few? Hogan replied, "Okay."

I was shocked. Evidently, Faldo had charmed Hogan beyond my wildest imagination. Hogan never watched *anyone* hit balls, except for Kris Tschetter, the winsome, blonde-haired LPGA professional whose father was a member at Shady Oaks. Hogan never watched any PGA Tour players hit balls, not even Hogan Company staff pros like Tom Kite, Lanny Wadkins, or Davis Love III. He probably knew any one of them would have been thrilled at the prospect, but he abstained all the same.

This being the case, I could not help but take it as presumptuous and brazen when Faldo then said, "That's great. And I would really appreciate it if you would make some comments about my swing."

Hogan shook his head. "No," he replied.

Faldo persevered. "Really, Mr. Hogan, I would so appreciate hearing anything that you might have to say."

Hogan then looked him straight in the eye, pointed his right index finger at him, and said, "Nick . . . right, it's Nick?" Faldo nodded. "You are a pretty good player aren't you?" Faldo shrugged his shoulders in the affirmative and nodded yes again. Hogan continued, "You need to dig it out of the dirt yourself. Whatever I tell you, you will forget. If you dig it out of the dirt yourself, it is yours forever."

Hogan pushed back from his desk. We all stood up and got ready for the short drive to the Shady Oaks grillroom. Once we arrived, we gathered around Hogan's table, which is situated in the corner of the room just behind the 18th green. I had asked the head pro, Mike Wright, to have a golf cart waiting outside the back door in the event Hogan might watch Faldo hit some balls after lunch. I had also retrieved Hogan's overcoat from the coatroom to protect him against the chill of what was a cool November afternoon. Hogan might not say anything about Nick Faldo's swing, but he did promise to watch. I was intent on having everything ready.

The Shady Oaks grillroom is an unfailingly pleasant place for any group of golf-knowledgeable males to gather. The food and the service are first-rate. We all had a pleasant conservation and a fine lunch. Hogan, who had recently turned eighty, looked tired. When the plates were cleared, Faldo, his agent Simpson, and friend Vasquez, excused themselves. Faldo said something like, "I am going to go hit some balls now, and I look forward to seeing you up at the range." Faldo then looked in my direction and gave me the nod. His meaning was clear: I was to go over and get Hogan to do what he had promised to do—watch Faldo hit balls.

I slid into the seat next to Hogan, feeling a little word-weary, myself. "You said that you would watch him hit some balls," I reminded the great man.

"Yes, I know." There was a pause, but this time not an awkward one. I knew his fatigue level and wanted to relieve him of any further obligations. I think he sensed that. "He seems like a very nice young man," Hogan said of Faldo.

"Yes he is," I said, "and I believe that he made a special trip here on his way home to England, just to come and meet you." Hogan had been served a glass of Chablis and was holding the wineglass by the stem and swirling the wine in it.

"It's pretty cold out there, isn't it?" he asked.

"It's not all that bad. I have your overcoat right here, and the golf cart is parked just by the door."

Hogan continued to swirl the wine. "David, does he play our clubs?"

"No, Mr. Hogan. He plays Mizunos."

Hogan looked up from the table and said to me, "You know what to do. Explain things to them."

I walked out the back door of the grillroom, got into the golf cart, and drove up the hill to the driving range where Faldo, Simpson, and Vasquez were waiting. Nick was lofting wedge shots up into the brisk Texas air. He put the club on his shoulder and looked at me. "Where's Mr. Hogan?" he asked.

"It's Gary Player all over again," I said. (I was referring to the fabled incident in which Gary Player kept calling Hogan for swing advice, until he finally asked Player what brand of clubs he used. Player reportedly said, "Dunlop," upon which Hogan said, "Then go ask Mr. Dunlop for swing advice.")

Perhaps this was my moment to be obtuse, but in all honesty, I made this remark thinking all heads would nod, and nothing further would need to be said, given the famed Player precedent regarding a similar request. Faldo would be able to put his disappointment into the proper perspective.

Faldo looked at me quizzically. "What do you mean?" he asked.

"If you want a golf lesson, you are playing the wrong equipment," I said.

Faldo began to smolder. He turned to Simpson and said, "Go into the golf shop and buy a bloody set of Hogan clubs."

I held up a hand. "Nick, that won't be necessary. It is a little too cold for him. I was very surprised that he even agreed to watch you hit balls in the first place. You have spent more time with Hogan than anyone that I have seen—more time than he has ever given to any of his staff players including Kite, Love, and Wadkins. Be grateful for the time that was given."

Without answering, Faldo slammed his wedge into the bag and then walked in the direction of the parking lot. Vasquez and I watched him move off. Our eyes met for a moment; neither of us felt the need to say anything. Evidently "Sir Nick Faldo" was not quite up to the knightly standards of his title. It had been an afternoon each of us would long remember.

There is no doubt in my mind that if Hogan had gone out there to watch Faldo hit balls he would not have said anything. So when Hogan told me, "Go explain it to them," it represented no great turn of events. This was a cold, raw day for a man who didn't have much blood circulating in his legs. Meanwhile, the advice seeker—champion though he was—did not even play Hogan clubs. I went back into the clubhouse to find Hogan already in the locker room getting ready to take a shower. I reported to him his visitors had left and had asked me to express their appreciation once more for the time he'd spent with them.

Hogan looked up quickly. "Okay," he grunted.

2

NONE OF THEIR GODDAMN BUSINESS

One Sunday evening in April of 1991, I was playing golf alone at Shady Oaks Country Club. I was walking the golf course with a light carry bag and noticed Hogan out on the back nine walking as well. He had a golf club in his hand and seemed to have a spring in his step. He was limping, but it wasn't as noticeable as usual.

The next day we were in his office having a cup of coffee, and I commented that I had seen him at Shady Oaks walking on the course. He said, "Yes, I am feeling a little better and wanted to stretch my legs." I noted that he was carrying a golf club with him, and he said, "Yes, I was practicing my grip, using this weighted golf club." He then handed me the weighted Hogan driver, and I held the club in my hands, noting the reminder on the cord grip that was open at least two degrees.

"Are you going to start hitting golf balls again?" I asked him.

Ignoring my question, Hogan said that every club professional could maintain his golf game, keep it in shape, if he just practiced his golf grip every day for ten minutes with a weighted golf club. He then told me to have Gene Sheeley, his master clubmaker, make me up a weighted club, just like his, so that I could do the same thing at my office.

"Make sure that he puts some lead in the shaft so the swingweight is about the same as a regular driver," he said. "You don't want to practice your grip or swing with a sledgehammer. David," he added, "I want you to figure out how to make one of those clubs for every member on the Hogan club professional staff. Do you understand? This is important."

After getting this new assignment, I then tried to redirect our conversation to his playing golf again. "Since you are feeling a little better now and practicing your grip, are you planning to start hitting some balls again?"

"Probably not," he replied. "My knee and shoulder are both really bothering me. I need to get some arthroscopic surgery on both, but probably won't."

"Why not?"

"Because I couldn't see the ball even if I could hit it, and controlling the ball flight is the art and enjoyment of hitting a good golf shot."

"What do you mean that you couldn't see the golf ball," I asked. "Are you having vision problems?"

"I have cataracts, especially in my right eye," he said.

"What about your left eye?"

"Can't see much out of that eye at all," he said.

Noticing that he had bifocals in both of his lenses, I then asked him, "How long has that been, since you had good vision in your left eye?"

"Since the accident." (In the movie about his life, *Follow the Sun*, there is a bandage over Glenn Ford/Ben Hogan's left eye during the first scenes at the hospital.)

I was stunned, knowing how important good vision and depth perception were back in the days before yardage books pinpointed the distance for the pros. My first thought was the obvious one when I said, "Mr. Hogan, you never told *anyone* that you lost most of your vision in your left eye in the accident—the media, your fellow competitors—no one knows about this?"

"It was none of their goddamn business!"

Hogan wanted no chinks in his armor. You need two good eyes in order to have good depth perception. Since he did not have good vision in his left eye, it would be difficult to line up a putt at address for a right-handed golfer. It is also a plausible explanation for his poor putting after the accident. Hogan didn't want to show any weakness to his fellow competitors. He went to great lengths to create the mystique of a mechanical man who could not be beaten. He had even discovered the Secret and wasn't going to tell anyone what it was.

3

HOGAN ALWAYS FELT SORRY FOR RICH KIDS

Ben Hogan was never one to feel sorry for himself. The notion never even occurred to him. Interestingly, he once told me that he felt sorry for rich kids, implying that it was more difficult for them to develop the mental toughness needed to become a successful professional golfer.

William Ben Hogan was nine years old when his father, Chester Hogan, shot himself in the chest with a .38 caliber revolver on February 13, 1922. He died on Valentine's Day at age 37. He had long suffered from depression. The *Fort Worth Star-Telegram* reported that his twelve-year-old son, Royal, witnessed the suicide. Ben and his sixteen-year-old sister, Princess, then rushed into the room. Their father was reported to have uttered, "I wish I hadn't done that." It was a tragedy that forever changed the lives of the Hogan brothers; their older sister, Princess; and their mom, Clara.[1]

Royal quit school to go to work delivering office supplies on his bicycle. Bennie first sold newspapers near the Texas and Pacific Railway Station and then started caddying at Glen Garden Country Club. The Hogan family was dirt poor; they no longer had a primary breadwinner and had to eke out a living. Even if their dad had not committed suicide, both boys might have had to go to work. They lived from day to day, without the comforts which we take for granted.

Most great golfers of Hogan's time, with the notable exception of Bobby Jones, came out of the caddie yards. This "school of hard knocks" in the 1920s and 1930s had both kids and adults trying to earn a living to feed their families. Not only did the caddie yard toughen up its graduates, it gave the caddies a hunger for a better life. At the country clubs, they had a bird's-eye view of how the other half lived. There was an old television commercial for Cadillac that really captured this notion. It showed a caddie admiring the club member driving a luxury car. The caddie promises himself, "Someday *I'll* own a Cadillac."

These aspirations often led caddies toward golf, and some got pretty good at the game. Some even tried to earn a living through golf, even when there was not much of a living to be made. Both Ben Hogan and Byron Nelson were the same age and caddied at the same nine-hole Glen Garden Country Club in Fort Worth. Nelson usually bested Hogan in the caddie tournaments and also beat him most of the time during their early days as professional golfers. As a matter of fact, Nelson was awarded an honorary membership at Glen Garden over Hogan, setting up a rivalry that would last a lifetime. Nelson enjoyed early success on the pro tour, while Hogan continued to struggle with his game until he found a swing that worked for him.

One story illustrates the competitive mind-set forged in the caddie yards back then. It was told to me by Ben Wright, the former golf broadcaster for CBS Golf. At the time, I was president of the Ben Hogan Company. I was having dinner with Ben Wright and the president of CBS Sports, Peter Lund, during the Colonial National Invitation Tournament in Fort Worth. We were advertising on CBS in those days, and I was being wined and dined. Wright was talking about the competition in the old days when he told me about the time he interviewed Sam Snead, who also happened to be the same age as Hogan and Nelson.

"And," Wright cautioned me, "if you don't believe this story, I have it on videotape, even though we never aired that segment."

He described the interview as somewhat lighthearted until they got to the rivalry between Snead and Hogan. Snead said Hogan never beat him when they were playing together—one-on-one, face-to-face, so to speak. Wright said that was not true and reminded him of the *Shell's Wonderful World of Golf* episode at the Houston Country Club. Snead said that didn't mean "diddly shit"; it was one of those made-for-TV programs that meant nothing. (As I recall, it was a match where Hogan hit 18 greens in regulation and turned a 66 into a 69 with bad putting, while Snead scrambled to shoot somewhere around par.)

But the details really do not matter; what did matter was that Snead's mood changed, as did the tone of the interview.

Wright tried to get Snead to open up as he pursued the rivalry, much to the ire of Snead. At that point, Snead was ready to end the interview. He then said to Wright, "You know, I don't think that Hogan was really hurt that bad in the accident." Keep in mind that Snead made a cameo appearance in the movie about Hogan called, *Follow the Sun*. Snead played himself in the scene when he visited Hogan (actor Glenn Ford) in the hospital.

For the few readers that don't know the story regarding Hogan's comeback from a near-fatal car crash, the following explanation is provided. In 1948, Ben Hogan was the best player in the world. He had won both the U.S. Open and the PGA Championship and was the leading money winner on the tour for the fifth time. After he won two of his first four events out West in 1949, he

Marvin Leonard, Ben Hogan's friend and early sponsor, towed Hogan's totaled Cadillac to Fort Worth in the spring of 1949. It was displayed in front of Leonard's Department Store for a short time. *Courtesy of the Historical Preservation Committee, Colonial Country Club, Fort Worth, Texas.*

and Valerie were driving back home to Fort Worth. It was a foggy morning on February 2. Just outside of Van Horn, Texas (near El Paso), a Greyhound bus crossed the center line and collided head-on with Hogan's Cadillac. Instinctively, Hogan leaned toward the passenger side to shield Valerie, just before the crash drove the car's steering column into the back seat. This may have saved both of their lives.

Valerie escaped with minor injuries, but Ben was critically injured. His left eye was swollen shut; he had a fractured left collarbone, a chipped rib, a double fracture of his pelvis, and a broken ankle. There were complications that followed from internal injuries. Hogan had trouble breathing and excruciating chest pains. Blood clots formed in his legs, and one had traveled to his lung. Abdominal surgery was performed to tie off a large vein (vena cava) from the lower half of the body to the heart. That led to the chronic pain, swelling, and fatigue that plagued Hogan the rest of his days. Hogan was in the hospital for fifty-nine days; the prognosis to walk, much less play golf, was uncertain. His steely determination to recover and to play professional golf embodied his legendary quest for excellence both on and off the golf course.

In January of the 1950 season, Hogan returned to the PGA Tour and played in the Los Angeles Open. At the end of seventy-two holes, it was Snead who tied Hogan at Riviera. The playoff was delayed, and it was Snead who beat Hogan a week later. Professional golfers in those days neither asked for, nor gave, any quarter.

One evening as my wife Cindy and I were having dinner with Valerie and Ben Hogan at Shady Oaks, I asked Mrs. Hogan how she liked *Follow the Sun*. In the movie, Valerie was appropriately portrayed as a loving, dedicated wife and life partner, but her reply revealed the moviemakers could not capture it all.

"It was a nice film," she said, "but they really missed how difficult the recovery was for Ben. Almost daily, I was afraid for him, even after we returned home [Fort Worth]. Sometimes I wasn't sure if he was going to make it. The pain was terrible for him, but he persevered. I guess that isn't something that people really wanted to see in a movie, but that's how it was."

The trials and challenges of his childhood were what enabled Hogan to deal with these even more difficult trials and challenges later in life. Early on, he and Valerie had little. One morning, as Hogan was leaving his motel to play the next round in a tournament, he saw that the back of his car was jacked up—someone had stolen the rear wheels off his car.

Many might have packed it in after the horrific collision. Many would have heeded the doctors' advice. He was told not to play golf because his legs could not stand the wear and tear of tournament competition. But if Hogan had packed it in, he would not have won the 1950 U.S. Open just eleven months later. He also would not have won three of the tournaments in the Modern Grand Slam in 1953: the Masters, the U.S. Open, and the British Open, making a Career Grand Slam.

Hogan was a product of his environment and circumstances. He understood that challenges made him tougher mentally and enabled him to improve his game. He knew that opportunities handed out on a silver platter are not savored or appreciated. Mental toughness is not genetically passed down from parent to child; it is earned through hardship and hard work. He understood much of his success was the direct result of dealing with adversity. He felt sorry for the rich kids, because he viewed their advantages as being a disadvantage in becoming great golfers.

That philosophy, borne out of adversity and tested at every turn in life, enabled Hogan to battle his way out of the caddie yards and become one of the greatest to ever play the game. And, "digging it out of the dirt" was what drove him to start the Ben Hogan Company with the singular purpose of making perfect golf clubs. He didn't know any other way to do it.

4

GROWING UP
IN GOLF

Growing up in the 1950s and 1960s was a comfortable existence. We were the first American generation not to have to worry about food and shelter. The American dream was ours if we wanted it and were willing to work for it. In Ben Hogan's terms, we were all *rich kids*. For me, growing up in golf meant making a few pars, bogeys, and birdies in the game of life.

I grew up in a family of seven children in Fort Wayne, Indiana. We lived in a century-old brick home in a lower-income diocese of the Most Precious Blood Catholic Church. The house had three bedrooms and one bathroom. It had no heat source upstairs other than the grates my father cut into the flooring to allow the warmer air from downstairs to rise upstairs. It kept our bedrooms at just above freezing in the wintertime.

Although neither of our parents went to college, six out of seven of us kids graduated from college with honors, and four have advanced degrees. The one who did not go to college ended up more successful in the corporate world than the lot of us. Each of us had a specialty where we shined in the eyes of our parents. My specialty was golf, and golf was the basis for the special bond I shared with my father. I wanted to be a professional golfer as he once was, and if I could not do that, then I wanted to work in the golf business. As it turned out, I was not good enough to play golf for a living, but I eventually was able to earn a living in the golf industry.

Perhaps my most cherished golfing moment with my father was when I arranged for the Ben Hogan Tour (now the Web.com Tour) to come to Fort Wayne. This was the new PGA Tour circuit for up-and-coming players. John Daly and Tom Lehman were in the field that year at the Orchard Ridge Country Club, where my dad had once been the club professional.

Playing golf with my dad in the pro-am could not have been a more poignant experience, except for the four golf clubs he broke in two separate attempts to drive the golf cart under the gallery ropes. (I did not know that a nylon gallery rope could snap the heads right off golf clubs in that manner. The clubheads were flung back and skyward as if launched from a slingshot.) Fortunately, no one was hurt. My son Ben, who was about seven at the time, was riding with his grandfather and wore a look that was either fear or mortification. I told him that it was okay; we still had a whole bagful of clubs.

One of the more memorable moments that day came when Dad ran into a childhood buddy who had caddied with him around the time of the stock market crash. We had just finished playing in the pro-am, and this fellow called him over. Dad didn't recognize him, and his friend would not have recognized Dad except that our names were in the tournament program. I invited him to join us on the clubhouse patio for a drink, and the two former caddies reminisced about golf in the late 1920s and early 1930s.

Naturally, the former loopers fell to talking about various golfers for whom they had caddied "way back when." One got a particular going-over. My dad punctuated it by saying, "There's a guy who *never* had a bad lie in the rough." They shared a rueful laugh, remembering someone who had cheated at golf some sixty years ago. It was an unfortunate epitaph for the man, because it revealed more about his character than any of a thousand good deeds he may have done over the course of his life. "Golf gives you an insight into human nature," Grantland Rice once observed; "your own, as well as your opponent's."

Thanks to my father, I realized my childhood dream. While I never played golf professionally, I did make golf my profession, working my way from one exciting challenge to another during the golf industry's most compelling era ever.

My dad, Bud Hueber, turned pro when he was sixteen. In those days, the United States Golf Association (USGA) rules concerning amateur status didn't offer any choice. If you worked in a golf shop after the age of sixteen you became a golf professional whether you were planning to or not. My father did not make much of a living in the golf trade, but with the Great Depression bogging everything down, he was always proud he had a job—even one that paid a dollar a day. If the job had any perks, they came in the form of shop talk and the occasional tall tale.

Dad was a skilled clubmaker who kept the old Scottish craft alive. He worked with raw hickory, malleable iron, and long strips of tanned leather. I loved hearing him describe how a pro knew how to build a club *and* how to swing one. If you got both sides of the equation right, there was no greater satisfaction than the sweet, true feeling of a properly struck one iron coming up the hickory shaft into the player's hands. He told me step by step how he built a custom set of golf clubs, wrapping the leather grip and sanding down the hickory shaft to make it flexible in just the right spots. Golf equipment felt lighter and whippier in your hands back then, requiring golfers to make a slower swing and use their hands and wrists more actively.

New Pro Here

FRED (BUD) HUEBER.

HUEBER PRO AT NO. HIGHLANDS

Succeeds Jim Wagner; Takes Over Monday

Fred (Bud) Hueber, one of the best young golfers in the city, will be the new pro at the North Highlands golf course, it was announced yesterday by Godfrey Gladbach, secretary of the North Highlands Golf club. Hueber will succeed Jim Wagner, who is leaving Sunday for San Antonio, Tex., and will take over his new duties Monday.

Ever since Hueber graduated from North Side high school in 1935 he has been actively interested in golf and has had considerable experience in the last four years. He was assistant to Sam Wearley when North Highlands first opened in 1932 and later was assistant to Dewey Sommerville for three years. Last year he was with Sommerville in Rockton, Ill., until the latter part of the season when he returned here to work with Porter Pace, who was then the pro at North Highlands.

Hueber is a fine golfer and is popular with the younger players in the city which should prove a valuable asset to North Highlands. Hueber plans several improvements at the course, particularly in the condition of the layout. He plans to clean up the course in general, mow the rough and to place it in the best condition possible.

At twenty-two, my dad got his first job as a head pro at North Highlands golf course. When I asked him about the two-tone golf shoes in the picture, he said he also had a pair of black street shoes, but used the two-tone shoes (sans metal golf spikes) for swing dancing with mom. *Originally published in the* Fort Wayne News-Sentinel, *July 1939.*

But the men who made the clubs and taught you how to swing them had some hard conditions to bear. Golf professionals were not even allowed inside the clubhouse at private clubs. To the elite members of a private-club world, pros were considered hired help, no matter what their skills as players might be. Walter Hagen, the charismatic playboy golfer, instigated a change in those attitudes and paved the way for golf professionals to eventually be allowed inside the clubhouses. He was once quoted as saying, "I don't want to be a millionaire; I just want to live like one."

My dad told me of a time from his early club professional days when he walked alongside Walter Hagen during an exhibition in the summer of 1938. (Back then, the top pros made more money playing exhibitions, because there was not enough to be made in tournament prize money.) Hagen wanted to hit his approach shot into a greenside bunker so he could demonstrate how to play a proper sand shot. He missed the greenside bunkers on two consecutive holes, however, landing his ball on the green both times.

"The Haig" turned to my dad, very frustrated, with beads of sweat on his forehead, and obviously suffering from the rigors of the previous night's misadventures. He said, "Buddy, I have some advice for you."

Of course, Dad perked up for any wisdom his idol might impart (Dad was a twenty-three-year-old club pro at the time) and replied, "Yes, Mr. Hagen?"

"Always drink Scotch," Hagen replied. "You'll never get a hangover like you do with that god-awful gin."

Bud Hueber only drank Scotch from that day forward.

***

Dad introduced me to the game when I was very young. He took me to the Goodwill store to pick out a set of old Walter Hagen clubs that he could cut down to my size. They had steel shafts painted a mustard-yellow color to make them look more like wooden shafts. He refinished the woods to reveal the grain and luster. I thought they were the most beautiful golf clubs that were ever made.

He would not let me play on the golf course right away. So I put some cans in the ground to make golf holes in my backyard greens and fashioned my own course. There were three holes; the longest was twenty "kid" paces. I wasn't strong enough to push the mower and cut the greens down to a puttable length, but that didn't matter. As far as I was concerned, my first golf course rivaled Augusta National.

My introduction to golf was as a caddie at the Elks Country Club in Fort Wayne. I was a rotten caddie. I was more interested in playing golf. Often, while caddying, if it was not my turn to tend the flag, I would go ahead to the next tee to hit shots while the golfers were putting. My dad scolded me more than a few times about this, but I never paid much attention. I was such a bad caddie that the assistant pro at our club, Dick Leiszer, christened me with the nickname "Hazard," remarking that as a caddie I was just like any other hazard on the golf course. The nickname stuck. Everyone called me Hazard or "Haz" for short, until I finally went away on a golf scholarship to Florida State University (FSU). I never told anyone at FSU what my nickname was.

My cousin Bill Hinga (who later grew to be six-foot-nine and play basketball for Notre Dame during the Austin Carr era) and I managed to get into more trouble than anyone should in the subdued environment of a golf club. On one occasion, we climbed atop the roof just above the pro shop for a better view of the few girls our age that played golf on Mondays (kids' day at the Elks). We tossed things, never intending to hit anything, but bouncing a golf ball toward Leiszer's white Corvette in the parking lot seemed dicey. We were genuinely surprised they heard us from the pro shop below. Leiszer ran out, yelling at the top of his voice. Bill and I jumped off the roof and took off. Leiszer usually couldn't catch us, but Bill stumbled and fell. I kept on running but started laughing so hard it slowed me down. Meanwhile, Leiszer passed by Bill (on the ground) and caught me with a diving tackle.

The laughter stopped once I realized how angry he was. His twenty-something strength certainly overpowered my twelve-year-old body. At that point in my life, I thought that I was faster than anyone my age, with a strength well beyond my years. Now, as my arm was twisted behind me and my head and face were pushed into the ground, I learned there were certain limits I just had to accept.

"Hazard!" the winded and cigarette-puffing assistant pro yelled, "I am really tired of your shit. You need to straighten up or I am going to tell your dad. No . . . I am going to tell your dad anyway."

I pleaded with him not to say anything, and I promised to change my ways, if he just wouldn't tell my dad, which he never did.

I cleaned up my act, at least as well as I could, but I never did get much better as a caddie. I had motivational problems. I liked to play golf, mess around, and hunt for golf balls in the creek and weeds, and like most kids, I would rather play than work. Being a caddie was just a way to get some spending money. On Wednesdays and weekends, I usually caddied for a group of regulars—Macedonians. They were men of Macedonian descent and worked primarily in the restaurant business. They played a particularly demonstrative version of the game.

The Macedonians had ways to communicate their scores with their teammates in the foursomes either ahead of or behind them. The signal for help was to raise both hands to the sky and look upward to the heavens, or to wave a white towel in a dramatic fashion, as if trying to signal an airplane high in the sky. The signal for making a birdie was to place your right or left hand over your balls and do a few short, knee-bending squats. If someone happened to make an eagle, that squat turned into a frog-hopping, ball-grabbing jump for joy. With this system, they never needed scoreboards to know how they stood on all of their bets by the round's end.

My cousin Bill and I knew how much each of them paid their caddies. Most of them were pretty cheap, paying between two dollars and two dollars and fifty cents for 18 holes. They all had their quirks. My favorite was Mel Hayes, an imposing man, some six foot two and well over 220 pounds. He prided himself on how far he could hit the golf ball and constantly complained that the only reason the pros hit it so far was they had better golf equipment. Hayes's best trick was to take a nine iron or some other high-lofted club and hood it to de-loft the clubface to make it go farther. Then, he could impress everyone with what little club he needed on a par-3 hole. Usually, he hit a low, boring hook over the green and lamented to his playing opponents that he couldn't believe a nine iron was too much club. Everyone else used a seven iron or more and was duly impressed with Hayes's golfing prowess. He also hit very few par-3 holes in regulation, never putted for birdies, and almost never had a skin against his shorter-hitting opponents.

Hayes's biggest problem was his temper. He threw his clubs in fits of anger. Sometimes those tossed clubs came your way, and if you got hit, he felt guilty and would give you a tip over his standard fare of two dollars. I was pretty good at dodging golf clubs, having had a good deal of experience as a pin setter in the wintertime at my grandfather's bowling alley. I knew how to get out of the way of an errant golf club. But I also knew that I could *take* a hit. Getting hit by one of Hayes's tosses was worth at least a buck or two, especially, if I rolled over, winced in pain, grabbed my leg, and feigned a limp for the rest of the round.

My cousin and I also constantly vied to caddie for Bill Eschoff, the one big spender among the Macedonians. He paid three dollars and bought you a hot dog and a soft drink at the turn. Some thirty years later, I ran into Eschoff at the Fort Wayne Ben Hogan Tour event and thanked him for his kindness and generosity. I bought him a drink, which he seemed to appreciate.

I knew my days as a caddie were numbered when I almost killed my dad.

As a special treat, my dad occasionally rented a golf cart, and I worked as the forecaddie. They had the old Cushman electric golf carts at the Elks— maybe a dozen or so—steel tanks that could survive a demolition derby. If they had a heavy charge the night before, they might make 18 holes. They had three wheels and a steering column with a metal bar in the shape of a shoe-string bow. Officially, I was not allowed to drive the golf carts because of my age, but once I got out of the view of the golf shop, I considered my training as a vehicular driver underway.

The 15th hole at the Elks is a downhill par 5 with a creek crossing the fairway about 100 yards short of the green. From there, the green is perched high up on a hill. My dad hit his shot onto the green from 110 yards out. My uncle Bill (young Bill's dad) had already played his shot to the green. I jumped into the golf cart and started driving. As I crossed the narrow bridge across the creek and started up the steep hill, my dad yelled, "Wait and let me take the cart up the hill." I didn't listen and pressed the gas pedal to climb the hill. There wasn't much of a charge left, however, and the golf cart only made it three-quarters of the way up. Next, my dad yelled, "Don't take your foot off the gas, and just put your other foot on the brake!"

Of course, I did just the opposite. The golf cart started going backward down the hill. I jumped out and watched the steering bar swing sideways, back and forth, as the cart veered backward down the hill toward my dad and uncle. Dad jumped one way; my uncle dove in the other direction. The golf cart barely missed them. It ended up in the creek, just missing the bridge I had crossed moments earlier.

My dad stormed up the hill where I lay and asked if I was okay. I was. I then started apologizing, but he interrupted, "It wasn't your fault, I should not have let you drive it in the first place. I am just thankful that no one was hurt." I was so shaken by the incident that I really do not remember how it turned out, except that I had to carry doubles for the last three holes. No one said anything about it, but it was quite a while before I was ever again allowed to drive a golf cart.

My early education as a golfer was fraught with the trials and tribulations that every young person who dreams of being a sports star has. I just knew that I was going to be a pro golfer—it was my destiny. I was as unsophisticated in my quest as Gilda Radner in her *Saturday Night Live* skit, "The Judy Miller Show." In retrospect, my delusions of grandeur were humorous in their naïveté and sad in their sincerity.

Our Monday junior program at the Elks was the cradle for those dreams. By the way, the Elks Junior Golf program was run by Dottie Wiltse Collins, who was none other than the model for the fictional Dottie character on whom they loosely based the movie, *A League of Their Own*. The real Dottie was a pitcher for the Fort Wayne Daisies, which was one of the teams in the All American Girls Professional Baseball League. She won twenty or more games in her four years, with a career ERA of 1.83. In her best year, 1945, she had a 29-10 record with seventeen shutouts. She was also quite a golfer, winning many Fort Wayne Women's City Championships, and she was partly responsible for my initial understanding of the Rules of Golf and how to compete and conduct myself on the golf course.

***

As a kid, I feared the Sisters of the Providence, wardens of the Most Precious Blood Grade School. They were relentless in their pursuit of order and discipline. Hidden within their habits, beneath their medieval veils and draped layers of gray and black cloaks, were beings with eyes in the backs of their heads and supersonic hearing. Their ability to spot bad behavior and hear the slightest mischievous noise can only be explained as one of the Mysteries of Faith (a tenet always cited to explain the unexplainable in our catechism classes). Most nuns carried a ruler in their oversized sleeves. The purpose of that ruler was not to be able to measure something or draw a straight line at a moment's notice; the purpose was to enforce the rules without mercy. My knuckles were rapped for crimes that I did not commit, but if I dared to withdraw my hands during the meting out of punishment, that punishment was doubled until I finally submitted.

As scary as the nuns were to me, I was even more afraid of the lioness down the street. Believe it or not, four doors down from my house on 535 Huffman Street lived a female lion. All the neighborhood kids saw the sign on the chain-link fence bordering the alley that read, *Beware of Lion*. The gas man verified it. He told our mother to keep us far away from that house, and he refused to read the meter there.

Reportedly, the lioness spent most of her adolescence in the basement until she got too big to manage. Supposedly, she was tame and used to people. I saw her one day from the alley behind the house. The lioness had a thick leather collar with a chain leash that was attached to a steel cable, which also served as a clothes line. I was both intrigued and terrified of this lioness tied precariously to that perilously thin steel line. Defying the gas man's warning, I stood in the alley, mesmerized by this boy-eating beast. I began to reason that this lioness had to be tame and was apparently a docile animal, just out for a little sun.

Then the lioness turned and looked at me. She growled the deepest and most penetrating sound I had ever heard. I turned and ran. I ran home on that cinder-track alley faster than I had ever run before. I didn't stop until I was upstairs and safely in my bedroom with the door locked behind me. Not even Leiszer could have caught me that day. A couple of weeks later, the police were all over our neighborhood with rifles. The lioness had broken free from her tenuous confines. After that day, the lioness was gone. Just for effect, they kept the Beware of Lion sign on the chain-link fence.

From the age of eight through thirteen, I managed to have some sort of physical accident every year or so. At eight, I fractured my tailbone when I parachuted off my cousin Bill's swing set and landed on my backside. When I hit the ground, it hurt so badly that at first, I could not scream. I made up for it later and was so embarrassed about falling off a kiddie swing set that I lied and told the doctor and nurses I had fallen out of a tree.

I broke my thumb and wrist playing baseball when I was struck by a pitch while batting; a year later, I fractured my skull as a catcher in Little League when the batter swung around and clubbed me in the head. This was before they put helmets on catchers. I remember stumbling down the first-base line, holding my head, with blood spurting everywhere. My GE (General Electric) Little League team was playing Allen Dairy, and my mom was on her way to the game when the ambulance passed her car. She turned to my sister Becky and said, "I hope that's not David on his way to the hospital again."

About a year later, I got hit by a car and was thrown twenty-five or thirty feet. Fortunately, I was riding my sister Julie's bike. It was a girl's bike, without the bar a boy's bike has. Instead of catching my leg on the bar, I was pushed past the bike and missed being crumpled under the car along with the bike. Not too long after that, I broke my leg playing football in the Catholic Youth Organization league for Precious Blood grade school. I probably broke my nose more than most boys, because it was a large target, and I got into a few more fights than I should have. I can't say there was any benefit to any of these experiences, except to say I learned early on it was far better to fight, maybe even get hit, than be afraid to fight.

I often wondered why I was so accident prone during my youth. Perhaps it was because I never cared about getting in trouble, yet when I did, the worst thing that could happen from my vantage point would be for someone to tell my dad or mom. My brother and five sisters were all excellent students, and I almost flunked the fourth grade. My problem was I could not read very well, and my fourth grade teacher, Mrs. Falby, did not like me—or Gary Walker. I could understand why she didn't like Gary; I didn't like him very much either. We got into a fight after school at least once or twice a month. But she didn't seem to like me, and I felt her wrath on my backside more than once. She had one of those fraternity paddles that really stung. I usually got into trouble for talking or not paying attention, and I probably frustrated her no end. I was the student who stammered and stumbled across every word when reading aloud. Mrs. Falby always said I wasn't trying hard enough.

I finally learned to read in the fifth grade. I even remember sounding out my first word: *pen-man-ship*. My fifth-grade teacher, Mrs. Mahon, cheered me on as I read the flash card. I had finally unraveled the mystery of sounding out a word with more than one syllable. Mrs. Mahon, an elderly, gray-haired lady, told me I could be "row captain" with a little effort. Every night after school, I swept the classroom floor and cleaned the chalk erasers. When I finished, she and I would review flash cards and then read books aloud. She told me I was intelligent, and I was soon elevated to row-captain status. By the end of the year, I was one of the best students in the class. I felt better about myself, had a great deal more confidence, and had this wonderful lady to thank for it.

This might sound silly, but it was significant for me that for the first time my education in school was on par with my education as a golfer. Life went on. By the summer of 1965, I started caring about things that did not seem to matter much before. I even tried to be a better caddie. Once I knew that I could do something as well as my siblings, I had the confidence to give everything my best effort. The early teenage summers breezed by. Eventually, my dad got me a job working on the golf course maintenance crew at the Elks. He was responsible for hiring the course superintendent, Chuck Blumenhurst, so

Chuck owed him a favor.

The problem was I wasn't old enough to operate power equipment. The only thing I could do was physical labor: hand raking sand traps, sickling weeds on the hillsides where it was too steep to mow, pulling weeds, digging ditches, syringing greens, etc. Eventually, I was allowed to handle power equipment, but with caution. As everyone at the club knew, I had nearly killed my dad, and I was pretty sure that I killed the Cushman golf cart.

Actually, I really liked working on the golf course. I never minded manual labor and never got bored with mundane chores. I learned how to get lost in my own thoughts, and I took pride in my work. Once I was allowed to mow greens, I did my best. My fellow workers and I competed over who finished first and who had the straightest and best mower lines. After work, I would go to the clubhouse, take a shower, and begin practice. I usually hit several bags of shag balls and then practiced my chipping and putting. I played until dark. Before I could drive, I hitched a ride home. Usually, one of the members just leaving the bar gave me a ride. Later, I had a Honda 50cc motor scooter. Summers were great fun, just as long as there was enough sunlight to accomplish what I needed to do to become a tour pro.

Occasionally, I got to play in golf tournaments. I was getting better as a golfer, and I knew it. I copied my dad's swing, and he gave me tips when he could. My secret objective was to surprise everyone with my golfing skills. My ambition became a reality at the Elks Junior Club Championship. I was paired with Bill Schumaker, who was a couple of years older and would someday win the PGA Club Professional Championship. The other two in the group were Barry Wilkinson, a long hitter by virtue of his competitive baton twirling and physical superiority (you never kidded him about baton twirling), and Rod Butler, the world's greatest flop-shot artist (whose first job as an adult was being what is now known as a sanitation engineer).

My golf round on that tournament day was stealthy. I didn't say much, because if they noticed I was sneaking up on them, both Schumaker and Wilkinson could beat me handily. By the time we got to the last hole, Butler was well into a round in the low 80s, in spite of his artistry with a wedge around the greens; Wilkinson would shoot in the high 70s and had already broken his fancy Hogan Sure Out sand wedge after scalding a shot over the green; and Schumaker and I were both two over. I chipped in on the last hole for 73. Schumaker was pissed. He hit the green in two and missed a ten-foot putt for birdie to tie. When they gave me the trophy, Bill leaned over and said, "If I had known that the trophy was going to be that big, I would have never let you win." It was the greatest compliment he could have ever given me.

As my golf game continued to improve, I advanced from local to statewide events. One of the most memorable was the Indiana Amateur Championship at Otter Creek Golf Course in Columbus, Indiana. Mickey Powell was the golf professional there and would someday become the president of the PGA (our paths would cross again when I worked for the PGA Tour).

What was memorable about this tournament in the summer of 1968 was that the two finalists for the championship were Bill Schumaker (Elks Junior Golf Championship runner-up) and Bill Kratzert, who would go on to play the PGA Tour, win four tournaments, and become a golf commentator for ESPN. The interesting thing about the whole affair was that Schumaker, Kratzert, myself and two other friends, Pete Clarke and Kent Frandsen (a.k.a. "Fish") and I all stayed in the same Holiday Inn room. There were two double beds in that room with two of us sleeping in each bed. The fifth person (we took turns) slept on the floor, using the cushions from the couch as bedding. Our shared room rent, including taxes, was just under four dollars a day. Kratzert won that final, 36-hole match, soundly defeating Schumaker. Both Clarke and Frandsen later became lawyers, and Fish won the Indiana Amateur Championship in 1983. He was eventually placed in the Indiana Golf Hall of Fame, along with Schumaker and Kratzert.

That final match attracted many fans from Fort Wayne. Our hotel room arrangement had made the papers, and we were all celebrities of a sort. I remember walking the last nine holes with Dottie Collins, who had driven down from Fort Wayne with some friends from the Elks. As Kratzert was drubbing Schumaker, Dottie prophetically remarked, "Kratzert hits the ball like a tour pro; 'Shoe' [as we all called Schumaker] just doesn't have the game to beat him."

Before this event, Kratzert would have been considered the least likely among the five hotel roommates to win. He barely qualified for the tournament, shooting a 79 and winning a five-way playoff. Obviously, Kratzert was much better than we had all imagined, and winning the Indiana State Amateur Championship catapulted him to the next level.

Kratzert also won the Indiana State Open the next year, the youngest ever to do so. He proved himself to be a nationally ranked player. His dad, Bill Kratzert Sr., was the head golf professional at the premier country club in town, the Fort Wayne Country Club. After winning the Indiana State Open, Bill Kratzert Jr. went on the big-time amateur circuit. Occasionally, Kratzert and I roomed together at some state junior tournament, but he was now basically out of my league. One time Tom Kelley, son of Jim Kelley, the richest man in Fort Wayne, joined us. I roomed once with both Bill and Tom at the Indiana State Junior at the Purdue University golf course in Lafayette, Indiana. Jim Kelley drove us down in a Buick Riviera from one of his dealerships. It was the swankiest car I had ever seen.

Kratzert arrived later that day, and did not have a chance to play a practice round on the Purdue course. He was good and really did not need to play a practice round in order to qualify. Surprisingly, he barely made it into the match-play field. Both Kelley and I beat him, which had to bother him. Kratzert seemed subdued that evening at dinner. He was worn out. He had just finished the Sunnehanna Amateur, which was his third or fourth event in a row. The Indiana State Junior really didn't pique his interest as it did ours.

We all lost our first-round matches. Rocky Schooley beat me in a close match and went on to win the State Junior that year. When I got back to our hotel room, Kratzert was sitting on one of the beds, slouched over, looking downward, like he was about to throw up. He was mumbling something. I said, "Bill, how did you do today?" I noted that I had lost my match and said, "The guy I played was pretty good, but I should have beaten him." Kratzert then mumbled something that I just couldn't understand, so I said, "Bill, did you win your match today or not?"

Kratzert then said in what I can only describe as a weary gasp, "Hush Puppies."

"What did you say?" Kratzert didn't answer, so I asked him again, "What did you say?"

"Okay!" and almost shouting, Kratzert cried out, "The son-of-a-bitch who beat me wore Hush Puppies!" The indignity of such a cruel loss was more than Kratzert could bear. He had been beaten by a golf nerd.

5

EDUCATION
OF A GOLFER

Though somewhat exotic and definitely foreign to my family's socioeconomic status, I was an overseas exchange student in Bogotá, Colombia, during my junior year of high school. It was a private family exchange. My sister, Cindy, and my brother, Tom, had both stayed with the Marin family in Bogotá. One of their daughters, Marta, also lived at our home for about a year. When I think back on it, it was amazing we had room for Marta in our modest three-bedroom, one-bath, century-old brick farm house. My mom and dad had one bedroom; my brother Tom and I shared another; and the girls shared two double beds in the third bedroom. The girls slept two heads up and one head down in the same bed.

Marta became a member of our family during her stay, and we all loved her, especially my mom, who had someone to help with the housework. Marta liked me too, because I smelled so good. Actually, I smelled like a donut because every morning during my freshman year in high school, I worked before dawn at the bakery and then returned home. Marta always gave me a big hug, inhaling deeply to take in the sweet, lingering aroma of baked goods. Also, I usually had free samples.

By the time Marta left, it had been arranged for me to go to Bogotá and stay with the Marin family. I had minimal expenses and had saved money working summers on the golf course, at the bakery before school, and at the bowling alley setting pins in the winter. All I had to pay was the airfare and any incidental expenses. In the fall of 1967, I would attend the Universidad Javeriana to learn Spanish, and I'd play golf at the Los Lagartos Country Club. I would miss my junior year in high school and join the class behind me, which was fine with me since I was young for my grade.

I really did not have a clue what the journey would be like. I had never flown on a plane and knew very little Spanish. My folks drove me to Cleveland where I had a flight to Atlanta. In Atlanta, I took another flight to Miami, arriving around midnight. My flight to Bogotá the next morning was at 8:00 a.m. on Aero Condor airlines, which roughly translated means Buzzard Airlines. There would be one stopover in Barranquilla, Colombia, for refueling.

I spent the night in the Miami airport unable to sleep. I was afraid that if I fell asleep I might miss my flight. Back then, you picked your seat at the departure gate, so I had to sleep close by on the plastic seating affixed in rows to the floor. When it was time to check in, they had a picture of the plane's seating layout with a sticker for each seat. Once you had your sticker attached to your ticket, you were all set to go.

In those days, there was little airport security. The flight on the big-prop plane from Miami to Barranquilla was uneventful, except that we flew over Cuba. That was cool because American planes did not cross Cuban air space due to all the hijackings at the time. Also, in the late 1960s, we weren't too many years removed from the Cuban missile crisis.

What wasn't cool was the stopover in Barranquilla, perhaps one of the hottest places on the earth. It is located in the steamy lowlands of Colombia's north coast and not far from the equator. Upon landing at the Barranquilla airport, when I first reached the plane's doorway to exit I felt as if someone had just thrown a hot, wet blanket on me. The air was very warm, thick, and wet. As I stepped down the stairway to the tarmac and followed the other passengers, I could see their footprint impressions in the asphalt ahead of me. All I wanted was to get into the airport air-conditioning and get a Coke while they refueled the airplane.

Much to my dismay, the airport terminal was not air-conditioned. They had a few ceiling fans to stir the hot air. I ordered a *Coca-Cola con ielo* (with ice). They gave me one of the classic, eight-ounce bottles which was refreshingly lukewarm. I quickly gulped it down and then almost threw up. At this point, after no sleep and no opportunity to freshen up, my face felt sticky from the cola, and I could almost feel my oily, sixteen-year-old face breaking out. By the time we got back on the plane, it had been baking on the tarmac for almost an hour.

The stewards (all male) wore white shirts with epaulettes. They were sweating so badly their shirts turned translucent. You could see their tank-top undershirts. The passengers yelled for the plane to get moving and take off so we could get some cooler air into the plane from the higher altitudes. By the time we arrived in Bogotá on that elevated plateau in the Andes, we had all dried out, though none of us smelled very fresh. As I left the plane, I was greeted with a cool breeze.

I was worried my Colombian caretakers might not be there, so I had their address written on a piece of paper. As an added precaution, I had memorized it. My plan was to take a cab if they missed my flight. I rehearsed their address in Spanish so many times that I remember it to this day: *Calle trienta nueve B, con diez y ocho A, zero ocho.* As I left customs with my luggage and golf clubs in tow, I wearily walked out of a tunnel to the terminal waiting area and saw a very welcome face. It was Marta, dressed impeccably in a dark suit and high heels, along with her family. It looked like they were dressed for church. She ran over to me with a big smile and gave me a hug, saying, "David [accent the first syllable: Dah'vid] welcome to Colombia!" She then paused, took a big sniff and winced, "You don't smell so good. You always used to smell so good." She was right. I didn't smell like a donut, I smelled more like a gym bag, and my big adventure south of the equator was just beginning.

The Marin house had three bedrooms, a bathroom, and a small den upstairs. The three girls (Clemencia, Marta and Gloria) slept in one bed, like Marta did when she stayed at our house: two heads up, one down. Marta's parents, Esmiraldo and Eiuhenia Marin, slept in another bedroom. Her brother Jorge and I slept in the third upstairs bedroom. There was a grandmother who lived there, but she slept somewhere on the first floor close to the quarters where the two servants stayed.

The Marins were an upper-class family, but did not have much money. Mr. Marin had a small accounting practice. Their home was part of a series of what we might describe as attached red-brick townhomes with common areas sandwiched among them. Just adjacent to the kitchen was a communal area with what looked like a shallow, tiled swimming pool with faucets placed at various points around it. Here, the servants hand washed the laundry, rinsed the garments under a faucet, and then hung them on a line to dry. They would not let me go into the kitchen or the common area. After my first uninvited visit, I was briskly shooed away thereafter.

I spent my first week at the Marins in the bathroom. Evidently, I did not adjust very well to the bacteria in their water. Having thoroughly verified that the water in the toilet swirls clockwise south of the equator, I was eventually able to venture out and see how these people lived. Initially, I just walked around the block, gradually expanding my forays until I deciphered that the city was divided into numbered streets (*calles*) and avenues (*carreras*). Once I figured this out, I could easily navigate my way around the neighborhood. One day I came upon a bookstore that sold magazines, newspapers, and miscellaneous supplies. I bought a *Time* magazine and a spiral notebook. The notebook was actually my brother Tom's idea. He said I should keep a journal on my life and times in South America, which I started that day.

Living in Colombia with another family for about a year had a significant impact on me. I learned to be independent, more responsible, and self-reliant. I also learned to speak Spanish and experienced a different culture. At the Universidad Javeriana, there was a fellow there from Libya, maybe a year or two older than me. We struck up a friendship and played ping-pong at the college. He couldn't speak English, and I couldn't speak Arabic, but we communicated in Spanish and got along just fine.

I began reading voraciously for the first time in my life. I read everything I could find in English at that bookstore, from *Time* magazine to a used paperback collection of Shakespeare's plays. I would like to say I was pursuing academic excellence, but the truth was the Marin family only had a black-and-white TV, and everything was in Spanish. I needed other forms of entertainment. But I watched what I could and eventually began to understand what they were saying. The *Mission Impossible* TV show was dubbed into Spanish, and I could pretty much understand the dialogue. The really funny program was *Perry Mason*. The dubbed voice for Perry Mason was a baritone, which was okay, but the voice for Paul Drake, his private investigator, was very high and effeminate. I thought this was hilarious, but the Marins just could not understand why I thought it was so funny. The Marins also had a hi-fi, which is a fancy name for a crappy record player. I had one album, *Sgt. Pepper's Lonely Hearts Club Band*, that was purchased at a small market in downtown Bogotá.

There are only two social classes in Colombia: the upper and the lower. The Marin family was upper class even though they had a lower-middle-class income. Class distinctions were not strictly along economic lines. The Marins spoke a version of Spanish that they called *Castillano* from Spain, not *Indio* (Indian), or what they described as sounding the way the lower class spoke. One of the greatest compliments you could give a new mother about her infant child was that the baby was *so* white—again, not dark-skinned like the Indios.

There were so many things that were foreign to my life experiences as a Hoosier. For example, during holidays, the young people did not go their separate ways as is common in the states. They all celebrated together. It was not unusual to see a son dancing with his grandmother, mom, or sisters, while teenagers would be mortified to do the same back home. Also of particular interest to me was that teenagers were allowed to drink alcohol. They were served alcohol at family functions, and no one batted an eye. A family friend, Pablo Escobar (no relation to the drug lord) once invited me to join him at the country club for a teen dance. I was picked up in the family car. The driver took Pablo and me to the party. We danced with the girls, drank rum and Coke—probably too much—and then put all of the charges, including two bottles of rum (smuggling one for later use), on the family club bill. When the dance was over, the driver picked up two shit-faced sixteen-year-olds and delivered them home—nauseous but safe and sound.

The gap between the rich and the poor was most evident at the country club. The Marin family secured a special membership for me at the Los Lagartos Country Club—the finest club in Bogotá. It was so much cooler than the Fort Wayne Country Club. It had everything from clay tennis courts to wet and dry saunas, an Olympic-sized swimming pool, billiard and pool rooms, a great golf course, two practice areas with greens and bunkers—everything imaginable. My membership cost was about twenty-three dollars a month. I had died and gone to upper-class golf heaven. I went from raking sand traps and mowing greens at the Elks to a lifestyle well beyond my wildest dreams. I had a glimpse of what Tom Kelley's life (my wealthy Fort Wayne friend) was like. I may have had one foot in the front door, but I also had one foot stuck out the back. I had trouble reconciling the class disparity both at home and abroad. Sometimes everything isn't what it seems to be, and I had some difficulty simply looking away.

My daily trip to the Los Lagartos Country Club (except on Monday when the club was closed) involved taking the big Russian electric tram bus, then a transfer to another smaller bus. A special club bus took me the final four miles. The journey was about an hour one way. The things I saw along the way gave me pause. I remember being in back of the Russian electric bus watching ten-year-old kids stand on the bus's back bumper, hanging onto the cables for a free ride as the bus sped along. And I would see children sleeping in cardboard boxes. Just off to the side of the road, a young boy might be standing there in the open, pants down to his knees, peeing. No one paid attention or seemed to care. On one trip home, the Russian bus was so packed with people that we all kept getting pushed back beyond the back-door exits. I missed my bus stop. Not until some three kilometers later did I manage to fight my way back to the exit door.

At the Los Lagartos Country Club, though, I was in wonderland. The food was great and inexpensive, even by my standards. For a special treat, I might have some Argentine baby beef for lunch. You could cut it with your fork and it only cost about a dollar. It came with bite-sized, fried yellow potatoes and a salad. The yellow potatoes were delicious. One day, when I was playing golf with some friends, I noticed several men on horseback with M-16s strapped to their shoulders. I asked what they were doing and was told that they worked for the club and were "keeping the bad people out." I later learned that the bad people were the rebels, who later became the army for the drug lords. They were known to periodically plunder the playgrounds of the rich.

One day while playing golf with a friend, Henry (Enrique in Spanish), we took a break between nines and stopped for a snack and a soda. I sat with my golfing buddy, Enrique, and we both had a cold baked potato, which might sound odd, but is really good with just a little salt, like you might put on a hardboiled egg. For a drink, I ordered a *naranha postoban* (orange soda pop) and Enrique ordered a Coca-Cola. As we sat there, Enrique took a long drink of his Coke, turned to me and asked me in Spanish, "Tell me, Dah'vid, do they have Coca-Cola in the United States?"

I was flabbergasted and furiously said, "Of course we do. Coca-Cola is an American product. It's an original! We invented it!"

I said it with such fervor that it was unsettling for Enrique, and he said, "I am sorry, Dah'vid, I didn't mean to offend you."

At this point, I felt like a jerk and had my first lesson in ethnocentrism, although I didn't know what that word meant at the time. I was beginning to understand why Americans are not so well liked when they travel the world. We think that the world revolves around us. We don't understand that we are guests when traveling around the world. It was a lesson I would never forget, but it wasn't over.

The 10th hole at the Los Lagartos Club is a 187-yard, par 3 over water to an elevated green. That sounds long and intimidating, but in the high altitude of Bogotá, the ball flies farther in the thin air. It was never usually more than a six iron, even with my lifeless, British-size, Dunlop-65 golf ball and my Wilson Staff Dynapower blade irons. I managed to hit my shot onto the green, as did Enrique. I retrieved my broken tee and started to walk on the path alongside the water up to the green. My tee was bent and of no further use, so I tossed it into the water. Then, my caddie, who was probably just a year or two younger than me, waded into the cold lake for the tee. I looked over to Enrique; he shrugged his shoulders and said, "He will glue it together, wrap some string around it, and it will be as good as new."

The ugly American had struck again.

***

The Los Lagartos Open was a regular stop on the Caribbean Tour for those players who were not eligible for regular play on the PGA Tour. Also, a number of club pros ventured south to get a little competition while their northern clubs were closed for the winter; however, most of the players were either down-and-out veterans or young, aspiring tour professionals. The exception was Roberto de Vicenzo. He had won the British Open the previous summer. It was probably easy money for him to come to the Los Lagartos Open in February 1968 and not that far from his home compared to playing in Europe or North America.

I first saw de Vicenzo sleeping on a long bench in the men's locker room at the Los Lagartos Country Club. I immediately went over to the attendant to verify that it was him. It was. I sat down nearby and just watched him sleep.

He eventually became aware of my presence, snorted, and rubbed his eyes. "What do you want young man?"

"*Nada*," I replied. Then I said in Spanish, "I am just looking forward to watching you play and learning everything that I can from you."

Mr. de Vicenzo then grumbled something. I am not sure exactly what, but it sounded like, "Go ahead and learn what you can." I asked him if I could watch him practice and play, and he said, "That's why I am here."

Later that day, he and the head golf professional at the Los Lagartos, Miguel Sala, played a pretournament practice round. I kept my distance but watched every shot. Sometime during the latter part of the round, I started walking alongside Sala and de Vicenzo. I listened to their conversation, but my Spanish was not quite good enough to grasp the nuances of their golf talk.

On the 17th hole, a 160-yard, uphill par 3, de Vicenzo buried his 9-iron shot in the bunker, just short of the green. The golf ball looked like it was embedded below the surface of the sand. Mr. de Vicenzo took his sand wedge and pointed the toe of the club at the ball. He then took a short, but firm, swing and popped the ball out to about three feet from the hole. He looked over to me and smiled. My lower jaw was hanging open when he said in Spanish, "It is easier to do it this way, son. Come over and try it. I'll show you."

I looked over to Sala, who by this time had come to where we were, and he indicated without saying anything that it was okay for me to try. Mr. de Vicenzo had his caddie toss him a ball. He stepped on it, and handed me his sand wedge.

"Now, what you do is point the toe of the club at the ball and enter the sand about the width of the club behind the ball," he explained. "You do not have to swing hard, and that is the best part about it, because you are only moving a very narrow swath of sand."

I took his club and nervously did what he said. The ball popped out of the buried lie, just like he said. He only smiled and said, "Give me back my wedge." It was a magical moment.

For some bizarre reason I was able to enter the tournament and play with the pros. My previous best adult event had been the Fort Wayne Men's City Golf Championship, where I shot three rounds of 75 to finish in the top fifteen behind Bill Schumaker's older brother Dave (who also was then captain of the Purdue golf team and won the city championship). I was way out of my league at Los Lagartos. Because I could get around that course well enough, I had a one handicap, but I played like most kids played. Par was clearly within my grasp if I could get somewhere near the green in regulation and chip for a birdie. And if I happened to hit the green in regulation, there was a pretty good chance I could make the putt. And if I ever had a putt for an eagle, there was no doubt I would get the ball to the hole—or beyond—in order to give it a chance. "Never up, never in" was the motto for this sixteen-year-old aspiring pro golfer.

If the Los Lagartos Country Club was wonderland, then playing in the Los Lagartos Open was the pinnacle—an equivalent Space Mountain ride for me in that amusement park. I was paired with Al Besselink (once one of the glamour names on the PGA Tour) and a local club professional from the nearby San Andres Golf Club. To describe Besselink as colorful would be an understatement. "Bessie," as his peers called him, was also known as the "Golden Boy" for his shock of blond, wavy hair atop his six-foot-one frame. He was far more famous for his gambling on the links than for his golfing. I didn't know any of that at the time, however.

I only knew he was a famous golfer, and I was going to play 36 holes with him. When I met him on the first hole of the first round, I thought I was standing next to the Adonis of golfdom. He wore a cream-colored cashmere sweater, white golf shirt, shiny gold-colored slacks, and what looked like white with gold trim, leather golf shoes. He looked down at me in my gray slacks and practical blue wool sweater (my other sweater was green) and said, "Good luck, kid. Stay out of my way, stand still, and keep quiet when I am making a shot. I am playing for ten thousand dollars here, and I don't want to be distracted by any of your antics."

I did not know what those antics might be, and I wasn't going to get in his way, but I wasn't going to let him intimidate me either. My dad once told me that "everyone is tied on the first tee. What you do after that is what counts, and that's why they keep score." But even those words of wisdom did not settle the stirrings in my stomach.

The first hole at Los Lagartos was a par 4, some 419 yards long. There was a road down the left side that was out of bounds. The pro from the San Andres Country Club hit a decent shot down the right side. I took my Wilson Staff 3-wood (my persimmon driver was cracked and couldn't be repaired) and hammered it down the middle. Besselink hit it left and out of bounds (OB), and had to reload. His next shot was long and straight. I missed the green with my 175-yard-long second shot and chipped up close for a tap-in par. I immediately scurried over to the next tee, leaving Besselink to sweat over his three-footer for a bogey. He missed it. I was sitting on my golf bag when Besselink finally got to the tee. I was glad I was keeping the other guy's score, because I would have been afraid to ask Besselink what he made (a double-bogey 6).

The next three holes were pretty much the same, except Besselink made two pars and a three-putt bogey to my two pars and chip-in birdie on the fourth hole. He was three over par after four and had hit every green in regulation except for the first where he had hit it OB. I had yet to hit a green in regulation, and I was one under. I exited each green as quickly as I could and then went to the next tee, thinking I was staying out of his way. Besselink, however, was beside himself. His anger mounted with the completion of each hole. We had to wait on the fifth tee. Play was backed up, and this was just the opening Besselink needed to give me a piece of his mind.

He walked over to me and said, "What in the hell do you think you are doing out here?"

I was stunned by this rebuke and couldn't say anything.

"I am out here playing for ten thousand dollars, and you are out here playing high school golf. Whoever taught you how to play golf? Don't you know the first thing about courtesy? On two of my past three putts you were wandering around in the line of my putt!"

I replied defensively, "I was on the next tee."

"That's exactly what I am talking about," he said. "You shouldn't leave the green until all of the players have completed the hole. You don't know anything! Why in the hell did they even let you play in this tournament?" The fairway ahead had cleared and Besselink barked, "It's your turn to play."

By this time, I was shaking and almost in tears. I grabbed my three wood, mindlessly lined up my tee shot, and sprayed it dead right and out of play. I reloaded to play a provisional shot and did it again. By now, it was obvious to everyone how rattled I was. I asked my playing partners to play away while I retrieved another ball.

The group behind us was waiting and had seen all that transpired. I had my face in a towel to hide my tears. After Besselink hit his drive down the middle, he said sternly, "It's your turn, kid. Don't hold up play."

Just then, a fellow in a plantation hat playing in the group behind us intervened. It was PGA Tour player Butch Baird, who was not much bigger than me, but stood much taller and tougher when he said to my tormentor with a slight stutter, "Tha-a-that's enough Bessie. Leave the kid alone. You are playing like shit and blaming the kid." Then he turned to me and said, "Don't pay any attention to him, his bark is far worse than his bite."

I gathered what composure I had left and hit my shot down the middle. Besselink came over to me as we were walking down the fairway and clumsily said, "I am sorry kid. I should not have said what I said. I know that you didn't mean it."

I would have preferred it if he had punched me. I could take a hit because I knew physical pain passes, but I wasn't prepared for this type of emotional pain. I never regrouped mentally that day. In my journal, I noted I shot an 84. I shot a 76 the next day to miss the 36-hole cut by 14 shots. Besselink tried to be nice to me the next day, but I stayed as far away from him as I could, and I never left the green until everyone had completed play.

For the last two days of the tournament, I watched every shot that Roberto de Vicenzo made. The galleries were quite small—only Los Lagartos members and their guests. It was easy to get a good vantage point. Some acknowledgement from Roberto, maybe a wink or a nod as he passed by me several times, would have certainly been nice, but that never happened. What I found most remarkable about de Vicenzo's play was that every part of his game was good on most tees (even though his driver wasn't broken like mine). Obviously, he had other reasons for choosing his three wood: perhaps he hit it straighter or higher or the ball flew nearly as far in the high altitude. By the end of the tournament, de Vicenzo distanced himself from the field and won by about 12 shots.

I never bothered to see how Besselink finished. Baird finished well and made a check. There would be many more lessons to learn during my stay in Colombia, but none would be as cut-to-the-bone as that first day with Besselink. Quite honestly, what bothered me most about the entire matter was that I felt like I didn't handle myself very well. I was embarrassed by my own

During the third round of the Los Lagartos Open, Roberto de Vicenzo was two behind Wilf Homenuik, a Canadian PGA Tour player and winner on the Caribbean PGA Tour's winter season. *Author's collection.*

actions. I felt like I did when I fell off the kiddie swing set when I was eight years old.

After a couple of months or so, I was pretty comfortable in traveling around by myself, although I was told by everyone that I had to be extremely careful. "They will kill you," my brother once warned, "for the money in your pocket." So I kept my big bills in a money belt. Mondays were movie days, since the golf course was closed. I took the Russian tram downtown, saw a Spaghetti Western, bought a magazine or used book, and then headed home. The experience became routine once I was able to overlook things like small children approaching to show me their open wounds as they begged for money. Sometimes they would scratch open a sore on their hands or arms to make it bleed.

Other times they would take a small cloth and wipe my shoe while I stood in line to buy a movie ticket.

Back to High School

When I returned home to Fort Wayne, Indiana, I felt I had learned a great deal and was mature beyond my years. I also knew I was a much-improved golfer, and I looked forward to the next spring when I could challenge Kratzert, Schumaker, and whoever else might be lurking in my competitive future. I returned to school in Fort Wayne in the fall of 1969 as a junior and joined the class originally behind me. Because I had been to a foreign country, I was somewhat of a celebrity at Central Catholic High School. I was elected vice president of the student council. It was the first time in my life I was popular and well known. My fifteen minutes of fame soon faded, however, once the novelty wore off and everyone got to know me a little better.

During that winter, my Aunt Vi, who was the accountant at Lakeside Golf Course, got me a job. This course had the area's first Golf-O-Mat, which is an indoor golf facility with simulators. My job was to turn on the units, explain how they worked, and do some repair work on them. I worked every day. On weekdays, I worked the night shift until about 10:00 or 11:00 p.m., depending upon which industrial golf league or golf club was playing. While I was working, I could go to an empty booth and hit balls or putt most of the time. It was the best job imaginable for a seventeen-year-old stuck in a northern climate with ambitions to play professional golf.

The Golf-O-Mat simulators were unsophisticated by today's standards. The golfer would "hit" a golf ball into a screen that had a projected image of the shot to be played. A microphone underneath a teeing-area brush was activated when the golfer struck the shot. The computer calculated the time it took to activate the microphone and break the light beams along the screen. The distance was then relayed to the projector. It switched to an image of the next shot (at ten-yard intervals). Once the golfer reached the green, she/he could have a five-, ten-, or fifteen-foot putt. It was very high tech for the winter of 1969. We had three simulator courses: Pebble Beach, Congressional, and Doral.

I figured out how to beat the machines. The distance between the microphone and the light beams was shortest on the right-hand side. I got more distance if I hit a low shot on the right side of the screen. I also figured out how every putt broke. I had the record at all three courses, which was 54. You could not shoot a lower score. I knew that I was destined for greatness with those records, but there was a problem. When the snow melted, and I was finally able to hit some practice shots outside, I could not do anything but hit a low hook. The harder I swung, the lower I hit it, and the more it hooked.

It took me most of the spring golf season to straighten out my hook. I played well enough to beat Kratzert in the Indiana State High School Cham-

Among those pictured are (kneeling, second from the left) Kratzert, a five-time winner on the PGA Tour and ESPN golf commentator; (standing) me; Kelley, who roomed with Kratzert and me during the Indiana State Junior Championship (today he is a businessman and race car owner); and Butler, of noted wedge-play fame in the Elks Junior Club Championship. *Originally published in the* Fort Wayne Journal Gazette, *May 14, 1969.*

pionship and was bemused by the *Fort Wayne News-Sentinel* sports headline, "Kratzert Finishes Third in State Tourney." I played in whatever local tournaments I could and still keep my job at Lakeside Golf Course. In the summer, I was the starter there and took care of the golf carts. I also finished second to Bill Schumaker in the Fort Wayne Men's City Championship at the Orchard Ridge Country Club.

***

My senior year in high school was devoid of any significant golfing achievements. I had a pretty low scoring average, won a couple of unimportant events, but that was enough to capture the attention of some colleges. Kratzert deservedly received most of the attention and ended up at the University of Georgia. He later became an All-American.

I was recruited mainly by schools in the Midwest. Western Michigan, Miami of Ohio, Purdue, and Indiana all expressed some serious interest, but I wanted no part of it. I was determined to go to school in the South where I could work on my game all year round. Also, I figured that even if I didn't make it as a pro, I could find a job in the South after graduating. It seemed crazy to me that people worked their entire lives in the dreary northern climes and then spent their final twenty years in Florida. So I wrote every school south of the Mason-Dixon Line. Only a few expressed any interest: notably Vanderbilt, Alabama, and Florida State.

The cost to go to school at Vanderbilt was well beyond my means. Alabama had enough interest to fly me down for a visit. The golf coach there was Steve Sloan, who also served as an assistant football coach. Coach Sloan had been an All-American quarterback at Alabama, played for the Atlanta Falcons, and was an excellent golfer, as I was about to learn.

Alabama did not have its own golf course in those days; they played at the nearby Indian Hills Country Club in Tuscaloosa. I played a round with Sloan and two other members of the golf team. I broke 70, playing my usual round that was adequate from tee to green, but exceptional once I got on the dance floor. I had hand-ground my Ping model putter to exaggerate the heel-toe weight distribution and pretty much made everything. When we were finished and hanging around the clubhouse putting green, Sloan told me he was very impressed with my putting and short game, but that I would need to learn how to hit the ball a little higher.

Just then, an older man drove up in a golf cart. On the side of the cart was written, "To Papa Bear from all of the Baby Bears." The older man, in a plaid woolen Fedora, emerged from the cart and came over to talk with us. He said to me, "Coach Sloan has told me that you are a pretty good golfer, and I want you to know that we intend to have a great golf program here at 'Bama. My goodness, the entire golf team is even going to Scotland to play some great courses and we play the top-notch collegiate events."

I replied, "Yes sir, I would welcome the opportunity to come and play with the best."

Then he grumbled, "Well, then it's settled. I gotta go. Coach Sloan," he said, tipping his hat. Then he went back to his golf cart and drove away.

Sloan turned to me and solemnly said with some exaggerated emphasis, "David...you just met Coach Bear Bryant."

"Yes," I replied, "He seems like a very nice man. What does he coach?" My response was true to form for someone who had lived in South America, focused solely on golf, and only followed Notre Dame and Ara Parseghian football.

Sloan started to laugh. He couldn't contain himself. He fell to his knees laughing. Two members from our foursome (also players on the golf team) came over and asked him what was so funny. He told them, and they started laughing. Pretty soon, it seemed like everyone within earshot of the Indian

Hills putting green was laughing. I thought Sloan was going to start rolling down the hill laughing, but he was able to compose himself, stood up and wiped the tears from his eyes, and said, "I guess that you were really impressed in having met Coach Bryant, the greatest football coach of all time." He then started laughing again. I was embarrassed by my ignorance.

I ended up not going to Alabama. Sloan cut the scholarship offer in half, only leaving me with Florida State as an option for a school in the South. It turned out for the best. Florida State is a great university. To say that I was unprepared for the college experience, however, was an understatement. When I finally arrived a few days before classes, I had missed freshman orientation. I didn't know that you had to register for classes until the FSU golf coach, Scott Fletcher, asked me if my classes were all set. I thought it was like high school, and they just gave you a schedule of classes. It was the last day of registration when I went in to pick my classes. Unfortunately, available class times conflicted with the start of team practice three days a week, which did not endear me to the coach. And I didn't have a car and had to hitch a ride to the off-campus golf course, which made me late three days a week.

I also thought there might be some prejudice against Yankees at Florida, so I was careful not to stand out. The first day in line at the cafeteria breakfast, I patiently waited to be served by the wait staff on the other side of the food bar. When it was my turn, the black woman on the other side of the service line said, "You want some eggs?"

I replied, "Yeah, give me a couple."

Next she asked if I wanted some bacon, and I gave the same reply. Then she said, "Honey, you want some grits?"

"Yeah, give me a couple."

She turned to the woman working next to her and said, "That boy wants a couple grits." They enjoyed my ignorance and called me "Cupa Grits" for the rest of the year and laughed heartily every time. My stealthy profile as a non-Yankee was over before it started.

Later in my freshman year, I ran into Alabama Coach Sloan at the FSU Collegiate Invitational. He remembered me, and shook his head with a wry smile. He was surprised I wasn't playing in the tournament that week, thinking I should have easily made the first team. My college golf career can be summed up quite easily: I played without distinction. I tried my best and practiced hard, but I did not have whatever I needed to play at that level. There almost seemed to be an inverse relationship between effort extended and results achieved. Fortunately, I was smart enough to figure out that if I was not good enough to be one of the better players on the team, or good enough to keep my golf scholarship, then my chances of playing professional golf for a living were not so good.

In accepting my limitations, I looked for other ways to be involved in the game I loved. After graduating with a bachelor's degree in business and again after earning an MBA, I wrote every golf equipment company and golf association and asked for a job. Most did not bother to acknowledge my letter. Those that did, including the PGA Tour, said no thanks. I was willing to work for next to nothing and pay my dues for the privilege of having my avocation and vocation be one and the same. Eventually, I got a job working for the National Golf Foundation (NGF) doing golf course feasibility and operational studies. The pay was not very good, but the opportunity was just what I wanted-ed. Finally, I had my foot in the door of the golf business.

My unsuccessful pursuit to become a professional golfer did yield a significant dividend. While I was not playing golf for a living, I did have a golf game that was better than most, and this helped me achieve my career objectives in ways I never expected.

6

THE GAME CHANGERS

Armed with a freshly minted MBA, ambition, and more chutzpah than common sense, I started working for the National Golf Foundation (NGF) in Memphis. I then relocated to southern California to do golf course development consulting work. I was in the right place at the right time when I moved to Carlsbad. No one knew it at the time, but Carlsbad, California, would become the golf-club-making capital of the world, and I would learn about the business firsthand from some of golf's legendary entrepreneurs like Ping's Karsten Solheim and TaylorMade's Gary Adams. These contacts led to other contacts such as Tom Crowe of Cobra, Ely Callaway of Callaway Golf, and Deane Beman, commissioner of the PGA Tour.

My first golf job following graduate school carried the title Mid-Central Region Director. In that role, I promoted the development and profitable management of both public and private golf courses. Banks, developers, and municipalities were willing to pay a fee for my feasibility studies on golf course projects and my operational analyses for existing golf courses.

Back then, market analysis and economic research for golf course development were rather unsophisticated. The measures used in determining the feasibility of a project were very simplistic, with the rule of thumb being you needed a population of 25,000 to support the operation of an 18-hole golf course. The banks and developers liked my analytical and quantitative approach, which identified the number of golfers, rounds played in the area, competition, market share, and economic impact, etc. As the demand for this consulting work increased, I moved to southern California where more golf courses were being developed. My new job title there was Director of Facility Development.

In those days, the NGF was primarily funded by golf equipment manufacturers. Part of my job was to schmooze with upper-echelon, golf-company executives in my region, which I did gladly. It directly served my ambition to work my way into that part of the golf industry. In those days, there were only a few golf equipment companies in Southern California. Cobra Golf was a fledgling enterprise that only had the Baffler utility wood in its product line. Callaway Golf did not yet exist. Titleist had a small club-assembly operation in Escondido, and TaylorMade had just introduced metal woods to the golf industry, moving from Chicago to Carlsbad in the early 1980s. Over the next ten years or so, many of the top golf equipment companies located their businesses in this part of southern California because that was where the casting houses were first located for metal woods and irons (before the manufacturing of golf club components went offshore). As graphite became the preferred golf shaft, another advantage of locating in this area became evident. There were a large number of aerospace engineers there who had experience working with advanced materials and technology.

I had territorial responsibilities for California, Utah, Nevada, New Mexico, and Arizona. Soon thereafter, I handled golf course development assignments nationwide. Initially, my NGF consulting work required a lot of travel, mostly by automobile. On those long drives, I daydreamed about golf equipment inventions. I rarely turned on the radio, ever lost in contemplating ideas as the miles slipped by. Often, I would find myself at the next destination without realizing how much time had passed, naïvely pleased I had conjured up some fantastic innovation that would enrich me and the world of golf—or at least impress some golf equipment executive enough to offer me a job.

In parochial school, I was the student staring out the window until a nun pulled me from my daydreams with a Catechism question. If I had been born at a later time, they probably would have called it Attention Deficit Disorder (ADD) and prescribed Ritalin. My version of ADD allowed me to enjoy my solitude. When I was a teenager and worked on the golf course maintenance crew, it was almost as if those mundane tasks were a repetitive mantra that allowed my mind to stay on track and wonder wistfully. That served me well in productively passing time when I was by myself, but to this day, I have a difficult time adding a column of numbers, as my mind wanders.

So, with all of this transcendental time during my long drives, it was not long before I had a substantial number of ideas I was certain would bring me fame and fortune. In retrospect, only some of those ideas were marketable. I wrote a letter to Dick Tarlow, then one of the principals of FootJoy (with his brother Bill), just after General Mills had acquired a controlling interest in the company in 1975. Tarlow continued as president of FootJoy until Acushnet Company acquired the company some ten years later. I had played golf with Tarlow at an industry golf outing in 1978. He was a grouchy guy and had one of the shortest and quickest backswings imaginable. That quick swing mirrored his brief assessment and dismissal of the two ideas I presented to him.

My first idea was for golf shoes that provided a better foundation and functioned better when you swung a golf club. This golf shoe was lighter and more comfortable for walking than the traditional golf shoe—a heavy street-dress shoe with steel spikes. What I envisioned was an Earth Shoe and gym shoe combination. For those who don't remember, Earth Shoes were funky-looking walking shoes without heels from the 1970s. They were supposed to be ergonomically preferable to traditional shoes. The absence of an elevated heel, in my view, would promote better balance through the golf swing. In Sam Snead's book *The Education of a Golfer*, he described how he practiced barefooted because it helped him work on his balance during the swing. I figured this idea had to be a real breakthrough in golf shoe performance technology. Who in their right minds really wants to play golf sporting wing tips? Three decades or so later, this idea became the industry standard.

My second idea was for an improved, all-weather golf glove. I had long used Playtex Living Gloves when playing competitive golf in heavy rain. It enabled me to hold onto the club under the worst conditions. The golf club grips were made of a rubber material, as were the Playtex gloves, so the golf club never slipped when wet. My prototype was simple. I used scissors to cut the Playtex glove around the fingers and to outline the palm of the hand. Next, I used rubber cement to adhere that cutout pattern to the palm side of the leather FootJoy glove. It worked. The leather glove could be totally saturated, but the golfer could hold onto the wet golf grip.

I sent my ideas to Tarlow, president of the biggest and most important maker of golf shoes and golf gloves at the time (and my one-time golfing buddy). I was certain he would remember me since we won the scramble at the Sporting Goods Manufacturers Association (SGMA) industry meeting. He had to appreciate the Acushnet Bulls Eye putter each player on the championship team received as first prize. Several months passed. Eventually, he wrote me back to thank me for my letter, and to patronizingly explain that golfers were a very conservative lot, and they would "always want to have the support provided by traditional footwear." He did not bother to comment on the golf glove idea.

Karsten Solheim and Ping

In my eyes, Karsten Solheim, founder of Karsten Manufacturing Corporation (KMC), also known as Ping, was the preeminent entrepreneur in golf. He was my idol. I used one of his putters (69 model) and played the standard-bearer for all scratch golfers at the time, the Ping one iron. Solheim was the golf industry's Horatio Alger; he was the manifestation of everything anyone could aspire to accomplish in the golf equipment business. I was thrilled when he agreed to spend some time with me on an afternoon in the autumn of 1977. It ended up being the first of many visits to Ping headquarters in Phoenix, Arizona.

Before that first meeting, I researched everything about him I could find. This was before personal computers and the Internet. My sources were word of mouth and what was written in trade magazines or found on microfilm in the library. I learned Solheim was an engineer. When he was at General

Electric (GE) he had worked on jet fighter planes, ground-guidance systems, and even portable televisions; in one report, he was credited for inventing the rabbit ears television antenna.

He is famous in the world of golf for his innovations in club design. He pioneered heel-and-toe weighting for putters, revolutionizing putter design. He introduced investment casting to the manufacture of irons, and his perimeter weighting of irons forever changed how the game is played. Through sheer will, persistence, and the courage of his convictions, Solheim developed the preeminent privately owned golf equipment company in the United States (and the world)—all starting with his putter idea. He funded the development of his company without any backers, only borrowing $1,100 to buy a milling machine to make his first putters.[1] He stayed on at GE for two years after he founded Karsten Manufacturing Company in 1959. Solheim had been a shoemaker with his father, so I hoped he might be interested in my golf shoe idea, even though KMC was not in that business. I had a few golf club inventions as well, so I was eager to find out if he liked any of them.

Officially, my visit was made under the guise of my work at the National Golf Foundation. Solheim (everyone called him by his first name, Karsten) was on the NGF Board of Directors. It was a courtesy call on my part, but actually I was the one who was extended the most extraordinary courtesy. I was warmly introduced to the world of Ping by none other than Karsten Solheim himself. The first thing he did was take me on a personal tour of the Ping headquarters operation and then the factory.

The one observation I had regarding the factory was that it was cleaner than my condo in Carlsbad. They did not seem to have much inventory sitting around because it only stayed in the warehouse long enough to be sorted and shipped. Everything seemed made to order with UPS trucks waiting in a queue to be filled. They obviously knew what they were doing at Karsten Manufacturing. During the tour, Solheim introduced me to his son, Louis, described as a computer expert. He had created the Ping Man emblem used on their website and golf grips. Next, I met his son Allan, who was very quiet and very much his father's son in terms of his unpretentious demeanor and engineering expertise. Allan and I became very good friends over the ensuing years.

After we concluded my tour of the Ping plant, Karsten said he had to run over to their outdoor test facility to check something out and invited me to join him. I was whisked to the parking lot for the ride over to the test center. His car was not what I expected. It was an odd-looking foreign model, a Peugeot Citroën. As we drove over to the test center, Solheim said he wanted to show me something he had developed. I thought I might finally get a look inside his inventor personality. As we walked along the tee line at the driving range and watched golfers hitting shots, he said they had developed this property specifically to test their products. They did mechanical testing using Ping Man, their robotic club tester, but also wanted actual golfers to hit Ping clubs and give feedback. We went to the left side of the tee line where there were no golfers hitting balls and he said, "Do you see those small mounds on the ground about thirty yards out?"

I said, "Sure, what are they?"

A wry smile crept onto his face as he said, "They are lights . . . ground lighting. We were having some complaints from the neighbors about the brightness of the overhead lighting. We now illuminate the ball from above with the lighting on the poles along the tee line and from underneath with the ground lighting, which happens to be the side you see when you hit a golf shot at night. This enabled us to reduce the wattage of the overhead lighting, as well as the lighting projected across the field." He then had the golfers all stop hitting shots for a few minutes while he took me out to see the lights.

After quietly marveling to myself about the practicality and ingenuity of this innovation, I said, "Golfers can probably see the ball better with both over and under lighting. This idea will allow many driving ranges to stay open at night, which is important to freestanding driving ranges, in particular, because about seventy percent of their business is done at night." (I had just finished writing an NGF manual on how to build and operate a driving range.)

His response was simply, "That is why I showed it to you." We then got into his car and returned to Ping headquarters.

I could not help but notice he had no other business at the test center. I do not remember what we talked about on the ride back. However, I did manage to ask him for a little more of his time; I said I needed to ask his advice on a couple of matters. When we arrived at Ping headquarters, he led me into a small conference room adjacent to a maze of work stations.

We sat down and he said, "What do you want to talk about?"

At this point, I was overwhelmed by his generosity of spirit and felt somewhat of a cad asking him to opine on my ideas. After all, here I was, a twenty-six-year-old nobody sitting face-to-face with the preeminent mover and shaker of the golf equipment business. Undaunted, I told him about my idea for golf shoes and gloves, thinking it might engender some fond memories of Solheim's past work with his father.

He listened carefully, and a rueful hint of a smile emerged on his face. He did not say anything. I then related that I had written Dick Tarlow about both ideas, but that he had rejected them. Solheim then said, "Do you still think that they are good ideas?"

"Yes," I said.

"Well then," he said, "you need to develop them further. Also, you need to obtain some patent protection before presenting your ideas to anyone." He then explained to me the difference between utility and design patents and which offered the best protection. He also said most companies will not even speak with you about an idea unless you have your idea protected, and you should be careful about companies who will speak with you under any other circumstances.

I asked him if he was interested in either of those ideas and he simply said, "No, I am not in that business. You asked me for advice, and that's what I gave you."

Being one who can overlook an obvious inference, I then told him about two of my better golf club ideas. Once again, he listened patiently and did not interrupt. The first idea related to a golf shaft that would generate more club-head speed. The second idea was to put a plastic or graphite insert into an iron clubface, which would change the feel of an iron and, theoretically, push the weight of the club farther back from the clubface; both were desirable characteristics. There were two drawbacks regarding the latter idea. One, it was not permissible by the Rules of Golf (it would be eventually); and two, there were technical issues that made this task difficult.

Solheim looked at me and said, "I am going to give you the same advice as before. Obtain some patent protection before you present your ideas to anyone." I then wisely decided not to present any more golf equipment ideas.

Karsten seemed to sense my disappointment and said, "Come with me. I have something that might help you." We left the small conference room and went to a room adjacent to the factory. It looked like an R&D (research and development) workshop. He went over to a cabinet and grabbed a few iron club waxes out of a box. They were the blue-colored wax molds from one of his early Karsten iron designs. He handed me half a dozen waxes for a five iron and said, "See what you can do with these."

These wax molds were used in making the Ping irons via the lost-wax process. Wax molds are covered with a ceramic-sand mixture, which is then heated until hard. The wax melts and drains away, leaving a negative mold. Molten steel is then poured into the space formerly occupied by the wax. The steel is cooled and the ceramic coating is removed, revealing the steel clubhead, which is then polished and painted. This was the investment-casting process he brought to the golf industry.

I thanked Solheim for his time and advice. As I walked to my car in the visitor spot, I could not help but feel at home with the Solheim family. Over the years, I would see less of Karsten and more of Allan, who replaced his father on the NGF Board of Directors. My education in the golf equipment business was just beginning.

Innovation in Design, Engineering and Marketing

Solheim rose from a tinkerer just trying to make a better putter to changing how golf clubs were made. His club designs turned golf into a power game and challenged golf establishment's control of the game. He had more impact on the game over the latter half of the twentieth century than any player, commissioner, golf company, or golf association executive. He simply changed the tools of the trade and forever changed how the game is played.

Solheim did not start playing golf until the age of forty-two. He was terribly frustrated putting with the popular designs of the day. Most putters had a shaft at the heel (end) of the club; newer innovations, such as the Acushnet Bulls Eye putter, had the shaft in the center.

When golfers mis-hit a putt by hitting the golf ball off-center, the putter-face twists, and the putt rolls off line. Solheim discovered he could significantly improve a putterhead's resistance to twisting, also known as the moment of inertia (MOI), by positioning lead weights at either end of the putterhead. With this greater stability, the putterface would stay square and on target even with off-center hits.

That original Ping putter resembled a rectangular box with a shaft mounted in its center. The first prototype models made a distinctive "ping" noise, almost like a tuning fork, which Karsten's wife, Louise, thought might be a good name for the putter. In 1966, the Ping Anser was introduced. It proved to be the most-copied putter design. The idea of having weight at both ends of a putter is a standard design principle utilized today by every golf equipment company. Ping enjoyed the top market-share position in the putter business for three decades due to the design and continues to be among the companies dominating that business segment.

Before Solheim started making irons using investment casting, irons were made by a forging process. Rods of carbon steel were hammered into the rough shape of an iron by forging houses. Then they sent these raw forgings to the golf equipment manufacturers who milled, polished, and shaped them. They then chrome plated the heads to keep them from rusting. It was a very expensive process, and there were only a handful of golf equipment companies who could afford to manufacture clubs. Back then, the biggest costs for entry into the club-manufacturing business were in the equipment, know-how, and people required to produce the product.

Solheim changed the way the manufacturing game was played. He first decided to use investment casting to improve the consistency of his iron clubs. The investment-casting process was also less costly than forging. Karsten originally outsourced the casting of his early iron designs (notably, the K1 model in 1969). In 1972, KMC purchased a Phoenix foundry called Dolphin Inc. to cast Ping irons. The number of golf equipment companies went from about six companies in the 1960s to more than five hundred by the turn of the century.

Prior to Solheim's utilization of investment casting, there were two types of iron clubs: blade irons, which had a flat, elongated clubhead that twisted significantly with off-center hits; and game-improvement irons, which had more weight on the heel and toe of the clubhead, like the Ping putters. However, there were limitations on how the weight could be distributed using the old forging technology. Investment casting opened up a world of new iron design and manufacturing technologies. More funds could be invested into R&D as the revolution commenced.

When a golfer mis-hits an iron and strikes the ball off-center, the golf club twists and the shot strays off line just like it does with a putt, but to a greater degree because of the force of the impact of the clubface with the ball. The MOI of an iron with perimeter weighting is much greater than a traditional blade-type club or even the heel-and-toe-weighted game-improvement models (without perimeter weighting). As a result, the sweet spot on a perimeter-weighted club is much larger; this means perimeter-weighted irons are more forgiving and easier to hit.

One year during the Masters I had lunch with Solheim under the big tree by the clubhouse and asked him how he came up with the idea for perimeter weighting when everyone else was putting more weight behind the sweet spot (what we then called muscle-back irons). Karsten's reply was succinct: "A golf club is like a tennis racket. You do not need any weight behind the ball; you will have a more stable clubhead if the weight is around the perimeter of the clubface."

The traditional, forged-blade iron could not compete with the perimeter-weighted iron from a performance or technical standpoint. Eventually, many pros and practically all amateur golfers switched to perimeter-weighted clubs. Perimeter weighting for irons would have a profound influence on how the game is played.

Interestingly, Solheim's irons also had a lighter swingweight than what was considered standard among the golf equipment manufacturers. (Swingweight is a measurement of the clubhead's weight relative to the club's shaft length so that each of the clubs in a set has relatively the same feel as the others. Longer clubs have lighter clubhead weights; shorter clubs have heavier clubhead weights.) Ping irons were designed to feel lighter, and many golfers therefore believed they could generate more clubhead speed and hit the ball farther. The design of perimeter-weighted irons made it more difficult to work the ball (deliberately curve a shot) but enabled golfers, particularly the pros, to hit the ball higher and farther.

Most golfers were not concerned about working the golf ball. Most golfers sliced the ball and did not want the club to curve the ball at all. The result was golfers came to rely less on finesse and more on power when they played the game. Rather than curving a golf shot around a tall tree with a five iron, the power golfer might choose to hit a seven iron over the top of the tree. Solheim perfected his design with the development of a series of six Karsten models that reached its peak with the development of the now-infamous Ping Eye2 in 1982.

Critics of Solheim often pointed to his advertising as unsophisticated and unattractive, but no one can argue that it was ineffective. His print advertisements all had his Colonel Sanders likeness emblazoned onto the ad with an obtrusive yellow-colored background demanding the reader's attention. The ads typically featured the Ping color-coded fitting system.

Using a color-coded chart, customers could fit themselves and order their own personalized, custom set of clubs. The simple self-fitting system used the golfer's static measurements. All golfers received stiff shafts, regardless of how hard or easy they swung a golf club (going against the conventional wisdom that golfers with slower swing speeds needed a shaft flex that would bend more easily). The Ping system only had options in terms of the lie of the clubhead (angle of the golf shaft relative to the clubhead), the shaft length, and the grip size.

I asked Solheim at that same Masters why he did not offer different flexes (they do today). Solheim said, "It's not necessary." He then took out a chain about a foot long, like one that holds a St. Christopher's medal or a soldier's dog tags. He started to twirl it around like a helicopter blade, and said, "Once a golf shaft is in motion, it doesn't make any difference in the velocity of the clubhead. We have tested golfers with various swing speeds, and they all have better results with a lightweight, stiff shaft."

Whether the fitting system worked or not, it did not matter because customers thought it did. Mass marketing custom-fitted irons was a Karsten Solheim innovation. No one has come close to duplicating his success.

On another occasion under the big tree during the Masters, I had lunch with Solheim and again took the opportunity to ask him a number of questions. First, I wanted to know why he used a yellow background in his print ads. He said a yellow background catches a person's eye better than any other color, and then cited a study that showed the most eye-catching color was a yellow background with black lettering, followed by a black background with yellow lettering, followed by a white background with black lettering, followed by a black background with white lettering, and so on. I had always thought a red background with white lettering caught our eyes best, like a stop sign; but he said that was not the case: "Stop signs should be yellow and black—like the Yield signs. People would see them better."

When Ping introduced steel-headed versions of the Ping putters, I asked him why he charged more for them since steel costs less than brass. "Because we can," he said. When Ping entered the woods club business, they changed the shape of their woods to be more aerodynamic, but they did something even more unusual from a marketing standpoint. Every wood was custom-built on a back-order basis. They had a six-week time delay built into the order and delivery process, creating an artificial, latent demand for their woods. Distribution was tightly controlled and restricted to golf-course pro shops. Off-course shops usually had to buy Ping products through on-course shops or green-grass accounts.

While Ping was late in entering the metal woods business, they became the leading seller of woods (before metal woods eventually replaced them). Allan Solheim told me they actually had developed a metal wood long before anyone else, but they were not satisfied with its performance and quality. He said once they believed they could make a better metal wood, they would.

The one innovation that eventually led to a great deal of controversy was the development of the L-Wedge with its square grooves, which purportedly enabled lesser-skilled golfers to more easily hit high-spinning, short wedge shots that landed softly on the green. I sat next to Solheim for two hours at a private industry luncheon during the British Open at Troon, Scotland, in 1989, where he explained why the entire "groove" controversy was absolute nonsense. At the time, I was president of the Ben Hogan Company, a competitor with Ping. He drew pictures on a paper napkin of U or square grooves versus V grooves and explained, from an engineering standpoint, exactly how the distance between the grooves should be measured.

Solheim said the main function of the groove had little to do with spacing and more to do with the disbursement of moisture from wet turf conditions, very much like tire treads channel water when the roads are wet. He said the USGA had already approved U-shaped grooves, and it was nonsensical for the spacing issue to be raised because the spacing between the grooves on the clubface didn't make any difference in the performance of the golf club. He insisted the measurement should be made from the interior walls of the grooves, not where they curved over into the U. Solheim said the USGA didn't even know how to measure the spacing between the grooves, and he would never make an illegal golf club. Ironically, the one person who engendered the most attention for using the L-Wedge and came to be seen as benefiting most from the square grooves was none other than Mark Calcavecchia, the winner of that year's British Open. He beat Australians Wayne Grady and Greg Norman in a four-hole playoff.

Gary Adams and TaylorMade

Gary Adams pioneered the first commercially successful metal wood (driver) in 1978 when he founded the TaylorMade Golf Company in McHenry, Illinois. In those days, real wood-headed clubs dominated the market, and most were sold in sets. Northwestern Golf Company had developed a metal wood prior to Adams, but it never enjoyed much acceptance. Everyone considered it to be in the class of the cheap, aluminum-headed golf clubs found at many driving ranges. Adams had to fight that perception with a golf club that performed better than the gold standard of drivers—the classic persimmon driver with matching fairway woods.

The ball just seemed to jump off the face of a TaylorMade driver with a greater velocity. And due to greater weighting around the perimeter of the clubface, somewhat like the perimeter weighting of an investment-cast iron, the metal clubhead twisted less than a real wood-headed club. But there was a difference. TaylorMade's clubhead had much of its weight in back, around, and behind the clubface; therefore, it was even more stable at impact and had a lower center of gravity. This created a higher effective loft, enabling golfers to hit TaylorMade's metal wood, with a nine-degree loft, higher than they could hit a wooden club with the same loft. They could also control the direction of the shot better because there was less torque and sidespin with off-center hits.

Adams introduced the metal wood at the 1979 PGA Merchandise Show. He sold enough clubs to take a chance and mortgage his house to fund a six-thousand-square-foot plant in McHenry, Illinois. He then did something no one had done before. He personally went out to the PGA Club Championship and other PGA Tour events to sell these innovative drivers directly to the players. Everyone paid the $39.95 "pro price." The tour players liked Adams, and did not mind him charging for the clubs. In a world where everything is given to you, it almost made the product seem better because the pros had to dig into their pockets and pay for it. PGA Tour players liked the fact they could hit the ball farther with the metal drivers off a good fairway lie than with their three woods. Some stopped carrying a three wood and added an extra wedge or utility wood to their bags instead.

Soon a revolution was underway in the golf equipment world. Everyone had to have or at least try a metal wood. Seemingly overnight, many of the top players on the PGA Tour had TaylorMade metal woods in their bags. The drivers came in different lofts. The fairway wood came in both strong and weaker lofts. Adams also introduced utility woods to hit out of the heavy roughs. Sales went from a modest $1.2 million in 1981 to about $12 million in 1982 and $15 million the next year. Adams moved his manufacturing operation from McHenry to Carlsbad to be closer to the California-based casting houses. The move also coincided with the acquisition of TaylorMade by Salomon S.A., the French sporting goods company and noted maker of snow skis.

Prior to TaylorMade, woods were sold in matching sets. Even the tour players sought clubs that matched. They might have a MacGregor Eye-O-Matic driver or a couple of backup drivers, but they always looked and played differently from the woods in a matched set. Regular amateurs always bought their woods in sets of three or four clubs.

TaylorMade metal woods were very consistent from a quality standpoint because the clubheads were cast from a mold, as opposed to wooden clubheads that were crafted by hand, shaped, and then sanded into their final form. With metal woods, a tour player might still carry a backup club or two, or even have some drivers with different lofts, but it was never a disaster if the primary driver was lost or damaged because an exact duplicate could be procured. Amateur golfers bought a metal-headed driver, and after having some success, bought additional metal fairway woods, one at a time. Metal woods were not sold in sets.

The sale of metal woods became a "loose club" or "barrel" business. This was a breakthrough from an inventory and sales standpoint for both the retailer and the manufacturer. Retailers no longer had to have sets of clubs on display (carrying a higher total price tag). Instead, they had inventory that turned over much more quickly, since the price for one club (instead of three) had a lower discretionary-purchase threshold. A golfer in the mid-1980s might not mind spending $69.95 for one golf club, but to spend $209.95 for three clubs represented a greater discretionary-purchase decision.

Retailers liked selling clubs out of barrel because they did not have to worry about having slow-moving inventory just sitting on a shelf. They could invest less into their inventory and see that inventory turn more quickly. So they could invest more with less risk and move more of the same product with fewer SKUs (stock keeping units). It was better for TaylorMade, as well. The company could make a batch of drivers at various lofts, then make three woods or utility clubs but in direct proportion to market demand. Like the retailer, TaylorMade could increase its inventory turns because the retailer was enjoying more turns. It was a marketing, distribution, and sales revolution.

Adams also pioneered direct promotion on the PGA Tour. Most established golf companies at that time had tour reps, but those reps catered to that company's contract professional staff. In his earlier days, Solheim was out there promoting his putters, but no one developed the relationships and personal following Adams enjoyed. Eventually, after establishing his company on the tour, he quit selling clubs to the players and developed TaylorMade's own PGA Tour professional staff. Soon thereafter, Adams developed a line of irons. It was about this time that I visited Adams at his new headquarters. I knew Adams from my early days working for the PGA Tour. I had even bought one of his Pittsburgh Persimmon drivers for the tour players' price of $39.95.

I visited Adams in the early summer of 1984, just a few months after I became president of the National Golf Foundation. His offices were on the mezzanine level of the assembly plant. He took me over to the railing of an interior overlook that looked down on the club assembly and warehouse areas. It was probably about twenty thousand square feet and was quite impressive. There was a great deal of activity, and like the Karsten Manufacturing facility I first saw a few years earlier, the UPS trucks were lined up in the back waiting for their share of that day's production. As we went back to Adams's office, I remember seeing the classy Bernie Fuchs *Art of Golf* advertising print campaign mounted and framed on the hallway walls. I was so impressed with what had been accomplished in just about four or five years. Adams went from mortgaging his home to heading up the fastest-growing golf club company in the business. I was not aware of it at the time, but not everything was going as well as it seemed.

We sat down in his office and talked about the many PGA Tour players using TaylorMade metal woods—from Mark O'Meara to Lee Trevino. There seemed to be no stopping the changeover from wood to metal, and Taylor-Made had the pole position in the golf equipment race. Adams liked the racing analogy. He asked me if I wanted some coffee or a drink. I said I would have whatever he was having. We had bottles of chilled water. I know it's common today, but in 1984 it was not. This was during one of many droughts in California, when you did not automatically get water at a restaurant unless you asked for it. Perrier was popular, but snobby. Usually people drank coffee or had a soda of some kind in the office environment. Perhaps I remember this detail because it represented the nouveau nature of the California experience.

I complimented Adams on what he had achieved in such a short period of time and said, "The development of the metal wood is destined to change how golf will be played, as well as how the business game will be played." Adams looked puzzled as I paused and then continued, "Certainly, metal woods will be a significant hallmark in golf club technology. But as great as that innovation is, I have always considered the way that you marketed and sold clubs to be even more revolutionary."

Adams then asked, "Really, why do you say that?"

"Because you changed the dynamics of the golf club business. By selling clubs one at a time, you lowered the cost of inventory for the retailers and increased their turns. You put the average green-grass shop back into the golf-equipment business and enabled the off-course shops to once again start making money selling golf clubs. You did the same for yourself, which enabled you to take the club market by storm."

Adams replied, "I never really thought about it that way. Quite frankly, we kind of backed into that business strategy because we had no other choice. I only had one driver at first, and that's what I had to sell. I then had drivers of different lofts and a three wood, then other metal woods. That's just how it all worked out. I would be lying if I said that this was deliberately planned. Sometimes you get lucky, especially if you are desperate enough and willing to work hard enough at it."

After this candid and self-effacing revelation, I really did not know what to say, but asked, "I do have one question for you. I was curious as to why, after having so much success in selling clubs one at a time, that you then went into the business of selling sets of irons. It seems to me that you might start selling wedges, putters, utility clubs, etcetera, or even sell short sets of irons. Selling full sets of irons certainly requires greater resources and more risk for both you and your retailers because it would require having larger inventories and fewer turns."

He replied with surprising aplomb, "David, the reason I got into the iron business was that I had some tour staff players that wanted to play our irons. I wanted to take advantage of that exposure on the PGA Tour and leverage that investment by going into the iron club business. In retrospect, I know that it was probably a mistake to do it at that time, especially with the [metal wood] price war that is going on today. Perhaps I might still own this company today [instead of Salomon], if I had done otherwise."

That admission was shocking, and I did not know what to say.

He continued, "Sometimes you are successful, but don't recognize all of the reasons why you were successful. That missing ingredient is called luck. Maybe it's timing, maybe it's hard work, and maybe it's just a good product or some combination. In my case, our situation left us no alternative but success. We were successful because we had a better product and sold it the only way that we could, as you say, one club at a time. If we had understood more about why we were successful, it might have been different."

About five or six years later, Adams and Salomon parted ways. Adams sold his interest in the company and formed a new company called Founders Club. Around that time, I saw him at a Christmas party hosted by Gary Wiren, the famous PGA golf instructor, in Palm Beach Gardens, Florida. Adams cornered me and said, "I still remember what you said to me back in Carlsbad." I looked at him somewhat quizzically, not knowing what he was talking about, and then he said, "I am starting a new company [Founders Club], and this time I am going to do it my way, the way that I know it will work, and sell clubs one at a time." I wished him the best of luck and sincerely hoped he would succeed.

Tom Crow and Cobra Golf Company

In the summer of 1978, Australian Tom Crow had recently launched Cobra Golf in the United States, and his lead product was the Baffler—a real wood-headed fairway club with two metal bars traversing the clubhead's heavy soleplate. It was innovative because it lowered the center of gravity and helped golfers hit the ball higher out of tough lies. However, Cobra's success in the golf business was not due to any particular innovation. Cobra made its mark because Crow was a genius in retail marketing. He was simply the best at what the golf industry calls sell-through.

All golf equipment companies must be marketing oriented and build brand awareness and distribution. This is sell-in. However, the key to success is to turn the inventory at retail—in other words, get the consumer to buy the product at the retail point of purchase. This is sell-through. It sounds simple, but it's not. No one was better at it than Cobra Golf.

Cobra spent its limited marketing dollars on sell-through and creating customer service excellence. Crow knew that Cobra could not compete with the big boys on their terms so he rewrote the rules in terms that gave him a fighting chance. Cobra really didn't have any innovative products after the Baffler to spontaneously drive sales. Cobra generated sales by outperforming in other areas where they could beat the competition.

In the fall of 1978, I first met Mark McClure, who later became Cobra's president and CEO. At the time, he was a product manager and a former ski instructor who had made friends with one of the company's investors. I just happened to be visiting with him one day at Cobra's San Diego offices when he received a Federal Express package (of course today, we all call it FedEx). He excused himself from our meeting, saying he had to turn around a mistaken club order. He had to send it back to the customer before the Federal Express 4:00 p.m. pickup time. The cost of sending the order FedEx exceeded any profit they would have made on the order. So I asked McClure why he was returning it so quickly.

"Our business is all about creating customers with our superior customer service," he said. "We might not make anything on this order, but we will on the next." His response floored me.

What Cobra did about ten years later that transformed them into a much bigger player was to segment the market into senior, men's, and women's clubs, and target-market its product line. They color-coordinated the clubs to those market segments and converted the entire Cobra golf club line over to graphite-shaft clubs. None of the bigger companies could do this at the time, and due to their smaller size and flexibility, Cobra redefined customer service and took it to the next level.

Cobra placed demo sets with Cobra-logo golf bags in golf shops and stores for customers to test on the golf course. The tactic was to have those demo sets at the golf shops to shorten the golfers' purchase decision timeframe and to increase sales velocity. Cobra put those demo sets out at no charge to the retailer. At the end of the year, that retailer could return the demo set or buy it at 50 percent off the wholesale price. Very few sets were ever returned. This selling tactic was an unequivocal success.

When oversized drivers became the rage in the early 1990s, Cobra was quick to join the bandwagon, but on its own terms. Once again, Cobra had programs to induce trial use and priced its products below the market leaders. While Cobra might not have been the innovator of new product designs, the company was more innovative in how it marketed products. Most importantly, Cobra focused on sell-through, not the more risky and expensive sell-in tactics of the big boys. When oversized irons came into vogue, Cobra advertisements featured the top golfer at the time, Greg Norman; it was a prime example of the sell-through strategy. Norman gave them the visibility and credibility to sell irons. Cobra's print ad headline simply said, "If you like oversized woods . . . you'll love our oversized irons."

In terms of marketing, Cobra always encouraged product trial; this is what ensured success over much larger competitors. Because they were smaller and more versatile, Cobra could provide a level of turnaround and customer service that the bigger companies could not match. Cobra found the weaknesses in the underbelly of the big boys and exploited it tactically. In 1996, the Acushnet Company acquired Cobra Golf Company for more than $700 million. Cobra was projected to have revenues in excess of $200 million that year.

Ely Callaway and Callaway Golf Company

Long heralded for his Midas touch and success in the textile and wine businesses, Ely Callaway invested in a small golf business, Hickory Stick USA, that made hickory-shaft golf clubs with a steel rod running through the length of the wooden shaft. He founded Callaway Hickory Stick USA in 1982 and changed the name to Callaway Golf Company in 1988 when he introduced the S2H2 line of irons and woods. Callaway was the first in the golf equipment business to recognize the emerging popularity of the Champions Tour, then known as the Senior PGA Tour. He saw the aging of the golfing population and geared his product offerings and promotions accordingly.

During the 1985 PGA Show in Orlando, Florida, I remember walking the show aisles with PGA Tour Commissioner Deane Beman. Callaway had a nice display of the Callaway Hickory Stick product line (mostly wooden-shafted wedges and putters). They also sold sets of irons and had a few players on the Senior PGA Tour using their clubs. Callaway cornered Beman and pitched him pretty hard concerning his support of the Senior PGA Tour. Callaway noted the changing demographics of the golf market and how well he was positioned to take advantage of it. Beman was impressed with his insight, but not the Callaway product line.

As we left the Callaway booth, Beman commented prophetically, "That product line is crap, but Ely knows what he is doing. As soon as he has a decent product, he is going to be a big player in this business."

At the PGA Show in 1991, Callaway Golf introduced the Big Bertha metal wood, named after the World War I cannon; it was the first oversized metal wood in the marketplace. He took out full-page ads in the regional issues of *USA TODAY* and the *Wall Street Journal* and had copies delivered to the hotel rooms of the PGA Show attendees. All of his competitors, including the Ben Hogan Company, which I was running at the time, were working on oversized drivers, but Callaway beat everyone to the punch.

At the time, I also headed Ben Hogan Properties, which owned Pebble Beach. The next week, I went out there to play in the AT&T Pebble Beach Pro-Am. Every celebrity in the tournament had a Big Bertha driver. Jack Lemmon, the actor, was even touting its benefits, vowing to make the cut for the first time. To make matters worse, the rental golf clubs at the Pebble Beach, Spyglass Hill, and Spanish Bay courses were all Callaways. I fixed that problem, but had to admire how well they had executed their marketing plan. They were selling circles around us and everyone else, with fewer assets and very limited resources.

The Big Bertha metal wood was Callaway's breakthrough product, but it would not have enjoyed the extraordinary success it did without the marketing, promotion, sales, and distribution ducks all in a row. Overnight success does not occur without a great deal of planning and hard work.

Callaway Golf Company became a formidable force, because Ely Callaway was a visionary and strategic thinker. The company's meteoric rise to the number-one clubmaker spot was interrupted only occasionally. He was sensitive to the ups and downs of the business, and overcame each challenge with the sense of style, panache, and flair everyone admired.

Callaway was the first to successfully take his company public in 1992, which provided him with the resources to market his company and distance Callaway Golf from the competition. Also, Callaway rewrote the rules of engagement with the company's PGA Tour pros, giving them generous compensation, performance bonuses, and company stock. As the company stock rose, some of the players made more on it than by playing the golf equipment. They became stakeholders in the success of the company, which prompted them to be more assertive in their endorsement of the Callaway Golf product line.

Taking Callaway Golf public did provide Callaway with the resources to take the company to the next level, but there were costs. Callaway's shareholders had an insatiable appetite for revenue growth, profit, and capital gains. Dancing with the devil is fine, just as long as he lets you lead. In Ely Callaway's case, he was Fred Astaire, always a step ahead, and he made his dance partners look good. Callaway seemed to always have something in his bag of tricks. It would be myopic to characterize Callaway's success as the result of being good at dealing with his shareholders or being a better marketer of golf equipment than his competition. Ely Callaway was better at most everything. He was product oriented and knew what the consumer wanted, even if he or she didn't know yet what that might be. His marketing credo, which became the company motto and philosophy, was to make products that were "pleasingly different and demonstrably superior" in performance. Products with those attributes are easier to sell.

Callaway often decried his salesmanship capabilities, but one has to be leery of someone who says he is not good at something when the opposite is so apparent. His success took on mythic proportions because no one really understood why he was so successful in the first place. His sense of style, his Brioni suits, and his toys, including a blue Rolls-Royce, only added to his mystique as a marketing genius and successful entrepreneur. He created a persona that befitted his celebrity status. He made the "friendliest golf clubs," but when sales sagged or slid, he made dramatic moves to appease investors.

The company acquired Odyssey Golf in 1997 which immediately made Callaway Golf the number-one putter company in the game, and importantly, it pushed company revenues up a big notch when they had been heading in the other direction. When the golf club business looked like it was going to level off, Callaway decided to enter the golf ball business. Because Callaway was a product and manufacturing guy at heart, he built his own golf ball plant rather than source the product from a competing manufacturer. He hired the best golf ball executive in the business, Chuck Yash, who had headed that business for Spalding and who also happened to be the president of Callaway's main competitor in the golf club business, TaylorMade.

Callaway always knew what he wanted to do strategically, but he was not always right tactically. In April of 1999, I met with the top executives of Nike Golf at their headquarters in Beaverton, Oregon. They were astounded and joked about Callaway investing nearly $200 million to build a golf ball plant in Carlsbad, California. Of course, Nike thought it was ridiculous to do such a thing, since they outsourced *all* of their products.

When Nike went into the golf ball business, they had Bridgestone Golf manufacture their product line. Bridgestone had the expertise, the patents, and the underutilized manufacturing facilities. Nike had the brand, the marketing expertise, and the money to do whatever Nike wanted. It was a match made in heaven. I understood the reasoning but thought it might be just as smart to acquire a company that already made golf balls and owned the intellectual properties, which is what happened in 2003 when Callaway acquired Top Flite Golf Company. This included the Top-Flite, Strata, and Ben Hogan brands, obtained through the sale of Spalding Sports assets.

If Callaway wanted to grow his business beyond golf clubs and accessories, going into the golf ball business was the right decision. It was the only avenue available to meet Callaway's shareholders' appetite for growth. How Callaway chose to do it was the problem. They started from scratch and tried to do it all by themselves. With that strategic miscue, Callaway learned he could not profitably manufacture and market golf balls. Yash became the sacrificial lamb to the shareholders.

When driver sales stalled on the way to Y2K (year 2000), Ely Callaway had to stir the stew in the marketing pot one more time. This time, he went counter to his roots. He was a distant relative of Bobby Jones and revered the traditional elements of the game, but in 2000, Callaway introduced a driver with a super-thin clubface and a high trampoline effect that was nonconforming, according to USGA Rules. The illegal driver, the ERC II, exceeded the USGA's standard for the coefficient of restitution (COR), which meant the golf ball rebounded and was propelled off the ERC II clubface at a higher speed than permitted by the rules. Therefore, the USGA put the offending golf club on its "Non-Conforming List." The club sold well in Japan, which adopted either the USGA or R&A (Royal and Ancient) standards, depending upon what suited them.

Clearly, Callaway's development of a nonconforming golf club was deliberate—a marketing ploy to garner attention and further establish Callaway Golf in the minds of the golfing public as being on the leading edge of technology. Eli Callaway never denied the nonconformity of the ERC II; rather, he challenged the USGA's rules and suggested a bifurcation of the rules—one set of rules for the pros and another for the common man. Translation: Callaway was on the side of the little guy who enjoyed hitting the golf ball farther. The debate raged on between the USGA and Callaway.

In an ironic twist, Arnold Palmer (after shutting down his namesake golf-equipment company) endorsed Callaway Golf equipment. However, Palmer was also the spokesperson for the USGA Associates Program, which is the grassroots membership program for golfers supporting the USGA. Once again, it seemed Ely Callaway had all his ducks in a row. He had Palmer, who epitomized everything that was enjoyable and good about the game—and a justifiable cause. All Callaway was trying to do was make the game more fun for the average Joe. Who could argue with that?

The USGA, that's who. The debate was not about whether or not the ERC II driver was nonconforming. It clearly did not conform. In a sense, Callaway simply changed the subject of the dispute. His proposed bifurcation of the USGA Rules could fundamentally change the nature of the game; some might have even said undermine it. During a debate aired on the Golf Channel between David Fay, the USGA executive director, and Callaway, Fay summed up the impasse: "To us, there's one set of rules, and the first rule of golf is that you play by the Rules."

Recreational golfers could play any type of golf club they chose, but if they wanted to have a USGA Handicap or play in any competition under the USGA Rules, they could not use the ERC II driver. The battle lines were drawn, and eventually, Callaway retreated. But who was Callaway really fighting? Was it the USGA, or was Callaway firing another promotional shot from his Big Bertha marketing arsenal? The deliberate nature of this embattlement with the USGA, coupled with the high regard one must have for Callaway's promotional and marketing capabilities, leads one to believe the real battle was for market share and revenue growth.

7

MAKING THE CUT

While living in Carlsbad, I had a chance to get to know Ted Wooley, who moved his golf company, Golfcraft, from Chicago to southern California and later sold it to Titleist (Acushnet). Titleist wasn't in the golf club business in any meaningful way in those days, except for its Bulls Eye putter manufacturing operation in Phoenix. Titleist's initial entry into the club business was no more than stamping the Titleist name onto the former Golfcraft Continental forged irons and atop Golfcraft's handcrafted woods.

Wooley was an unheralded pioneer of the golf business. My boss at the time, Don Rossi, the NGF executive director, insisted I meet Wooley, which I was pleased to do. According to Rossi, Wooley was the person responsible for the NGF's funding plan. Back in the 1950s, Chicago was the epicenter of the golf equipment world. The famous golf writers, brothers Herb and Joe Graffis, founded the NGF in 1936 and were running it on a shoestring budget. Wooley stepped up with a plan to automatically secure funding from the golf equipment manufacturers by charging a few cents for every dozen balls or golf shafts sold. If Wooley had not done that, the NGF would have withered on the Graffis brothers' vine.

Wooley invited me to his home in the ritzy Rancho Santa Fe community just north of San Diego for a barbeque. His hacienda-style home was situated within a sixty-acre lemon tree orchard worth $30 million or so, even back then. We had dinner outside on a patio, perched atop a high point overlooking other citrus groves and homes on the western horizon. After a couple of drinks I needed to go to the restroom, but what I really wanted to do was go for a look inside his house. I had never seen such a place—marble and stone floors, oriental rugs, and there were master artworks that I knew had to be worth millions.

When the time was right, I asked the elderly Wooley how he came to be so successful, and his reply was succinct: "Well David, I certainly didn't make it in the golf business. I have made a few good real estate investments, and I started a savings and loan business that has done pretty well." Other than

Karsten Solheim, Wooley was the only really rich man I had ever met. I was easily impressed and wanted to follow in his footsteps, although deep in my heart I knew that if I stayed in the golf business I would never have any master artworks hanging in the hallways of my home.

I continued doing my consulting work for the NGF, traveling throughout California and the nation. Before long, I met David Price, founder of American Golf Corporation (AGC), the nation's largest operator of golf courses. My introduction to him was via E. C. "Sandy" Burns, AGC cofounder, and Gail Goodrich, the former UCLA and Los Angeles Lakers star and also an executive at AGC. I was becoming a resource for the two as they sought golf courses they could buy or lease. Also, I was trying to impress them enough so that they might consider hiring me.

But there was no reason to hire me when they already had those services for free. One day on one of my many long drives, I came up with an idea that might make driving ranges more profitable. I called it California Golf Learning Centers. The idea was to brand and promote a business focusing on creating customers, not just renting baskets of range balls. The gimmick was to get the golf professionals out from behind the counters and on the tee line, teaching and promoting the game. Short golf lessons could be given away during down times. A premium could be charged for practice balls—charging for the time on the tee, not just per basket of balls.

The business concept was that golfers would progress from free mini lessons, to group or personal lessons, to playing more golf. Thus, golf equipment sales would increase. The net result was that these once-unprofitable enterprises—driving ranges—would be able to generate greater income over what they did just renting out baskets of range balls. I figured this concept could work at golf course driving ranges as well as freestanding ranges. I had a bunch of ancillary ideas that really enhanced the business concept. Burns liked the idea and said they should be doing something like that at all of their facilities.

Almost serendipitously, I received a call from Art West, who worked for the PGA Tour. I had done some consulting work for them a few years earlier about a kid's golf course at Firestone Country Club in Akron, Ohio. It was never built, but the PGA Tour was interested in developing prototype golf courses for kids. West came out to La Costa, which was near my home in Carlsbad, and interviewed me. I was invited to go to Ponte Vedra Beach, Florida, for another interview and to meet with Deane Beman, the PGA Tour Commissioner.

Deane Beman and the PGA Tour

No one had a greater impact on the game and growth of the golf industry during the last twenty-five years of the twentieth century than PGA Tour Commissioner Deane Beman. When I first met him in the summer of 1979, he had been commissioner for about five years and had moved PGA Tour headquarters from Washington, DC, to Ponte Vedra Beach, Florida. At the time, the PGA Tour offices were temporarily housed in a few vacant houses in a real estate development owned by the Fletcher brothers. They had sold the land for one dollar to the PGA Tour to build a new headquarters and a Tournament Players Club (TPC) stadium golf course; both were under construction when I first visited Beman in his temporary office.

The PGA Tour was looking for someone to launch Beman's junior golf course idea, then called The Wee Links. The idea was for the PGA Tour to promote junior golf by fostering the nationwide development of low-cost public golf courses for kids. It was an innovative and noble idea, but ill-conceived in terms of its practicality and economic viability. I knew that going into the interview, but I was desperate to get my foot in the door at the PGA Tour. When I walked into the commissioner's office and sat down in the chair across his modern, glass-topped desk, Beman asked me point blank if I could get this program off the ground.

I looked him in the eye and said, "No, not as it is presently conceived." I said that BOR (the former Bureau of Outdoor Recreation in the Department of the Interior) no longer provided matching funds to municipalities for the construction of recreational facilities. And, due to the slowdown in the US economy, municipalities did not have any discretionary funds and were not building sports facilities at the time, not even baseball diamonds or soccer fields.

Furthermore, the last thing these municipalities wanted to do was build golf facilities for kids where they might be unsupervised and use the clubs to hit projectiles at each other. Keep in mind that the Wee Links concept was Beman's idea, so my preliminary take on this was that what I had to say about this would not be well received by the commissioner. But he did not take it personally, even though he was passionate about the the cause. His reaction was, as I would learn, very typical.

He looked at me and said, "Okay, you got a better idea?"

I said, "Yes, as a matter of fact, I do." I then pulled out a proposal for what I called PGA Tour Golf Learning Centers—a variation on the Wee Links concept. It looked a lot like my proposal for the California Golf Learning Centers. I proposed pursuing an economically viable business, which did not rely on government funding. The promotional concept focused on introducing the game to beginning golfers—kids and their families—and provided a great place for existing golfers to improve their games. Most golfers were introduced to the game by family or friends, so this marketing approach made some business sense.

After I finished my presentation and answered his questions, he simply said to me, "Well, I think that your approach is better; let's go with it."

We then got into his Jeep Wagoneer and drove over to the golf course construction site to talk with Pete Dye, the famous golf course architect. We went out to a location on the golf course that looked like an open-pit mining project. There, the scoured-out, sandy wasteland would someday become a lake with a bulkheaded island green. We went to the edge of that open pit and peered across the divide. It would someday be the TPC's famous 17th hole. We stepped back another fifteen to twenty yards to ponder an even longer shot to the green.

Beman explained, "The bulkheaded green is big enough to accept a middle-iron shot from about one hundred seventy-five yards, and I have been thinking about putting the tee back here, but it would be too intimidating at this point in the round. The tee should be at the edge of the lake for a short iron from about one hundred thirty-five yards out. It will be great TV." Actually, it was still intimidating for a short-iron shot, which is exactly what Beman and architect Dye had in mind. Beman then introduced me to Dye as *one of the new guys working for the PGA Tour.*

From the Wee Links to the First Tee
Back then, Disney sponsored a PGA Tour event in the fall. Card Walker was a director on the PGA Tour Tournament Policy Board, and supported the Wee Links concept. Disney created the new PGA Tour logo, as well as the cartoon "Birdie" character for the PGA Tour to use in promoting junior golf. With all of the hoopla around the grand opening of the first Wee Links at Walt Disney World in Florida, there were great expectations that many new facilities would follow and have a positive impact on junior golf development. It didn't happen.

A brochure was developed to promote the Wee Links concept. It received a great deal of media attention and was widely distributed. Brochure respondents received a 150-page booklet with detailed plans and development options for a stand-alone driving range or one with three holes, six holes, or nine holes, along with construction and operating cost estimates.

What started out as the Wee Links later evolved into the PGA Tour Family Golf Centres. Regrettably, the key marketing concept of creating customers and offering free golf lessons was never incorporated into any of the projects because the PGA Tour engaged entrepreneurs to develop, design, build, own, and operate the centers. And, not unexpectedly, each developer or owner had his or her own interpretation as to how to make it work.

Additionally, I encouraged the re-creation of the famous 17th hole at the TPC as the centerpiece of PGA Tour Family Golf Centres to piggyback on the fame of the Island Green. I thought golfers would enjoy hitting golf balls onto the Island Green emulating what they saw on TV. Golf shots would be directed to the center of the driving range. Balls hit into the water could be channeled into a central collection area and easily retrieved. But the idea was never incorporated as intended.

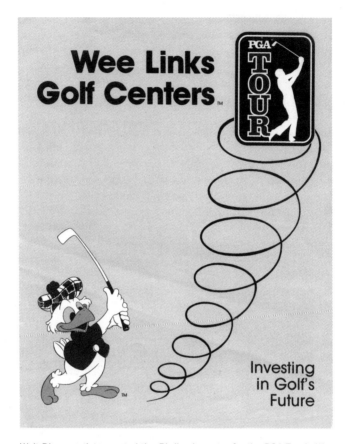

Walt Disney artists created the Birdie character for the PGA Tour's Wee Links Golf Centers. The tour created a costume of Birdie to promote golf to kids. Beman's nephew, Michael, was the first to wear it. The costume was so hot it could only be worn for fifteen minutes at a time. Fortunately, I was too big to fit into it. *Courtesy of the PGA Tour.*

An investor group (headed by attorney Fred Ridley, who had won the U.S. Amateur and would later become the president of the USGA) built a PGA Tour Family Golf Centre not too far from the famed Innisbrook Golf Resort in the Tampa area. By the time it was completed, however, I had left the PGA Tour to become CEO of the National Golf Foundation (only one of the original PGA Tour Family Golf Centres was built in Oakville, Ontario, of all places). Vernon Kelley, who was in charge of anything getting built for the PGA Tour, asked me to come by and take a look at what they had done in Tampa. I did, but it wasn't as advertised.

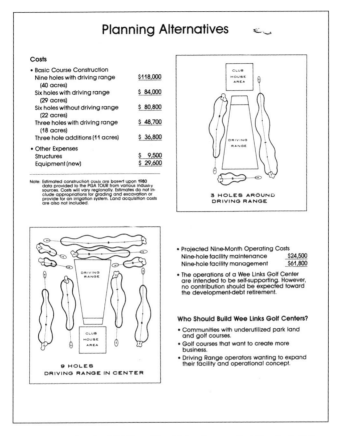

Planning Alternatives

Costs

- Basic Course Construction
  Nine holes with driving range ... $118,000
  (40 acres)
  Six holes with driving range ... $ 84,000
  (29 acres)
  Six holes without driving range ... $ 80,800
  (22 acres)
  Three holes with driving range ... $ 48,700
  (18 acres)
  Three hole additions (11 acres) ... $ 36,800

- Other Expenses
  Structures ... $ 9,500
  Equipment (new) ... $ 29,600

Note: Estimated construction costs are based upon 1980 data provided to the PGA TOUR from various industry sources. Costs will vary regionally. Estimates do not include appropriations for grading and excavation or provide for an irrigation system. Land acquisition costs are also not included.

3 HOLES AROUND DRIVING RANGE

9 HOLES DRIVING RANGE IN CENTER

- Projected Nine-Month Operating Costs
  Nine-hole facility maintenance ... $24,500
  Nine-hole facility management ... $61,800

- The operations of a Wee Links Golf Center are intended to be self-supporting. However, no contribution should be expected toward the development-debt retirement.

Who Should Build Wee Links Golf Centers?

- Communities with underutilized park land and golf courses.
- Golf courses that want to create more business.
- Driving Range operators wanting to expand their facility and operational concept.

The brochure for the PGA Tour Wee Links (later called Family Golf Centres) offered planning alternatives for a nine-, six-, or even three-hole golf course with a central driving range. Estimates were offered, but costs varied across the country. *Courtesy of the PGA Tour.*

They had built an Island Green, but it wasn't surrounded by water; instead, it was surrounded by sand. Disappointed, I turned to Kelley and asked, "Why did you use sand? Islands are surrounded by water. Hitting balls into a sand trap isn't much fun, and you are going to need to hand pick the balls. Why didn't you put in a shallow lake?"

Kelley replied, "Well, it would have cost too much; we just didn't have it in the budget."

At this point, I could tell my remarks were not well received, but I couldn't help myself and said, "Vernon, I hate to say this, but if you didn't have the

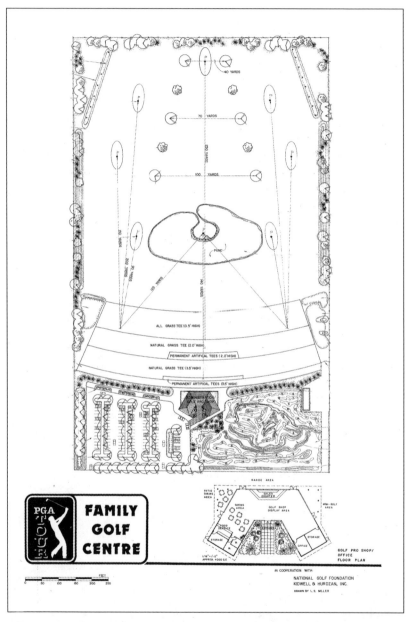

The proposed Family Golf Centre design for a stand-alone driving range featured the TPC 17th hole Island Green, target greens, and trees. The trees were set apart to allow mowers and ball pickers to do their jobs but still created the illusion of a fairway. This facility also had a 36-hole putting course. *Courtesy of the PGA Tour.*

money to do it right and go all the way, it would have been better to do nothing."

The Tampa PGA Tour Family Golf Centre fared poorly and died a natural death. Regardless of the fact it wasn't built or operated as intended, we proved unequivocally that any venture in this vein needed to be subsidized. If the objective was to promote junior golf or create a place for people to begin playing the game, it was quite evident it could not be made into a profitable, or even breakeven, enterprise.

After four PGA Tour Family Golf Centres proved to be unprofitable, the idea was shelved for a number of years and eventually resurrected by PGA Tour Commissioner Tim Finchem in 1997 as the First Tee, which now has over two hundred facilities nationwide introducing golf and life skills to (primarily) inner-city kids. The First Tee is subsidized through contributions, so it does not need to be profitable. The First Tee wasn't about promoting and growing golf participation; it was about extolling the virtues and values of the game to youngsters who otherwise would never have a chance to learn how to play. That's what made it different and successful.

Ironically, my introduction to the PGA Tour was based upon my expertise relative to what eventually became a failed enterprise. Fortunately, Commissioner Beman saw something in me. I joined the PGA Tour as a twenty-eight-year-old marketing executive in October of 1979. I had the right qualifications, but I also had good luck and timing. What I found on my arrival in Ponte Vedra Beach that fall was a small organization with a very big future. It had strong leadership, the will to succeed, and a creative approach to problem solving, and it was all wound together in the sport and culture that meant everything to me—golf.

8

THE PGA TOUR YOU NEVER KNEW

The PGA Tour's first commissioner, Joe Dey, was the former executive director of the USGA and initially served as the mediator in the rift between the PGA and their prodigal stepchild, the Tournament Players Division, also known as the PGA Tour. When Dey resigned on February 28, 1974, he was replaced by Deane Beman, a former U.S. and British Amateur champion and winner of five PGA Tour events.

Beman was known as a gritty player both as an amateur and as a pro golfer on the PGA Tour. He was a short hitter, often needing fairway woods to reach some of the longer par-4 holes, though fellow competitors were hitting irons. Yet he was a tough-as-nails competitor and was his fellow players' choice to be their commissioner—the first time in any sport that a former professional athlete was elevated to such a lofty executive position. Beman's competitive and entrepreneurial spirit permeated the entire PGA Tour organization. This led to the creation of a myriad of commercial enterprises intended to promote professional golf, grow the business, and increase tournament prize money. Most of these ventures were very successful; some were not; and a few were very controversial.

No single person did more to elevate golf's status in the consumer culture and media marketplace than Beman. During his twenty-year reign as commissioner, the PGA Tour's assets grew from about $500,000 to over $500 million. Operating revenues soared from $3.9 million a year to nearly $230 million in 1993. As anyone who follows golf knows, tournament purse money increased exponentially. This robust growth helped fuel the growth of golf participation at clubs and courses around the country and, in turn, fed off that grassroots excitement.

Looking back on what Beman achieved, I'm still amazed by the simple fact he was both perceptive enough to see the PGA Tour's future as a massive, multifaceted organization and passionate enough to drive so hard toward that end. He had been a successful businessman and insurance broker, a world-class amateur golfer and PGA Tour player, but hardly a star. By rights, he should have taken the standard attitude of a middle-of-the-pack player. He should have been in favor of a tour that stuck to basics—gathering purse money (from tickets, broadcast rights, and sponsors), setting up the golf courses for tournament play, and paying out checks on Sunday night. Such an average player would see anything beyond that as diverting potential prize money toward unnecessary causes.

The star players tended to want the very same thing. That is, until they became stars. As stars, the desire to accept big-money playing offers (non-PGA Tour) was in conflict with the PGA Tour's rules and requirements. But here was one solitary athlete-businessman who fell into neither of these predictable categories but who forged a compelling vision for the men's pro golf tour as a uniquely powerful commercial entity.

Assuming the reins of the PGA Tour at age thirty-five, Beman had the intelligence, mental toughness, and obvious tenacity, but no administrative experience. He was passionate about growing the business of the PGA Tour, but probably unsure how to do so. In retrospect, it's clear the man was a visionary. Problem solving was his stock and trade, and he saw solutions where others only saw problems. He had a different way of looking at the world. Beman spotted opportunities that were often hidden in plain sight. He also took advantage of any opening that presented itself.

Hidden in Plain Sight

Sometimes the most significant milestones, achievements, and breakthroughs are overlooked because they are not glamorous or sexy. The boldest and most significant act Beman undertook—the conversion of the tour from a for-profit to a nonprofit entity—was one of those breakthroughs hidden in plain sight. For the six prior years of its existence (following the PGA Tour's split from the PGA of America), the organization was a for-profit Delaware corporation paying taxes on its net income. Beman took office and immediately laid the groundwork for conversion to 501(c)(6) nonprofit status.

Many close observers of the tour don't realize it was Beman who accomplished this. Few, if any, appreciate what a challenge it was convincing the US Treasury Department to grant the change of status—the feds don't like saying good-bye to a taxpayer. Even a highly successful enterprise can be a nonprofit, as long as no distributions go to any individual member; that's what precludes income tax liability. Beman had to reorganize and start a new, not-for-profit corporation called the Tournament Golfers Association and then transfer the board, officers, and assets of the existing tour to this new entity. In a single stroke, the PGA Tour set itself up for probably a billion dollars in tax savings over the years.

The PGA Tour's greatest asset was its visionary leadership. It was a no-holds-barred approach that opened up doors of opportunity (formerly closed by a more traditional mind-set) in the marketing and promotion of professional golf. This went against the grain of many of the old guard and led to previously inconceivable and highly controversial marketing efforts such as the Vantage (cigarette) electronic scoreboards, stadium golf courses, the development of the Tournament Players Club (TPC) network of golf courses, the commercialization of the PGA Tour, the Senior PGA Tour, the Web.com Tour, the All-Exempt Tour, the player pension plan, etc. I had the extraordinary opportunity to work in marketing and administration for the PGA Tour when the organization was just glimpsing its potential to refashion professional golf and the business game into a bold, robust organization—what we now know the PGA Tour to be.

The PGA Tour today is unrecognizable from the organization I joined in October of 1979. At that time, the PGA Tour had fewer than sixty employees, including the tournament officials and tour agronomy staff. The tour had thirty-eight official events, plus the four majors run by other golf organizations. What I found on my arrival in Ponte Vedra Beach that September was a very small outfit with a big future, although no one really knew just how big.

In the late 1970s, the PGA Tour was still in start-up mode and about to sever the umbilical cord with its parent company, the PGA of America (officially, the Professional Golfers Association of America). This was when the tennis boom was in full swing, and golf was decidedly uncool. Golf's image was that of a sedentary game played by overweight white guys in plaid pants. Tennis was just then ascending to its peak of popularity, and we wanted to remake golf's image to appeal to the large baby boomer population segment. A cult-like sliver of the population revered the game of golf, but the mass marketplace did not.

Sunday telecasts of PGA Tour events were often preempted by reruns of *Old Yeller*; professional golf was a tough sell to prospective advertisers and tournament sponsors. If we could navigate our way there, our future was surely in television coverage and the support of corporate America. However, most of our tournaments still had celebrity associations—the Glen Campbell Los Angeles Open, the Sammy Davis Jr. Greater Hartford Open, or the Andy Williams San Diego Open. We knew the PGA Tour had great potential, but we were not quite sure where to start.

In 1979, the first year of the new television contracts with the three networks, the ratings were down from 1978. Overall, through the first half of the year, the ratings were down 11.6 percent. Back then, the total household viewing audience was 74.5 million; with the average ratings for golf events going from 6.0 to 5.3, that meant that the average number of households watching golf went from 4.47 to 3.95 million. Thirty percent of the revenue from the networks funded PGA Tour operations, and the balance went to fund tournament prize money. How the PGA Tour fared in the television marketing arena would determine the PGA Tour's future.

The only marketing advantage was the pro tour's following among top corporate decision makers—the aforementioned white guys in plaid pants. They played the game and watched it on TV (when it was not preempted), and their customers did as well. Judging by the few deals we were able to make early on, it was clear the executive passion for the royal and ancient game could uphold our cause when cold analysis dictated against golf as a marketing vehicle. Sometimes it was a stretch as we worked to discover value in our corporate relationships beyond the advertising minutes and title-sponsorship identification. It was a scattershot approach, and more often than not, we missed. But we kept shooting. Occasionally, we hit something.

Building a Management Team
At that time, the PGA Tour's inner management circle included some of Beman's trusted friends from his playing days. Steve Reid handled the early television negotiations. Bob Dickson did most of the advance work in selecting Sawgrass Country Club as the PGA Tour's future home. Labron Harris Jr. handled tournament administration. Serving as Deane's personal assistant and wielding considerable influence was Judy Beman, his wife. Clyde Mangrum and Jack Tuthill were holdovers from before the PGA-PGA Tour split, but they were trusted specialists charged with the vital task of conducting competitions and managing tournament officials. Outside the inner circle were professionals like Vernon Kelley, who was Beman's right-hand man when he needed to get anything built—be it the new headquarters building, the TPC clubhouse, or the infrastructure of the TPC club network. Chip Campbell headed communications and later took over television negotiations from Steve Reid, and Art West was the marketing ace and the man who originally hired me.

When I walked in that first morning, I said hello to our one-and-only secretary in the marketing department, Phyllis. Next, I went looking for the department's senior man, West, who had hired me based on my MBA, my recent consulting work for the PGA Tour, and my three years as a California-based field representative promoting new golf course development for the National Golf Foundation. "Where would you like me to park?" I asked West.

He motioned down the hallway, "Pick any spot you like." Our headquarters, though tiny by comparison to today's two thousand-plus-employee, sprawling multi-building complex, was new and spacious at that time. Down the hall, where West had pointed, were five empty offices from which the new guy could choose.

West, who had somehow tempered his freewheeling style over a lengthy tenure at IBM, was a pleasure to watch in action. He could sell ice to an Eskimo. A few weeks into the job, I was planning my first out-of-town trip. Phyllis asked me what kind of car I would like to reserve from "Hertz, the Official Rental Car Company of the PGA Tour." I replied, "Oh, something small," thinking it would be in my interest to appear budget-conscious.

West overheard our conversation and yelled down the hall for me to come see him. "David, you need to think bigger," he told me. "You are going to be out there seeing potential clients. What kind of impression are you going to make driving up in a Gremlin?"

I went back and said, "Okay, order me whatever Art usually gets."

In a matter-of-fact voice Phyllis asked, "Would you like a driver as well?"

I would like to say the breakthroughs in marketing the PGA Tour were the result of insightful analysis and planning, but the truth was we were winging it. In a sport where tradition and propriety are paramount, this wildcat approach was very much against the grain of how professional golf was (and there were those who thought *should* be) managed and promoted. Our tactics bordered on sacrilege, regularly displeasing the game's old guard. What we had going for us was attitude. We were willing to consider any and every avenue to grow the tour's business.

This approach fed on itself—like sharks who smell chum in the water. Sometimes these opportunities were obvious and right in front of us; sometimes they were under a rock. The real business breakthrough was simply our attitude and our willingness to consider everything and do whatever it took. We were not bound by tradition or by how we were supposed to act. There were no sacred cows as far as we were concerned.

Before this time, no one ever really viewed the PGA Tour as a business. No one even considered the notion of commercializing it. That would have been seen as an intrusion into the sanctity of professional golf. Our approach, however, enabled us to take advantage of opportunities when they presented themselves. We were willing to be whores if the price was right, and if the deals we cut furthered our cause.

"Art" of the Sale

One night in the fall of 1980, Art and I were at his house watching *Monday Night Football*. A player on the sidelines was shown taking a long drink of Gatorade. West turned to me and said, "David, our players get thirsty, too. We ought to have Gatorade on every tee at every tournament. Tomorrow, when you get to the office, check the Red Book [a directory of corporations and executives] and find out who at Stokely-Van Camp [then corporate owner of Gatorade] handles that brand. Give whoever it is a call."

The next day I did as requested and dug up the name. When I made the call I was told that this executive—we'll call him John Jones—had died just a couple of weeks earlier. I went into West's office to pass along the news. "Okay, what did you do next?" he asked me. I shrugged and told him I hadn't done anything, except to come and tell him. He held out his hand for the legal pad with my notes. "Give me the phone number," he said. "Now listen and learn from the master." West had an amplifier on his phone to offset some hearing loss, and he also spoke plenty loud, meaning if you were in the room, you could generally pick up the conversation at both ends.

He dialed the number and asked for John Jones, whom we both knew, was deceased. Informed once again of this sad fact, West said, "Oh no, I cannot believe this. John is dead? When did it happen? Did they have any warning? That's just terrible." (Cynical readers may be able to guess the rest.) "Look, this is Art West with the PGA Tour," West then paused for effect and continued, "John and I were working on a special project together. Could you tell me who is taking over for him?"

The voice on the other end of the line answered, "His name is Bill Brown [fictitious name]. And, his title is…vice president of Brand Management."

West then asked, "Look, could you connect me with Mr. Brown? Thank you so very much."

Before long, we were speaking with Bill Brown, to whom West stated authoritatively: "Bill, I just heard about John, I can't believe he had a heart attack. This is all so sudden. I know how much he will be missed by everyone." After a respectful pause, West continued, "Bill, are you taking over John's accounts?" West once again paused for effect, and asked, "Well, I would like to ask you if you are the right guy to talk to about this idea . . . if you are the decision maker on forming a relationship with the PGA Tour."

Brown seemed to take an inordinate amount of time to answer West's question, but the response was favorable.

West said, "That's great!" He continues, "Now Bill, are you a golfer?"

Bill answers.

"Okay, you're a thirteen handicapper, well then you'll have to give me a few strokes when we play at Sawgrass." (West was about an eight handicap at the time.) He then moved in for the close: "Basically," he crooned, "What we want to do is make Gatorade *the Official Thirst Quencher of the PGA Tour.*"

Brown clearly liked the idea.

"Oh, that's just great," West said, and then softened his voice to a faint lament. "I'm sure John would have wanted it that way."

I had the eerie feeling this was not the first time he had employed this sales tactic. West switched back to an up-tempo tone of voice. He did not want Brown to have the chance to grow skeptical. "Well Bill, it's wonderful of you to follow through on this project for John," West said. "My associate, David Hueber, will be up at your office in Indianapolis tomorrow afternoon. . . .Can you see him?"

Brown indicated he could.

"That's just great; we'll see you tomorrow."

And that's how Gatorade eventually became the Official Thirst Quencher of the PGA Tour. It was a good deal for everyone involved, and one of many more deals to come. And yes, in those early days, we were ad-libbing, with West as the self-described master ad-libber.

Our team had a work hard, play hard ethic in those early days, and a lively camaraderie went along with it. Nothing was sacred for long. At Christmas, Beman gave each member of the executive team a golf bag with a TPC logo on it. These were tour-size Wilson Staff bags with matching vinyl headcovers. I suspect Pete Davison, the TPC director of golf, had ordered too many of them, and this gesture was a good way of paring down inventory, but that did not matter to me. I loved my big Staff bag emblazoned with the TPC logo and was most grateful to the commissioner for presenting it to me.

A few weeks later, West and I were playing golf at the stadium golf course. It was a raw, cold Saturday morning in January. West didn't want to play, but I talked him into going nine with me. By the time we arrived at the ninth tee, West was miserable. His stocking cap was pulled over his ears. His hands were frozen because he did not have gloves and always insisted upon driving the golf cart. He was so bundled up he could hardly swing his driver. He hit his usual low, veering slice off the ninth tee. Unfortunately this time, his shot found the water down the right side of the ninth fairway. He stormed over to the golf cart. It was now my turn to hit my tee shot. Addressing the ball, I heard a ruckus over by the golf cart. It got louder and louder. West was over there in a battle with his new TPC Staff golf bag and headcovers. He was trying to replace the headcover on his driver, but the vinyl was so stiff from the cold it wouldn't fit over the clubhead. He was already fuming about dunking one in the lake, and now this equipment problem was putting him over the edge. The cart was actually rocking as West struggled for some control over the situation.

I stepped away from the ball and tried to sound irritated, asking, "What in the hell are you doing over there?"

To which, West replied, "Goddammit! You don't see Pete Rozelle [NFL commissioner at the time] giving his people stiff footballs do you?"

Selling Our Souls for a Lot of Silver

Beman never quite figured out how to maximize West's creative salesmanship skills. West was a maverick marketer. One of the first large-scale commercial sponsorship deals, R.J. Reynolds Tobacco Company, was made by Beman, but West reeled it in and orchestrated its implementation. We sold our souls for a pile of cigarette money and were able to roll out a new, onsite communications tool. I'm referring to the first-ever electronic scoreboards for golf events, those fondly remembered Vantage cigarette scoreboards.

The PGA Tour had an unwritten policy against involvement with tobacco (the same went for liquor and feminine-hygiene products), but the dollars in this Vantage deal were too big to walk away from. Pro golf could never have gotten away with a move like that even a few years later. It was so flagrant—the Vantage cigarette logo was plastered on all the side panels of these huge, electronic scoreboards which we set up at most of our events around the country. I have to say, it was a real innovation that truly did enhance the spectator experience and heighten fan enjoyment of the event. For those reasons, we felt the ends justified the means. So what if Vantage had a tent with an exhibit and passed out mini-packs of Vantage cigarettes to adults attending the tournaments? We were only committing a venial sin and would not burn in hell forever for it.

Golf's old expression, "It's not how, it's how many," should rightly have applied to our sponsor-seeking efforts, but arrangements like the Vantage deal came in for sharp criticism. Players opposed it on principle, including many players from what we called the "God Squad," that is, the regular Bible-meeting attendees. And, as I pointed out before, pleasing all the players even some of the time was rarely possible. In the marketing department, if we wanted praise we had to dole it out to each other.

By September 1981 I had left West's tutelage in the marketing department and moved over to the commissioner's office, where I actually replaced Judy Beman, Deane's wife. I settled in as Beman's go-to person, although no one really knew what to think of me at the time. Was I an executive assistant or the assistant commissioner? I preferred the latter, but that was a case of letting my aspirations get too far ahead of me.

Quite candidly, I probably was not the best chief administrator ever to be employed by the PGA Tour. While I did fancy myself as second in command, and a few guys on the tournament staff had taken to referring to me as the "Junior Commissioner," the real commissioner knew I had plenty to learn about the entire operation. That's why he sent me into the field to observe the crucially important work performed by our tournament officials. I hooked up with them at the Southern Open, an event then held not far from Ponte Vedra Beach in Columbus, Georgia.

My initial field observation was that a tournament official's workday is long. They start before daylight, marking the spots where the pins and tees will be set for that day's competition. Then, they roam the course and scoring centers all day, solving whatever problems may arise. They finish well after dark, but only after they've completed pairings for the next day's play. While the players are out competing, the day is tediously long. "Hours of boredom interrupted by moments of terror," as the commercial airline pilots like to say. It's the kind of job where you check your watch at 9:00 a.m., and when you check it again two hours later it says 9:20 a.m. So they broke up the long days however they could. Practical jokes were the preferred method.

Having the Junior Commissioner in town gave the crew at the Southern Open all the more reason to dig into the magic bag. Wade Cagle, a veteran official who would later spearhead formation of a union for tournament offi-

cials, reached in and pulled out a beauty that made the second day of my trip
an amusing one for all concerned. It began with the ring of a telephone—my
5:30 a.m. wakeup call at the Columbus, Georgia, Holiday Inn. I showered,
shaved, and dressed, and then sleepily headed to the golf course in my rental
car. I drove along thinking what a long and tough day these guys had, getting up before daylight and working until long after sundown. My throat felt
scratchy, so I pulled over to a convenience store to buy a bottle of juice. As I
waited at the counter to pay for my juice I asked the clerk: "When does it start
getting light around here?"

He looked at me with a raised eyebrow. "In about four hours," he replied.

Cagle had changed my wakeup call to 2:00 a.m., and I had crawled from
the bed in such a groggy state I had not bothered to check either my watch
or the clock in my room. Having transferred out of West's department, I was
back to reserving low-end rental cars, which in those days had no clocks on
their dashboards. Standing outside the store, I felt the loss of those three-and-
one-half prime sleeping hours like a child feels the loss of a helium balloon he
can still see floating above the fairgrounds. I went back to the motel and tried
to sleep, but there was no hope. When I finally got to the tournament I congratulated my tormentors, which gave Cagle and the boys no end of amusement. And I suppose that having fallen for the ruse, I passed my initiation, but
this was one fraternity you really would not want to pledge.

Later on, when I was handling routine administrative matters, I would receive two or three résumés a week from high-level retiring executives who
wanted to work as PGA Tour tournament officials. They were willing to work
for free—"just pay my expenses," their notes would say. I always wrote them
back to thank them for their interest. I was tempted to add a note in the rejec-
tion letters telling them that if they ever tried working one of those jobs they
would soon discover it wasn't nearly as fun as it looked on TV.

Another example of my lack of seasoning comes uncomfortably to mind.
I had been the commissioner's assistant for only a short time and was called
in from my adjacent office to pick up my marching orders for the day. I had
always had a knack for remembering everything I heard and prided myself
on my ironclad memory. This talent served me well in college and graduate
school, where I never needed to take detailed notes. On this particular day
Beman had quite a few matters he wished me to look into, and he was listing
them at a fairly rapid rate. After a while he said, "Aren't you going to write any
of this down?"

In my foolish bravado I said, "No, I don't need to. I'll remember it all."

He rattled off the remainder of his requests in a somewhat dubious tone
and then waved me off. I returned to my office in a mood that began with
confusion and then turned to regret. I chastised myself for my display of hu-
bris. Whether I had a good memory or not was not the issue. By writing down
whatever the boss was saying, you send the message that you consider his

instructions important and intend to carry them out. If I could, I would have kicked myself in the backside for this stupidity.

In working directly for Beman, I was able to see a side of him that probably eluded most. He appeared to not take things personally, and he seemed to be very calculating and professional in his responses. However, not everything was what it seemed. He did take things personally; he was just mentally tough. He didn't reveal his feelings, especially when it did not help in dealing with the issue at hand. Often the media, business associates, or underlings misconstrued his honest, straightforward and no-nonsense approach.

His forthrightness was often interpreted as a brusque demeanor. There were times when disgruntled players voiced criticisms—especially if it was related to fines issued for unprofessional behavior. There would be no discussion on the matter from the commissioner's office—even if the players involved pleaded their cases. The media, in these instances, stoked the fires of controversy to make the story more newsworthy. Sometimes the issue would be minor, such as not giving a star player a conflicting-event release; sometimes, however, it could involve matters of great consequence, such as the development of the TPC stadium golf courses or corporate support for promotional programs and title sponsorships for PGA Tour tournaments.

Beman was always a gentleman. He gave people the benefit of the doubt, whether they deserved it or not. But he also had some of the street fighter in him. He had an agile mind that at times forced him to wait while others puzzled out the strategy he had already formulated. He was a born innovator. He had political savvy in that he could read a situation and recognize motives—he just didn't let people know what he was thinking. The corporate culture at the PGA Tour when I worked there was tough and no-nonsense, a reflection of Beman's personality. That approach had real advantages, but it also presented an ongoing challenge to certain values and attitudes within the genteel game of golf.

Eventually, I learned how to deal with the commissioner when difficult issues arose: you never presented a problem without offering a recommendation or a solution. And, more often than not, your recommendation was approved and you had two new projects to do.

Tournament Players Clubs
In trying to parlay the PGA Tour image into sponsorship deals to compete in the professional sports marketplace (as well as grow the game and generate charitable income for PGA Tour events), it was critically important to continually improve the basic product—even down to electronic scoreboards that gave fans in the gallery instant updates on the competition. Most important was the concept for a fan-friendly TPC stadium golf course. Stadium courses were Beman's idea from the start. He realized that professional golf events had never really provided decent venues for the fans. In those days, it was

common to see a gallery filled with spectators looking at the action through cardboard periscopes. I remember one staff meeting when Beman pointed out the absurdity of this: "You know you have a real problem," he said, "when your fans have to look through cardboard periscopes to see the action they have paid money to watch. We've gotta get rid of the periscopes, and stadium golf courses are the answer."

Commissioner Beman was ahead of his time. He envisioned the greenside terrain and other vantage points that sloped to form amphitheaters, so that fans could comfortably sit and watch the greatest golfers play. Most importantly, by building a stadium course, the PGA Tour would have a permanent site (like Augusta) to host its very own tournament, which would hopefully, someday, become the fifth major. To put the execution of Beman's stadium golf concept in perspective, imagine Pete Rozelle, then commissioner of the NFL, deciding back in the 1960s that the stadiums for football were inadequate and then devising a prototype stadium-of-the-future, complete with sky boxes and fan amenities—all without any public funding.

Beman risked all his political capital on the TPC concept and won. But there were times when the effort appeared doomed. In constructing the golf course and clubhouse at TPC Sawgrass, we knew the entire golf world was watching, and mediocre reviews would kill us. No corners were cut, but when the course opened for play, barely any budget remained. Thick, unsightly stands of gnarly brush bordered the entire layout, and we had no money left to clear it. Pete Dye, the ever-creative architect who designed the course, suggested we bring in a small herd of goats to eat away the brush. I guess when you present a problem to someone from Indiana that is the kind of answer you can expect to get. However unconventional, Dye's idea worked. The goats were turned loose on the brush and the brush had no chance. Any branch, root, or shoot under an inch-and-one-half in diameter was swiftly consumed.

In point of fact, they were not turned loose, but penned into a prescribed area and left alone until their work was finished. Then, the maintenance crew would return to take down the barrier and herd the goats into another fenced-in parcel. The only problem was the goats, after devouring everything in sight, often turned to the wire-and-wood fencing in which they were enclosed and ate that as well, thereby escaping confinement. There were times when the escapees sought the highest ground, which happened to be the site of the TPC clubhouse. The goats positioned themselves in single file on the roof, with their patriarch, Old Prunes, at the summit.

Often, goat by-product was deposited in places where this fertilizer is really not all that useful. But the goats were doing their job cleaning up the perimeter areas. In time, the goats became "fruitful and multiplied." They also increasingly became a nuisance—stealing snacks and candy bars out of the golf carts and occasionally head-butting a golfer when threatened. On one occasion, Labron Harris Jr., a former PGA Tour winner and then director of PGA Tour Administration, was playing the first hole at the TPC when his tee shot strayed into the fenced-in area with the goats. He stepped over the barricade to retrieve his ball, but the biggest and baddest goat, Old Prunes, was protecting his latest stash which now included the ball and would not move. Harris wanted his golf ball, even though Titleist sent him four dozen a month for free. Holding his iron in hand, he lightly tapped Old Prunes on the head—bad idea. That was the last straw for Old Prunes, who then charged Harris, whose six-foot-two frame wasn't as sleek as it was during his playing days on the tour. After the first butt, Harris took flight, and Old Prunes took chase. As Harris lumbered away, he didn't bother to step over the barricade, taking the wood fence in tow.

Eventually, most of the cleanup work was done, and it was time for the goats to go. However, the saga of the TPC goats was not over. One day the goats once again escaped their confines and were grazing on the grass around the pond near the practice putting green, in full view of the lunchtime crowd in the clubhouse. One of Old Prunes's progenies was getting a drink of water from the pond when suddenly an alligator's head surfaced, eying this appetizer. The horrified crowd watched as the gator closed in on its prey. With a leap out of the water and swipe of his tail, the gator swatted the goat into the water. But the wee goat swam for his life and somehow escaped. Inside, the clubhouse crowd cheered. After this incident, the goats were gone but not forgotten.

The TPC stadium golf course was built on a swamp. With real estate prices rising, the Florida swampland had been renamed a "marsh" so that housing lots offering marsh views could be sold at a premium. Dye had to drain the land before he could start building the golf course. He dug a moat around the property to drain the swamp, and at one point nearly lost an $80,000 backhoe in the muck. At one of our regular Friday staff meetings, it was decided after much discussion that the drainage trench should be designated on the site map inside the brochures as the "Chain of Lakes." Personally, I favored calling it a moat. It seemed rather medieval and foreboding. Though Chain of Lakes probably sounded better, it never really caught on with the golfing public.

When they played the first TPC Championship at the stadium course in March of 1982, the fans loved the layout, and the players hated it. It was one of the hardest golf courses in the world at the time, even though Jerry Pate managed to shoot 12 under par in taking the title. The players thought it was too tricky and too penal. Sometimes good shots would not only be in awkward positions; they would end up in unplayable lies. The scores at Sawgrass Country Club—across Highway A1A—were all higher, but the wind proved to be less of a factor at the TPC because of the large trees that provided a buffer.

Readers might remember that back in the early 1980s, Jerry Pate was known for diving into a nearby lake after winning a golf tournament. When it appeared Pate might win at the inaugural TPC in 1982, we were unofficially advised that he would throw Beman, as well as the architect, Dye, into the greenside lake at the 18th green before taking the plunge himself. By then, I was serving as the commissioner's assistant. I had just brought the new Waterford trophy down to the 18th green for the presentation ceremony and was standing beside the commissioner as Pate hit an amazing five iron that stopped two feet away from the pin. It was obvious Pate would sew up this victory. Looking at Pate's tap-in putt with the obtrusive orange-colored golf ball, I began to think how uncomfortable a fully clothed person would feel once submerged in the cold waters of the greenside pond.

Beman leaned toward me and said, "It looks like I might be getting wet." He then handed me his watch, wallet, and other valuables, which I placed in my jacket pockets. Pate putted out for victory, and both Dye and Beman received their chilly baptisms. In his dread of getting dunked, Beman had forgotten to remove from his blazer breast pocket a sheaf of three-by-five cards containing some handwritten notes. He had a habit of making notes in ink from every conversation or meeting of importance. After his plunge, all that was left was a week's worth of blurred and smudged blue ink, containing not one legible word.

***

By this time, a major new player had joined the executive team on the business side of the PGA Tour. He was Kay Slayden, former president and chief operating officer of Fuqua Industries, later to become president and COO of Norrell Health Care, both of which were major public companies. Slayden had more business savvy than anyone who had ever come to work for the PGA Tour. He had managed billion-dollar businesses, served as an engineer on the Saturn rocket project, and even helped produce the first *Walking Tall* movie (when Fuqua teamed with Bing Crosby Productions). Just as impressive was his ability to offer a colorful story or provide an explanation on just about every subject or question that ever came up.

One day, a group of us were playing a round at the stadium course—Slayden, West, me, and Ruffin Beckwith, who worked the communications department. Beckwith was in constant amazement of Slayden. On the second hole, I hit a towering drive that seemed to hang in the air forever. Watching it climb to its apogee and slowly begin its descent, Slayden remarked: "Damnation, that ball was in the air long enough for the Coriolis effect to come into play."

Beckwith turned to Slayden and shook his head in disbelief. "Okay," he said, "I'll bite. What in the hell is the Coriolis effect?"

Slayden explained to him: "Dr. Coriolis was a famous French mathematician who figured out why water drains differently north and south of the equator. He also figured out why long-range cannons often missed their mark, because the people aiming them would neglect to factor in the rotation of the earth as the projectile headed toward its target."

Beckwith's jaw hung open as he asked, of no one in particular: "Is there anything this guy doesn't know?"

Slayden was the right person, at the right time. He enabled the PGA Tour to step up to the next level of corporate marketing and licensing in developing its commercial interests. Beman had an unusual ability to surround himself with talent, to inspire people and challenge them, then get out of their way and let them do their jobs. Also, it did not matter to Beman who got the credit. He only cared about getting the job done. Over time, he built his management team out with new recruits, moving beyond the inner circle of trusted friends from his playing days. He hired to his weaknesses, not to his strengths, which is an important characteristic of leadership that is intent upon success.

Playing Hardball

As PGA Tour business interests continued to grow, previously addressed concerns sometimes resurfaced, such as the direction of corporate marketing or the increase in the number of Tournament Players Clubs. Interestingly, the PGA Tour's strategy for developing TPCs was to put the PGA Tour at no financial risk. The focus was to be more on the attractiveness of the deal, and less on the viability of the project.

By doing that, Beman continually strengthened his own political base. In many ways, his day-in, day-out task was to increase tournament prize money. Beman was so adept at upping prize money for professional golfers he was even able to increase the purses for events over which the PGA Tour had no authority of any kind. Yes, I'm talking about the four majors: the Masters, the U.S. Open, the British Open, and the PGA Championship.

In the late 1970s and early 1980s, these four marquee events were not keeping pace with the regular PGA Tour events in terms of prize money. Was the size of their purses a matter that lay beyond Beman's jurisdiction? Perhaps it was. But something didn't smell right to Beman, and he was inclined to do something rather than sit on his hands. With the lucrative television-rights fees given to each of the majors, it was clear that the sponsoring organizations were not paying a fair share of revenues to the stars who made the show possible.

Beman had reached the conclusion that the organizations in charge of the majors were colluding with each other to keep the prize money down. The more he studied the situation, the more clues he saw indicating there was a conspiracy. One day during the 1982 Masters at Augusta National, he secured the evidence he had sought. In a casual conversation with Hord Hardin, former USGA president and then the Masters tournament chairman, Beman asked nonchalantly about the size of the next year's purse. Hardin made a comment along the lines that he didn't know yet, because they (Augusta National) hadn't met with representatives of the other events—the USGA, the PGA, and the R&A.

Beman heard this and began to seethe. He kept his composure just long enough to finish the conversation and excuse himself. That was surely not easy. Somewhere at that moment, a Masters competitor had just bladed a bunker shot or three-putted for bogey. Be that as it may, the most torqued-off man at Augusta National right then was the PGA Tour commissioner. Now, however, he had material evidence of a conspiracy among the four organizations that controlled golf's major championships.

Three officers of the PGA of America—career club pros, not men who had competed in the top ranks—also served on the PGA Tour's Tournament Policy Board, and Mark Cox, the PGA executive director, also attended the PGA Tour board meetings. The PGA was culpable and had a major conflict of interest as directors. Beman could have pushed it as an antitrust matter, but chose to go a different route.

The PGA was in a precarious situation, and Beman explained it to them in no uncertain terms. He told them they needed to do the right thing, or there would be "hell to pay." They heard his admonitions and did the right thing— right away, that very year. In 1983 there was a huge increase in the purse money for the PGA Championship, which went from $451,000 up to $600,000. The following year, the other three majors followed suit. Beman played hardball when the stakes were high and principles were on the line, but he made every effort to play fair. His policy was never to take undue advantage because he knew that "whatever goes around comes around." One party may hold the upper hand today, but could easily be dealt a weaker hand tomorrow.

Once the PGA Tour had proved itself a premier environment for high-end consumer branding as well as business-to-business relationship building, we held the upper hand in most dealings with corporate sponsors. That said, the standing order was to make sure both sides in the negotiation came out winners. We were determined that each side should get as close as possible to what each needed and wanted. The corporate sponsor, no matter what size check they wrote, should always feel they received a good value. Otherwise, no matter how pretty the weather on tournament week or how exciting the finish, they would not renew when the contract came up again.

Building a Broad Base of Support

The building blocks for Commissioner Beman's base of support among the PGA Tour membership were twofold. First, he had to do everything possible to increase the tournament prize money. This meant getting more from the networks, getting more from corporate marketing, and getting more from other sources, including the licensing of the TPCs. Second, he had to do everything possible to enhance the welfare of the PGA Tour membership in general.

Sometimes, the accomplishment of the latter was not as easy as it sounds. For example, the PGA Tour retirement plan and the All-Exempt PGA Tour were not as easy a sell to the tour membership as one might think. In order to understand this, one needs to understand the mentality of typical PGA Tour members. They are independent contractors, deciding where and when they play. They are very competitive with each other. They all earned and played their way onto the PGA Tour, and they were not very interested in making it any easier for their fellow competitors to compete with them. They preferred to keep the old system of having the top sixty money winners exempted from Monday qualifying, because it provided them with some competitive advantage—an advantage they had earned with their golf clubs.

The PGA Tour retirement plan is not really a retirement plan in the sense that most people understand one to be. It is not a defined benefit or contribution plan. The PGA Tour could never offer such a plan, because the tour is a 501(c)(6) nonprofit association (no member/shareholder of that organization can derive any financial benefit such as a dividend or capital gain relative to membership interest). The way the PGA Tour got around this issue was to make its "retirement plan" a deferred-compensation plan. This deferred compensation was paid based upon the number of cuts made by a player. Each year, the PGA Tour funded the retirement pool from which each player earned a certain share. Over time, this share accumulated. A player could have access to those funds upon reaching a certain age or via buying an annuity.

When this concept was presented to the membership, they used an up-and-coming player, Mark O'Meara, as an example. They projected that if O'Meara continued to make the minimum number of cuts he already had, by the time he was fifty years old, he would have an annual retirement income in the range of $250,000. This was at a time without a Senior PGA Tour, so players were concerned about earning a good living after their golf skills had diminished. Most of the players liked the idea of having a retirement plan, but given a choice, they would still rather play for the money put into such a plan and worry about retirement later. Beman was a former insurance salesman in his amateur days, and he understood the need for such a program. He also had the salesmanship skills to close the deal.

The All-Exempt Tour had great appeal to the players who weren't in the top sixty. The biggest advocate of this program among the players was Gary McCord, best known today for working on the CBS Golf broadcast team, and then being asked to no longer be a commentator for the Masters telecast after his "bikini wax" comments. Believe it or not, McCord was crazier in those days as a PGA Tour player than he is today.

Ken Venturi once told me a story about Gary McCord when he first started working for CBS and met Ben Hogan for the very first time at Shady Oaks during the Colonial tournament in Fort Worth. Venturi and Frank Chirkinian, the legendary CBS Golf producer, were having lunch with Hogan in the men's grill. As McCord nervously approached Hogan's table and introduced himself, he said something along the lines of, "Mr. Hogan, I am Gary McCord and it is an honor to meet you."

Hogan nodded and said, "Have a seat. What do you do?"

To which McCord replied, "I am a PGA Tour player and I have just started doing some television broadcast work with Mr. Venturi on CBS."

Hogan, skipping over the television-work reference, then asked, "How long have you played on the PGA Tour?"

McCord replied, "About fifteen years or so."

Hogan then inquired, "How many tournaments have you won?"

McCord answered, "None yet."

"Then why do you play?"

McCord was speechless for the first time in his life.

When McCord first played on the PGA Tour, he was sponsored by Lawrence Welk, the quintessential bandleader of days gone by, which seemed an odd pairing, given McCord's irreverence for tradition. He was the typical journeyman PGA Tour player, making enough to earn a living, but having a tough time doing it. McCord wasn't a top sixty money earner; he was relegated to qualifying nearly every Monday before the tour event. He was known as one of the "rabbits," and if he didn't qualify that week, he was on to the next tournament to try again. It was a tough life, not the glamorous life that people imagine. It was impossible to plan a schedule and not very conducive to having any kind of personal life. The top sixty players, on the other hand, could plan their schedules and enjoy some semblance of a personal life, if that is possible when one is away from home for twenty-five to thirty weeks a year.

Gary McCord was most outspoken on this issue at the player's meeting. Beman quietly listened to McCord and a number of other players, and then remarked to me that this was really something we needed to address. At the time, we were already computing the formula for increasing the number of exempt players. We didn't know if it was going to be 100 or 115 or 125, but we were going to have an All-Exempt Tour.

9

PGA DIVORCE AND REMARRIAGE

The common law marriage between the PGA, an association of club professionals founded in 1916, and the tournament professionals, many of whom were PGA members, began around the time of the Stock Market Crash in 1929. It was a rocky marriage, surviving the Great Depression, WWII, and the emerging discord from postwar economic recovery. With the increases in income coming from televised golf in the 1960s, the tour professionals were becoming dissatisfied with the PGA's tournament management and its allocation of revenue.

In August of 1968, the tournament professionals created their own organization, the American Professional Golf Association (APG), which was independent from the PGA. After a few months of negotiation, the APG was abolished, and it was agreed to form the PGA Tournament Players Division. It was to be an automonous organization and have its own ten-member Tournament Policy Board. It had three directors who were the officers of the PGA, three independent directors, and four player-directors who were members of the PGA Tour. Joe Dey, the former USGA executive director, was elected the PGA Tour's first commissioner in 1969. In 1974, Deane Beman became the second commissioner.

Not surprisingly, all would not be well in Camelot. The Beman administration inherited a number of problems including the usage of the brand name it shared with the PGA of America, who seemed to be parlaying the PGA Tour's brand equity into deals for the PGA club professionals. So, in order to allay any confusion in the marketplace, the PGA Tour decided to change its name in 1982 to the Tournament Players Association (TPA Tour). It was anticipated this name change would define and distinguish each organization, which from the PGA's standpoint was tantamount to a final divorce decree.

From the TPA Tour's standpoint, it was anticipated that its business interests would be better served in the long run once the golfing public understood that the PGA was the association of club professionals, and the TPA Tour was the organization of tournament professionals. Further, it would help the Tournament Players Championship, now the Players Championship, develop into one of golf's major championships, simply because it was the preeminent event of the TPA Tour.

No one realized how pivotal this point in time was in the tour's history and in the development of professional golf. Perhaps the TPA Tour's executive team just couldn't see the forest for the trees. Perhaps they had too many irons in the fire with barely enough hours in the day to put out all of the fires of confusion between the two organizations called the PGA.

This issue with the PGA of America seemed easy to resolve with the name change, but that name change was disturbingly fluid. The signage outside PGA Tour headquarters, along with everyone's letterhead and business cards, changed three times. A bit shortsightedly, the TPA Tour neglected to save any of the PGA Tour signage and paper stock, believing that when the name changed to the TPA Tour, it was permanent—never to be identified that way again. At the time, I was the assistant to the commissioner. Here is what happened instead.

At the Boca Raton Hotel in November of 1982, Beman and I appeared on behalf of the TPA Tour to commune with our uneasy PGA of America brethren. The occasion was the PGA's annual meeting; the immediate context was our organization's forfeiture of "the three letters," as people came to refer to them. The PGA annual meeting is always well attended, seating delegations from forty or so regional PGA sections from throughout the United States. Entering the lobby, I had a portent of the reception we would receive and suddenly felt more like Beman's bodyguard than his assistant.

As we entered the ballroom prior to Beman's speech, the PGA faithful parted and made way. It was as a bit like Moses splitting the fairway of the Red Sea as we passed through the throng of PGA club professionals. There were not very many smiles in the crowd, and if looks could kill, the two guys from the TPA Tour were goners. Needless to say, Beman's speech was not warmly received. The question-and-answer period following ended up being more or less a series of speeches from standing PGA officers and the council of past presidents. One of the past presidents on the dais, Don Padgett, recited a particularly detailed series of complaints. The commissioner's only response was to blandly ask, "Was there a question somewhere in your commentary?"

Not too long after that meeting, the president of the PGA, Joe Black, made an effort to put the hatchet aside, if not bury it altogether. Black had seen the world from the vantage point of a politically squeezed former professional tournament manager; he served in that capacity for the PGA in the 1950s before there was any separate governing body for tournament play. Black and

David Hueber
Director of Special Projects

PGA TOUR
Sawgrass
Ponte Vedra, Florida 32082
(904) 285-3700

David Hueber
Assistant to the Commissioner

Tournament Players Association
Sawgrass
Ponte Vedra, Florida 32082
(904) 285-3700

David B. Hueber
Vice President,
PGA TOUR PROPERTIES, INC.

PGA TOUR
Sawgrass
Ponte Vedra, Florida 32082
(904) 285-3700

When the PGA Tour changed its name to the TPA Tour, it was a shot across the bow, forever changing the relationship between the game's leading professional golf organizations. Note the change in the logos from the fall of 1982 through the spring of 1983. *Author's collection. Logos used with permission of the PGA Tour.*

Beman decided it would be in the best interests of both organizations if the TPA/PGA Tour and the PGA of America shared the same three letters in their brand names.

The PGA then had over 22,000 member professionals, and Beman felt they were an important resource in promoting not just the professional tour, but the game of golf as well. However, there were still three officers of the PGA serving on the tournament policy board (think of that as equivalent to a board of directors), and they wielded considerable influence. The problem was the PGA officers still viewed the TPA Tour as their rightful property—going back to the days when Sam Snead and Hogan also had club jobs and affiliations while playing golf for a living. Beman, in fact, was introduced to the 1982 PGA annual meeting as "commissioner of the PGA Tournament Players Division," and his first words were, "Thank you for that warm welcome; as commissioner of the TPA Tour . . . ."

The divorce between the PGA and the PGA Tour seemed final to everyone in the executive group at our TPA Tour headquarters. Before the ink had dried on the divorce papers, however, the two estranged combatants were back in marriage counseling. Leading the negotiation for the TPA Tour was new general counsel, Tim Smith. Smith distinguished himself over the course of these negotiations. He was an experienced political operative with a résumé that included management of Jimmy Carter's Virginia presidential campaign, followed by a stint as special assistant to President Carter.

Smith served ably in that White House post and then moved on to a position within the Justice Department, so this golf stuff was not about to faze him. He had a somewhat unique negotiation style—the slow and deliberate demeanor of Jimmy Stewart in the movie *It's a Wonderful Life*, coupled with the ruthlessness of Joe Pesci in *Goodfellows*. Smith demonstrated his political savvy early and often in the tour's negotiations with the PGA, a performance that justified and eventually led to his appointment as deputy commissioner and chief operating officer of the PGA Tour.

The PGA never had much leverage in these discussions. They actually believed they were holding the better hand, but failed to realize a vital fact: we were perfectly content to continue on as the TPA Tour. My own opinion at the time was we should not even bother trying to get back our share of the three letters; we should simply remain the TPA Tour. Initially, it would feel like a sacrifice, but before long, this would be the recognized brand name of top-level men's pro golf in the United States. Meanwhile, the three letters, P-G-A, would gradually lose importance and be recognized as the club professional's trade union—not confused with the star players who competed weekly. I felt that once this distinction was understood by the golfing public, it would be easier to market the TPA Tour with much less confusion as to which group was which. Lastly, I thought it would help the TPC Championship to more quickly gain recognition as a major championship, possibly nudging past the

PGA Championship. Why wouldn't the public put more stock in the premier event staged by touring pros rather than the premier event staged by club pros?

Fortunately for the PGA, I didn't have much influence at the time. Commissioner Beman, believe it or not, turned out to possess a rather magnanimous attitude toward the club-professional faction. Unfortunately for the PGA, the TPA Tour had one tough lead negotiator in Beman, ably backed by Smith. The PGA guys were outmanned and outgunned from start to finish.

Negotiations took place in Los Angeles in an out-of-the-way hotel called the Bel-Air Summit. I was there and tried to assist at various points, but Smith wanted no additional cooks in the kitchen. At one point, he dressed me down privately for having brought a financial concern to the attention of our player-directors serving on the Tournament Policy Board. "What the hell do you think you were doing? You are only confusing those guys with that kind of information," he said. "Who put you on the negotiating team, anyway?" At the time, his title was still just legal counsel, and he had only been on staff a few months, so his rebuke for something that seemed fairly innocuous caught me off guard.

In the period leading up to these negotiations, there were some in the golf industry, notably *Golf Digest* founders Bill Davis and Howard Gill, who considered me a legitimate candidate to one day become the tour commissioner. After that brief interaction with Smith, any such delusions of grandeur on my part were put aside. I remained present for all the closed-door sessions, but mostly observed. I was also given some ancillary issues to work out with industry people who held certain PGA licensing rights to be used as bargaining chips.

When the dust settled, the PGA of America reserved its right to continue using the PGA mark in connection with the PGA Championship, the Ryder Cup, the PGA Grand Slam, and other PGA of America sponsored events. They also continued to secure the television rights fees for those events. The PGA Tour did the same for its tournament schedule and negotiated separately with the networks. Both organizations agreed to continue joint sponsorship of the World Series of Golf.

The PGA Tour agreed to create, fund, and operate a developmental professional tour to provide playing opportunities for PGA club professionals as well as aspiring PGA Tour pros. This tour, which I later coined the Tournament Players Series (TPS), would be funded from the net income of the PGA Tour qualifying tournament. It was a major compromise for both parties. It reduced the number of spots reserved each week on the regular PGA Tour for members of the PGA, but gave those players more opportunity to play professional golf on the TPS Tour. This new developmental tour was the forerunner of the Hogan-Nike-Buy.com-Nationwide-Web.com Tour, so its legacy was certainly significant. Ironically, I later became involved in the setup and launch of both professional golf tours.

The PGA also agreed to create and operate a grassroots membership program similar to the highly successful USGA Associates Program. This would financially benefit both organizations. Lastly, the PGA Tour would create, control, and operate a joint marketing company, PGA Tour Properties, to actively sell and license the respective trademarks for the PGA and the PGA Tour.

With the PGA and the PGA Tour married once again, Beman sat me down to discuss my role in the organization. He said there were a number of people who could handle my administrative responsibilities competently, and if I stayed in that job it would eventually become boring for me. He felt there was more value in placing me on the team that was building the tour's business interests. So I transferred back to my old department, only this time with the lofty title of vice president of marketing. I felt complimented, but wished I could have remained for a while in the mentor relationship I'd developed with Beman. It was such a catalyst in my professional growth.

In my new role as vice president of PGA Tour Properties, I developed the commercial- and sponsorship-side of the business. Initially, I was the point man on everything related to the PGA of America, including the licensing of the PGA and PGA Tour marks. Also, I was responsible for finding local sponsorship groups for the new Tournament Players Series circuit.

The PGA Tour would run the TPS and fund it out of the net proceeds from the PGA Tour Qualifying Schools, as well as from local corporate sponsorship and related tournament income. Beman never really had to sell this idea to the membership. PGA Tour members already believed there were too many spots taken by PGA members who were not competitive. The TPS was born out of the negotiations with the PGA. The PGA of America still felt like it owned the PGA Tour, and this was simply a PGA entitlement. However, Beman really believed there should be a development tour, although this notion might not have been shared by many PGA Tour members.

The commissioner asked me to work toward securing at least five TPS events for the inaugural year, and even though many dry wells were dug, I was able to almost double that first-year objective. The mission got off to an unmistakably slow start, however. I had a clear enough goal but not the first idea how to accomplish it. It was no easy task finding local groups and organizations with the know-how to stage a pro golf tournament and secure local commercial sponsors to underwrite the cost. One way or another, I built the prospect file to perhaps half a dozen solid possibilities. But as the weeks ticked by, I grew desperate to close on a tournament or two. Everything was still a "maybe"; the commissioner's objective of establishing five events for the coming season started to seem far-fetched. One event in Orange County, California, however, was shaping up very nicely. We were far enough along in our planning and negotiations that I flew to California to set up a press conference with my sponsor group to announce the first-ever event on the exciting new Tournament Players Series Tour.

After meeting with the principals and following up on a few critical matters, I began to see beyond the happy talk and recognized that the essential elements were not in place and would not be anytime soon—no way could we book this event on our TPS schedule for the next year. I cancelled the press conference. Now, I was back to zero. With considerable trepidation, I made my way to a pay phone to call back East with the news. I briefed the commissioner on what had taken place and told him I had scratched this event from the list.

His response was unexpected and empowering: "Sounds like you did the right thing," he said. "I put you in charge of this project to make those kinds of decisions. It's better to find out now rather than later that they can't carry the ball. Don't be in a hurry to get this done. It's better to be right than fast."

Eventually, I secured nine TPS events for the first year and added another event for a total of ten in the second year. We had successfully created an entirely new pro tour, the Tournament Players Series, where PGA members had greater access to playing professional golf. We had also succeeded in reducing the number of spots for PGA members on the PGA Tour.

***

Beman was not always complimentary about my work. He could cut through the bullshit faster than it could be created. When things were not going as intended, he responded in an uncritical way, and you always knew it was sincere. Part of my job as the tour's point man with the PGA of America was to help them develop a PGA Inner Circle program (the grassroots membership program similar to the USGA Associates Program). Aware of the major treaty just hammered out, the PGA staff people administering the inner circle program called for PGA Tour assistance with this initiative, but the PGA of America *leadership* wanted no help and resisted anything I had to say. I continued offering advice and ideas until one day Beman took me aside and told me the PGA was complaining about my interference. Specifically, it was Lou King, the new PGA executive director, whose nose was out of joint.

I responded by saying King and his staff had no clue what they were doing. They were not consulting any outside marketing sources with experience in these consumer-affinity programs, and the PGA Inner Circle was destined for certain failure. Further, I reminded the commissioner of King's presentation at the last Tournament Policy Board meeting, when Del de Windt, the policy board chairman, wisely suggested to King that he may want to back off on the PGA's sales projections, based upon their anemic performance to date.

King became visibly indignant, telling de Windt: "That's what we have written down, and those are our projections, period." (He actually said the word, period.)

Beman then said to me, "We all know they aren't going to make it, David. They know it, themselves—they just won't admit it. You don't need to point it out to them. Whatever happens will happen, regardless of what you say or do." The PGA Inner Circle went away quietly. Both the PGA and the PGA Tour lost money on this misguided venture.

***

PGA Tour Properties, the joint marketing and licensing arm for the PGA and PGA Tour trademarks, was created, controlled, and managed by the PGA Tour. It accomplished its purpose for another ten years or so, until the PGA of America and the PGA Tour figured out how to further delineate their joint marketing of the PGA brand.

The corporate marketing deals soon started to trickle in. West implemented the R. J. Reynolds/Vantage electronic scoreboard program, which was the biggest deal to date at $12 million over three years. Slayden oversaw PGA Tour Properties. We all had a number of plates spinning. Slayden had a very different management style from Beman's. He challenged his subordinates to excel but did it in an affable, almost paternalistic, manner. He demanded results, but took a personal interest in his employees and their success. Most people who worked for him didn't mind moving heaven and earth to get the job done. Perhaps it was his charming demeanor, or his purposeful storytelling.

10

THINK BIG AND GROW RICH

Meanwhile, the business interests of the PGA Tour began to emerge. We knew that we were making progress, but didn't really understand how to exploit it. In the midst of all this came a compelling comment, courtesy of Card Walker, one of the independent directors on our Tournament Policy Board. Walker was a sharp-eyed business strategist who had begun his career in the mail room at Walt Disney Productions. He worked his way to the top, serving as the CEO and chairman of Disney before the tenure of Michael Eisner. Walker pointed out we were taking our cues from the success of NFL Properties and trying to develop PGA Tour marketing using the NFL model. But, as Walker observed, football and golf were much different. The NFL leveraged a far broader audience, and pro football fans fit into a wide array of consumer product categories. This gave NFL Properties access to many more licensing opportunities than the PGA Tour would ever have.

Walker had been involved in hiring Peter Ueberroth for the 1984 Olympics and arranged for Slayden and me to spend some time with him out in Los Angeles. In doing so he basically handed us the key to a vault of opportunities. It is no understatement to say Slayden and I absorbed a series of excellent lessons in sports marketing from Ueberroth. What he told us and showed us had direct application to the marketing doctrine of the PGA Tour.

The essence of it was the recognition that carrying fewer clients and providing them more value in exchange for larger portions of their budgets can be markedly more profitable than having many clients who pay you less and receive less value. Furthermore, Ueberroth figured out a way to tie television advertising exclusivity to sponsorship licensing. What he did was very simple and very smart, and it became the standard operating procedure for future Olympics as well as for the PGA Tour.

Ueberroth created thirty or so corporate sponsorship categories, each representing a product licensing and advertising exclusive. For a minimum fee of $4 million, a company could tie up one of these categories and become the "Official X-Y-Z" of the Olympics. More importantly (and this element would take the program far beyond what Art West had arranged with Gatorade in our exclusive-thirst-quencher deal), the sponsors would secure category-exclusive rights to advertise their product on worldwide television. Ueberroth linked the exclusive licensing of the product to the exclusive right to advertise on television, thereby enhancing the value of both.

Ueberroth exuded confidence and was friendly enough, but it was clear from his demeanor that he was only spending time with us because Walker had asked him. The temperature in the room seemed to drop about ten degrees when we first met in his Los Angeles office, and he started his primer on sports marketing. He told us a story to illustrate how his approach worked: He had arranged a meeting with the president of Eastman Kodak Company to talk about making Kodak the "Official Film of the Olympics."

Hearing what the program had to offer, Kodak's president expressed interest. Ueberroth explained that he sincerely wanted an American company to have this category exclusively, and would not open the category for bidding if Kodak agreed to come in at the minimum fee of $4 million. He emphasized that no other film company would be able to advertise during the Olympic telecasts. Kodak would be the Official Film of the Los Angeles Olympics. All fine and good, but Kodak's marketing budget was not positioned to handle it. The company president said he would be willing to pay double what Kodak had paid before, but that amount would come to just $2 million. Ueberroth said he would rather close the camera/film category than compromise the integrity of the deals he had already made with other companies.

McDonald's had built the swimming complex at UCLA as part of its Olympic deal at a cost far beyond the $4 million minimum. Furthermore, Ueberroth still believed in the value of this exclusive category for some company in the film market. He made it clear that when he left Kodak headquarters that day, the exclusive offer to Kodak would be withdrawn. The president said good-bye, leaving Ueberroth with no clear read on whether he considered the matter concluded or whether a counteroffer below the $4 million level might be forthcoming. Ueberroth certainly had no plans to lower his price. He flew back to Los Angeles and immediately sent a cable to Fujifilm saying that the 1984 Los Angeles Olympics was opening the film/camera category. The successful bidder would be the Official Film of the 1984 Los Angeles Olympics and enjoy the exclusive right to advertise their film and photographic products on the worldwide Olympic television broadcasts. The minimum acceptable offer to be considered was $4 million.

Six hours later, Fuji submitted its offer, which was preemptive, to say the least. In a considerable up-sell from the $2 million number he had stood at with Kodak the day before, Ueberroth peddled his official film marketing package (to a non-American brand) for $6.7 million.

Kodak was blocked from television advertising during the 1984 Olympics. The company could only buy spot-TV time in the major markets and was forced to pay a considerable premium to do so. Kodak even bought billboard space along LA freeways, posting ads that gave the impression Kodak was an Olympic sponsor. The company was served written notice to take the billboards down and complied. The 1984 Los Angeles Olympic Games were the first modern-day olympiads that turned a profit. Typically, the host city of any Olympics operated deep in the red and defined success based upon economic impact and the permanent assets remaining in place when the games moved on. When the 1984 games were over, the organizing committee had to get to work figuring out how to give away about $250 million in operating profit. The Ueberroth model became standard procedure for marketing future Olympics. Meanwhile, we golf guys learned our own valuable lessons from Ueberroth's Olympic horse-trading.

The PGA Tour was emerging, slowly but steadily, as an important player in sports television. Our tournaments were evolving into premier vehicles for corporate image and brand building. When Beman became the PGA Tour commissioner in 1974, only one tournament, the Kemper Open, had a corporate sponsor. Back then, most had celebrity associations like the Andy Williams San Diego Open. Over the next ten years, the business game changed, making way for new corporate-title sponsors like the Shearson-Lehman Brothers Andy Williams Open. This new relationship with corporate America forever changed how major sports operated, and the PGA Tour led the way.

Most of the PGA Tour tournaments made the transition without a hitch because corporate sponsors paid big bucks to put their names on the events. Sponsors underwrote all of the advertising time in the telecast in order to gain exclusive advertising rights in their particular product categories. For example, if Honda was the tournament-title sponsor and television advertising underwriter, you would not see an ad for a Buick during the telecast. Eventually, the networks started to get greedy and forced some of the sponsors to make incremental buys above and beyond their tournament advertising commitments. In other words, Honda might be asked to make an incremental buy elsewhere on NBC as part of the network's agreement to broadcast the Honda Classic golf event.

A few events did not make the transition so smoothly. One such example was the Bing Crosby National Pro-Am. When it came time to partner up with AT&T, the corporate sponsor, Kathryn Crosby, Bing's widow, objected. The new title, the AT&T Bing Crosby National Pro-Am, apparently wasn't music to her ears. She declined the offer and disassociated the Crosby name from the event, moving the Crosby clambake all the way East to the Carolinas. Now the tournament name is the AT&T Pebble Beach Pro-Am.

Back at tour headquarters there was some disappointment, considering the great heritage Bing Crosby had established as one of the first friends of pro-tour golf in America. Card Walker, in a cynical moment, wondered aloud why Kathryn Crosby "didn't see anything wrong with auctioning Bing's clothes and personal effects after his death, yet she objected to having AT&T in front of his name?" Celebrity title sponsors, while enthusiastic boosters and promoters of their events, had at times caused concern for PGA Tour management. We were in a corporate environment now with all the heightened sensitivities that went with it. For example, Glen Campbell traditionally staged a benefit concert to raise money for charities connected to the Los Angeles Open, and the proceeds from it were deeply appreciated. However, I recall that a group of executives from Sony left a Glen Campbell concert at the PGA Tour's title-sponsor's party prior to the 1983 TPC, because Campbell was visibly impaired and behaved obnoxiously during the performance.

Eventually, every tournament signed on with corporate America, even if the tournament never appeared on television. Corporate sponsors wanted their week in the sun, as well as an opportunity to entertain clients. The old, low-key days were gone. There were still a few stand-alone tournament hosts, such as the membership of Colonial Country Club (for the Colonial National Invitation Tournament), or the Salesmanship Club of Dallas (for the Byron Nelson Classic), but no tournament could continue to offer a competitive purse much longer without some national corporate sponsorship. Eventually, even these holdouts succumbed to corporate enticements.

The TV money flowed in, and televised tournaments received a larger share of the network money than those not broadcast on television. The rationale was that televised tournaments had higher expenses, but this system only seemed to aggravate the gap between the haves and the have-nots. The principle of tying category exclusivity to television was applied wherever and whenever it was appropriate. My first direct experience with this principle came as we were selling the inaugural season of *Inside the PGA Tour* on ESPN. At that time, ESPN was a relatively new enterprise. They claimed a reach of 40 million cable viewers, but in reality their service was made available to 40 million cable subscribers, a modest segment of which actually watched ESPN.

Our task was to sell five category-exclusive positions with billboards to five separate companies and at three times the rate card (the normal advertising price). We went out to our prospects without a pilot to show them—not even a video promo. All we had to sell was the sturdy reputation of the PGA Tour as a class organization that would not produce anything that wasn't top quality. Campbell and Slayden struck first; they got Buick to come in right away as part of their overall deal with the PGA Tour as its "Official Car." That was certainly a boost to our efforts, but we had four more positions to sell. Selling the remaining four slots was as exciting for me as sinking a twenty-footer on the last hole to win the Masters.

The idea of tying category exclusivity to television was a way to leverage the value of the corporate sponsorship investment. It nullified our one disadvantage—the narrowness of our demographic—and turned it into an asset. It was like having a twenty-acre site to sell homes on, and wanting to sell forty half-acre plots for $1,000 apiece. Instead, you are told that zoning regulations call for a standard lot size of four acres. Now you only have ten parcels to sell. But it's no problem; out there in the market are people who want privacy and can afford to pay $8,000 each or more for the lots (like Fujifilm at the Olympics). This analogy with real estate would prove a logical extension of the concept later with the development of the TPCs.

When I started in PGA Tour marketing, we had NFL-type deals with mass-market brands, such as our arrangement with Timex to be the "Official Watch." For what they paid us, it wasn't worth the effort. However, our subsequent deal with Seiko as the "Official Timepiece" and sponsor of a special program or tournament did make business sense for them. There were simply more zeros in the deal. Meanwhile, the time and effort to construct a big deal was about equal to what it took to make the smaller, simpler deal. And so what Art West told me on my first day on the job—and what Slayden emphasized later—now applied more than ever: I had to think bigger.

Leveraging the TPC Brand

Overlapping and directly linked to the PGA Tour's evolving marketing strategy was the licensing and development of the Tournament Players Club(s), also known as the TPCs. They were intended to first serve as a permanent venue for the Tournament Players Championship (TPC), and that is probably one of the reasons for later changing the name of the tournament to the Players Championship.

The strategic concept of the Tournament Players Clubs was to create stadium golf courses able to host PGA Tour events on a regular basis. There were many advantages that have been noted, including having a lower tournament site fee for the event; having a facility designed as a tournament venue to offer a much better spectator experience; being able to control the golf course; and having a venue identifiable as an integral aspect of the PGA Tour experience. Additionally, the TPCs provided a profitable, real-estate-development related income for the PGA Tour, and the TPCs created synergism among the tournament title sponsor, corporate advertisers, real estate development, etc. To understand it fully, it is necessary to backtrack to the beginnings of the TPC stadium golf course and the TPC Championship.

TPC Championship History

The original justification for building the TPC Sawgrass facility was so PGA Tour members could have their own event, an event that would someday become the fifth modern professional major added to the existing four (Masters,

U.S. Open, British Open, and the PGA Championship). Keep in mind that the Masters, the most prestigious major, had only been in business for some thirty years, so this wasn't a preposterous proposition. The British Open had been around for a long time, but didn't become what it is today until Palmer made it a must-play event in the late 1950s. The PGA was the weakest of the four majors; they had only converted that event from match to stroke play during the same time frame.

The presumptive fifth major, the lady-in-waiting, a.k.a. the TPC Championship, started as a roving event, like the PGA Championship and the U.S. Open. The inaugural event was held at the Atlanta Country Club in 1974. Nicklaus won the first tournament and won again in 1976 and 1978. It was memorable at the presentation ceremony that Beman touted Nicklaus's three TPCs as three majors. Nicklaus's cryptic expression belied his chagrin at Beman's remark, because the TPC was in direct competition with plans for his memorial tournament to be included in that exclusive list of majors. In 1975, the TPC was held at Colonial Country Club in Fort Worth, and in 1976, it was hosted by Inverrary Country Club in Fort Lauderdale. The TPC finally settled in Ponte Vedra Beach (Jacksonville), Florida, in 1977.

From that time until 1982, the event was held at Sawgrass Country Club. The difficult Sawgrass golf course and the March ocean breezes aroused the ire of the players and captured the imagination of the fans. It was an unequivocal success. Still, it wasn't quite the success that Beman wanted. Ironically, the PGA Tour had an opportunity to purchase the Sawgrass golf course, the oceanside Beach Club, and undeveloped property on the ocean with 500 other adjoining acres for about $2 million. Ray Floyd, then a player-director on the Tournament Policy Board, reportedly suggested they host the event for a year or so to see if they liked it before they bought it. After the first event, Penn Central Railroad bought it for about $5 million and then flipped it to Arvida for more money.

It may appear that the PGA Tour had taken a pass on a wonderful opportunity, but that really wasn't the case. The PGA Tour had acquired a large amount of acreage on the west side of State Road AIA from the Fletcher brothers for one dollar and then spent about $6 million building the TPC course. It cost more to build the Pete Dye/Deane Beman designed golf course because they had to drain the swamp and move a lot of dirt. But what they built from scratch was a first—the prototype TPC stadium golf course. They laid the foundation for the future development of TPC stadium golf courses, and in the process established the value of the PGA Tour brand. That brand could be leveraged to sell golf on television, sell real estate, and generate income for the tour and its tournaments.

The first Tournament Players Championship, played on the new Stadium Golf Course in March of 1982, was extraordinarily successful. As noted, it captured the attention of golfers worldwide with the island green on the 17th hole and later, when the winner, Jerry Pate, threw Commissioner Beman and golf course architect Pete Dye into the greenside water on number 18, and then dove into the water himself. It was a baptism heralding to the golf world just what the PGA Tour was capable of doing.

If golf would ever accept a fifth major, the TPC Championship would be it. The PGA Tour demonstrated they could create a championship stadium venue and market PGA-Tour-branded real estate. The tour proved they could develop and profitably operate a golf course, tie it to a golf event, secure corporate sponsorship, sell advertising, and present it on television. Using the Ueberroth sports-marketing business model, the PGA Tour leveraged all of its marketing assets to prove that one plus one, plus one, plus one, equals ten.

In retrospect, if the PGA Tour had purchased the completed Sawgrass Country Club for $2 million, they likely would never have developed the TPC network that today totals some thirty-plus facilities. Notably, the Tournament Policy Board had set strict parameters for the PGA Tour's involvement in the development of future TPCs, with the overriding caveat being that the PGA Tour would not be at any financial risk with any TPC development. That makes one wonder how these golf courses were developed at all.

***

The answer was beautiful in its simplicity.

Essentially, TPCs were licensing deals for the development of PGA Tour planned communities, which included association with the PGA Tour and the TPC brands, the hosting of a PGA Tour televised event, and a host of related and required services provided by the PGA Tour. The marketing and licensing strategy for the TPCs mirrored the marketing and licensing concept of the PGA Tour. The PGA Tour was not the developer. The PGA Tour was not assuming any financial risk. It was a licensing deal whereby the PGA Tour leveraged its marketing assets for the financial benefit of the tour and its partners. This might be surprising, but the PGA Tour never undertook a feasibility study for the viability of a golf real estate project. Given the PGA Tour brand equity at risk, it seemed to me that such a study should have been required. And, given my background in golf course development, I felt this might be another area where I might advance at the tour.

When I made this point to Beman, he did not agree. He noted that "real estate developments will succeed or fail on their own merit," and added, "The association with the PGA Tour gives them a better chance for success and for the development to have a greater R-O-I. If they fail, it isn't the fault of the PGA Tour . . . and we'll pull the brand and disassociate the tour from the project."

As it turned out, I was both right and wrong in my assessment. The PGA Tour did attract some marginal developers that eventually failed. However, I

The TPC golf courses and the TPC Championship shared the same brand image and initials until 1988 when it made sense for the PGA Tour to change the name of its preeminent tournament to The Players Championship. *Courtesy of the PGA Tour.*

was wrong in thinking it would damage the PGA Tour brand. No one seemed to notice or care, except for some local interests who might have lost money. The assets of PGA Tour Golf Course Properties, Inc., continued to increase.

The Senior PGA Tour (Champions Tour)

It all started back in 1978 and 1979 when two *Legends of Golf* senior tournaments had back-to-back tantalizing telecasts that captured the imagination of golf fans nationwide. In 1978, in an exciting finish, legendary players Sam Snead and Gardner Dickinson prevailed by a stroke in the better-ball format over Peter Thomson and Kel Nagle. The following year, the two-man team of Art Wall and Tommy Bolt made five birdies in a row in a playoff, only to be matched and beaten by Julius Boros and Roberto de Vicenzo, who birdied the sixth playoff hole. These old guys could still play, and the television ratings were great. A new golf television product had been created. This led to the birth of the Senior PGA Tour.

In January of 1980, founding Senior PGA Tour members Sam Snead, Gardner Dickinson, Bob Goalby, Don January, Dan Sikes, and Julius Boros met with PGA Tour Commissioner Beman to launch what would later become the most successful sports venture of the 1980s. The modest beginnings of the Senior PGA Tour belied its eventual success. The first official season included two new cosponsored events: the inaugural in Atlantic City, New Jersey, in June and a second in the fall at Melbourne, Florida. The existing U.S. Senior Open and the PGA Senior Championship brought the new Senior PGA Tour season to four events. The groundwork was laid with the formation of the Senior Advisory Council. Sikes was named chairman, and Snead was the honorary chairman.

Executive management at the PGA Tour were somewhat bemused by the notion this would be anything but a short-term fad. We thought these old geezers were nuts if they thought there was anything more than a minimum amount of television revenue for this new senior golf tour. In our opinion, it was not much more than an exhibition tour, largely funded by the pro-am format and local corporate sponsorship.

We saw it as a pro-am/exhibition event where corporate executives hobnobbed with the celebrity old-timers, not as a real competition. The Senior PGA Tour players, unlike their younger counterparts on the regular PGA Tour, showed up at the pro-am parties, socialized with the contestants, told stories, gave them golf tips, etc. It was a better value than playing a regular PGA Tour event. First of all, you competed for two rounds rather than one; second, you probably knew the pro's name and reputation, and after a couple of days, you were drinking buddies; and third, the pros gave you tips when you played and appreciated your support.

We didn't know it at the time, but the Senior PGA Tour was about to become an overnight success. There were five events (seven counting the two cosponsored events) in 1981, and there were eleven events (thirteen) in 1982. Although the Senior PGA Tour was starting to realize its growth potential, it was still a hard sell. I begged the Western Golf Association to sponsor a Senior PGA Tour event. After all, they had the Western Open, the Western Amateur, and the Western Junior events, so it seemed entirely logical they could manage another golf event in the Chicago area. They gave me an emphatic, "No thank you."

The Senior PGA Tour continued to grow unabatedly. In 1983, the number of events reached eighteen tournaments with over $3 million in prize money. This was also the first year of the Ford Senior TPC (now the Senior Players Championship). Cognizant of Palmer's appeal, they lowered the minimum age for eligibility from fifty-five to fifty. In 1984, the number of events reached twenty-four, and the purses exceeded $5 million.

Significantly, 1985 was a hallmark year for the Senior PGA Tour, with

The Senior Tour was the PGA Tour's most successful venture of the 1980s. Arnold Palmer was one of the players with great appeal, and age requirements were lowered to include him in the group of eligible senior players. Back in 1978, the NGF gave Palmer its highest honor, the Herb Graffis Award. I was working for the NGF as director of facility development at the time and was lucky enough to get my picture taken with the "King." *Author's collection.*

twenty-seven events, prize money exceeding $6 million, and a cable television package on ESPN. The Senior Tour was now big enough to be a separate entity within the PGA Tour with its own board and a retirement plan. They had their own logo, marketing and licensing programs, corporate sponsors, Vantage scoreboards, etc., all modeled after the regular PGA Tour. The Senior Tour had arrived, and as long as it had the marquee names and personality, there was no end in sight. The number of events hovered around thirty-plus throughout the 1990s. There was even a time in the early to middle part of the decade when the Senior PGA Tour was gaining on the PGA Tour. With Arnold Palmer, Ray Floyd, Jack Nicklaus, Lee Trevino, Chi Chi Rodriguez, Sam Snead, etc., the older guys seemed to have more star appeal than what *they* called the "Junior Tour."

Anytime an organization changes its name to something that is presumably better, and said organization must explain its new name in terms of the

The logo on the left was used from 1980 to 2002 when it was called the Senior PGA Tour. The logo on the right is current and reflects the name change to the Champions Tour. *Courtesy of the PGA Tour.*

old—the name change probably wasn't warranted. The Senior PGA Tour, excuse me, the PGA Tour Champions, had a rollercoaster ride from nowhere to somewhere, and is now back to *who cares*? Perhaps the novelty of watching old guys play golf just wore off. Perhaps the marquee names that once made the senior circuit so popular became unavoidably less popular with the next generation of older players. Perhaps the guys who were boring on the regular PGA Tour some twenty years ago are equally boring as seniors playing today. Perhaps it was mismanaged by the PGA Tour or is just at the end of its natural product life cycle.

Unfortunately, every dog has his day, and as these golf greats were often not atop the leader board in the latter part of the 1990s, the original appeal dissipated. Less notable journeymen players, as well as players who never played the PGA Tour, replaced the marquee names. Many of the stars, like Jack Nicklaus, Tom Weiskopf, and Greg Norman, didn't play very often for their own reasons, and the remaining roster of players often shone less brightly. No one at the PGA Tour would ever admit this, but everyone knew it.

Regardless, the Senior Tour Cinderella story seemed to be ending, and it didn't help in 2001 that they entered into a new television deal with CNBC. Not only were the television rights fees higher, but the underlying rationale for the move to CNBC was flawed. Evidently, PGA Tour management theorized that many Senior PGA Tour fans also watched business news on CNBC; therefore, having the Senior Tour would expand CNBC's audience. The reality was that many fans couldn't find (who would expect to find it on a news channel, after all?) or didn't bother to look for the PGA Tour Champions on CNBC. Television ratings plummeted.

At the time, I was CEO of Cosmo World Group and served on the Japanese owners' management committee at Hualālai, Hawaii, the Jack Nicklaus Signature Design course and host for the 2001 MasterCard Championship. Our ratings on NBC had been around a five, meaning that we reached around five million households. This was high because of the time of year, the later broadcast time, and the allure of Hawaii when the winter weather wasn't so nice on the mainland. On CNBC, the rating was around a 0.5, meaning that about a tenth of the households were watching (compared to the prior network coverage). Hualālai was still a great entertainment vehicle for MasterCard's business customers, but its week in the sun was markedly devalued from both a viewership and promotional standpoint.

The Senior Tour never fully recovered. It could have been that this change in the broadcast strategy just coincided with the downturn in the popularity of the Senior Tour's product life cycle. However, the facts were self-evident: the marquee players were playing less often. Perhaps they had other interests or maybe their games were not—as Hogan put it when asked if he would play on the Senior Tour many years earlier—"No, my game is no longer good enough for public display." After all, what did they have to prove? They weren't going to get in the Hall of Fame based upon their play on the PGA Tour Champions circuit, and if they had other business interests and didn't need the money, why play?

From the Ben Hogan Tour to the Web.com Tour
As noted, the PGA Tour developmental tour, the Tournament Players Series (TPS), was created as result of the dispute resolved between the PGA and PGA Tour regarding the use of the PGA brand name and the PGA club professionals' access to PGA Tour events. From 1983 to 1986, the PGA and PGA Tour conducted the TPS Tour, a ten-tournament circuit with purses of $100,000 to $150,000 each. However, the original 1982 deal unraveled with the absence of an overall corporate-title sponsor, eventually ending the TPS.

Over the course of its twenty-two-year history, the Web.com Tour had five title sponsors. The Tour began in 1990 as the Ben Hogan Tour[1] (named for the legendary professional player). The corporate sponsor was Cosmo World, a privately held Japanese conglomerate and the new owner of the Ben Hogan Company. Nike took up the sponsorship three years later, followed by Buy.com until 2003, when Nationwide became the sponsor. After nine and a half seasons as the Nationwide Tour, the insurance giant bowed out to lend its full support to its hometown PGA Tour event near Columbus, Ohio: the Memorial. When the ten-year title sponsorship agreement with Web.com was announced in late June 2012, the tour's name was changed midseason.

Originally, the top five finishers on the Ben Hogan Tour graduated to the 1991 PGA Tour. In 1993, the top-ten money-list finishers on the Nike Tour received PGA Tour cards; in 1997, it became the top fifteen. It was increased to the top twenty in 2000, and then the top twenty-five when Nationwide became the title sponsor.

Starting with the 2013 season, the Web.com Tour had a structure similar to that of the PGA Tour, with a regular season followed by a season-ending series of four tournaments held during the PGA Tour's FedExCup playoffs. The Web.com Tour final had a total of 150 players competing. The field included the top seventy-five players on the Web.com Tour regular-season money list, plus the players finishing between 126th and 200th on the FedExCup points list. A total of fifty PGA Tour cards for the following season were awarded at the end of the final—twenty-five to the top regular-season money winners on the Web.com Tour and twenty-five to those with the most money earned during the final. And starting in 2013, the PGA Tour Qualifying School granted playing rights only for the Web.com Tour.

The Scorecard
Beman knew from day one that the secret to the PGA Tour's success lay with television because TV drives revenues and creates synergism among a myriad of marketing and commercial interests, powering the economic growth of the PGA Tour. Back in 1981, he told the *Florida Times-Union*, "Eight to ten years from now, our marketing program will produce fifteen to twenty-five percent of the prize money. Right now, it produces zero, but eventually it will make us less dependent on our number-one source of income, which is television."

Looking back on those early days, that was clearly the intent of the plan. It just turned out differently from what Beman envisioned. Marketing would play a major role, but it manifested itself as the oil keeping the financial engine—television—running on all cylinders. The big marketing deals like the electronic scoreboards and TPC Stadium golf courses enhanced the spectator experience at the tournaments and on television. Corporate America watched and played golf and wanted to rub elbows with the pros and entertain customers. There were some serendipitous business breakthroughs, however, such as the TPC network and the PGA Champions Tour.

As golf started booming in the 1990s, it became the darling of Wall Street. Golf equipment companies like Callaway Golf and Aldila had successful IPOs (initial public offerings of stock). PGA Tour revenues and tournament purses increased dramatically. Television provided the resources and the medium to grow interest in the game and professional golf by forging alliances with corporate America. The 1984 Olympic exclusivity business model worked very well. It created the brand and promotional synergism, fostering the development of the TPC network. In 1992, TPC royalties, licensing fees, management fees, and membership revenues were at their peak of approximately $63.5 million (which at one point were greater than television revenues). However, the golf course and real estate development market would slow as television rights, fees, and corporate sponsorships continued to accelerate.

There were a few bumps in the road, but Beman chose a road that no one had ever considered traveling before. When he retired in 1994, he handed the keys to the Mercedes, or perhaps it would be more appropriate to say, the Buick (the PGA Tour's Official Automobile), to new PGA Tour Commissioner Tim Finchem.

***

In the late fall of 1983, Slayden invited me into his office and shut the door. "David," he said, "I've wanted to speak with you about something, but before I say anything, I want you to understand that I am pleased with your job performance. So don't take this the wrong way."

With some apprehension, I said, "Well, what's on your mind?"

"David, I think that you have the potential to be a CEO of a public company. Does that idea appeal to you?"

I responded, "Of course it does. I made a decision long ago to try and get into the golf business because that is my passion. I figured that if I liked the subject matter of my work, and looked forward to going to work every day, then I might fare better in the full scheme of things."

"That makes some sense," Slayden replied, "but you need to make a decision, and it's not an easy one. Years ago, I decided to go back to Auburn and get an advanced degree in engineering. At a football game, I ran into someone who said that I might accomplish more outside of academia, and he introduced me to some of his business associates. My career went from working on the Saturn [rocket] project to president and COO of Fuqua. At times, Nancy [his wife] might have preferred that I had chosen academia and not to wait for me with our two boys for hours on the tarmac for us to leave on a vacation because I had to take care of business. But that was the choice that I had made. I don't regret it. You are at that point now in your career. You have a choice to make. What do you want to do? Do you want to be an association executive, and go to the Masters as an official? Or do you want to fly in on a corporate jet and attend the Masters as a member?"

"Put in those terms," I replied, "I would rather be a member of Augusta than an invited guest."

Slayden continued, "Well, David, if that is really how you feel, then you are headed in the wrong direction. If your goal is to be here," (raising his right hand and pointing upward) "then you can't expect to get there via this route," (raising his left hand and pointing to the left). "Right now, you are on track to being a lifetime golf association executive. That's okay. You can earn a good living. You can be an official at every Masters from now on. But don't expect to become CEO of a company on that career track. You just aren't heading in that direction. If that is what you want in life, that's fine. Nancy would agree and say that's a good choice; she has had to wait for me on too many tarmacs too many times. But if you really want to run a company, I can help you get on that track."

I didn't say anything right away, because I didn't know what to say. I was flattered, but in all honesty I wasn't sure if I really wanted to be a CEO of a public company. Just working for the PGA Tour had far exceeded my wildest career expectations. In my teens, I wanted to become a player on the PGA Tour, but wasn't good enough. I was fortunate to pursue my passion in golf, and here I was working for the PGA Tour. Now, here was someone whom I greatly respected telling me I had the potential to do much more professionally.

All I could muster for my new mentor was, "Kay, thanks for your advice. I need to think about it a little more."

As it turned out, a couple of weeks later, I was asked if I would like to interview to become the next CEO of the National Golf Foundation. In February of 1984, I accepted the job and moved from Ponte Vedra Beach to Palm Beach Gardens, Florida.

11

FLYING HIGH ON A WING AND A PRAYER

In late January of 1984, I went into PGA Tour Commissioner Beman's office to tell him I had just accepted an offer from the National Golf Foundation (NGF) Board of Directors to be the NGF's next president and CEO. Beman told me, "I figured that they would go after you, especially since you've been representing the PGA Tour at all of the golf industry meetings." Then he cautioned me and said, "Do you really think the foundation is salvageable? Frank Smith [outgoing NGF president] didn't leave you much to work with."

A few years earlier, as his assistant, Beman had me write a report evaluating the NGF. As a result of that analysis, he offered to take the NGF under the wing of the PGA Tour in order to save the organization from pending obscurity and likely dissolution. Tim Smith, then PGA Tour general counsel, and I went to an NGF Board meeting with our proposal. At that meeting they introduced Frank Smith, former CBS Sports president, as the new NGF president. About three years later, it was my turn.

When I took over in February of 1984, I did not realize how cloudy the NGF's future was. Essentially, I inherited a trade association that relied upon a handful of golf equipment manufacturers for 90 percent of its funding. Within two weeks of taking the job, three key golf equipment corporate members advised me they would no longer bear the lion's share of the financial burden, which meant that about half the NGF's operating budget was about to dry up. Something had to be done very quickly, or the NGF would be no more. When I discussed the situation with Beman, he asked me if I wanted my old job back. I thought about it. The urge lingered for a few days and then passed as I set to work solving the many problems facing the NGF.

Fortunately, with my experience at the PGA Tour, I had a pretty good Rolodex of contacts in addition to the support of Beman, who offered to provide some PSAs (public service announcements) on PGA Tour golf telecasts to help raise the NGF profile. However, it was not clear to me what that profile might be. I knew I had to make some draconian decisions if the NGF was to survive and play a meaningful role in the golf industry.

The biggest problem was that no one really cared if the NGF survived. I had to not only resuscitate this fifty-year-old institution but make it matter in the business world of golf. The NGF needed to become indispensable to the future of the golf industry—a pretty tall order under the circumstances. Golf, as a sport, seemed to be sliding and becoming less popular. Golf course development was stalled. Golf participation and rounds played were stagnant. It wasn't a pretty picture.

Compounding these unfavorable circumstances was the fact I had inherited an organization populated by retired military colonels and many other good people who were not highly motivated; most were not receptive to any change in the direction and role of the NGF. Further, if there was a new destination for the NGF, they were certainly in no hurry to get there and were content to drive below the posted speed limit all the way. With the fiscal cliff looming, however, it was clear that desperate circumstances required desperate measures.

Back then, the NGF tried to function as the chamber of commerce for the golf industry; unfortunately, the NGF's mission was too broad, particularly in light of the fact that the NGF did not have the resources and capability to fulfill that mission. The NGF tried to promote the game, foster new golf course development, teach teachers how to teach golf, and provide feel-good, but not very credible, golf-industry research. It was a scattershot business strategy aimed at many targets but hitting none. The NGF seemed content to define itself in terms of its good intentions. Instead of trying to do something measurable and deserving of industry support, the NGF was dysfunctional and in a desperate financial predicament.

Perhaps it was a blessing in disguise that I had no choice but to take some drastic measures to reposition and remarket the NGF in a way to attract new financial support and broaden its corporate membership base. What the NGF needed was more than just a makeover; it needed what we used to say in the school yards—*a do-over*. The NGF needed a new strategic vision and probably a new management team. We needed to redefine its mission and purpose, as well as its role in the industry.

The strategy was to focus on research—credible, quantitative, and qualitative research that would be of value to its corporate members and help shape the golf industry's view as to how to grow both the game and the business of golf. Most importantly, the NGF needed to learn the importance of focus—keeping the main thing (its research program) the main thing.

My first task was to sell this concept to the NGF Board of Directors, which at the time consisted of the leading golf equipment companies and national golf associations. Fortunately, I got some good advice from NGF Board Chairman Bob MacNally, who was a personal friend and president of the PGA Golf Company during the divorce and remarriage of the PGA Tour and the PGA. Back then, I negotiated a deal with MacNally to give up the PGA brand and change the company's name to Tommy Armour Golf.

Chairman MacNally insisted I prepare a monthly report for the NGF Board of Directors to keep them apprised of what I was planning, what I was doing, what was working, and what wasn't. I didn't like the idea at the time, because I viewed it as micromanagement. But I was wrong. More than keeping everyone updated on the NGF's progress, successes, and failures, this monthly report, unbeknownst to me, was building allies for the changes that needed to be made in developing a rescue plan for the NGF. By the time I presented the new NGF strategic plan at the next board meeting, everyone was pretty much on board.

There were some who doubted what I proposed to do. I remember overhearing Bob Rickey, with the Golf Writers Association of America, talking with Mark Kizziar, the PGA president, during a bathroom break at the NGF board meeting. Rickey asked Kizziar, "What do you think, Mark? A bit ambitious, don't you think?"

Kizziar replied, "It may be, but it's this way or the highway for the NGF. David's one of Deane's disciples, and I'm betting that he has figured out what he needs to do and the role that the NGF needs to play."

What I asked of the NGF Board was nothing less than a leap of faith. If I had not kept them abreast of the plan as it developed, they might not have approved such a major course change.

The first important hire in August of 1984 was Dr. Joe Beditz. I lured him to the job with a once-in-a-lifetime opportunity to become the "guru of golf." He would be the leading professional research authority on the golf industry. That was an appealing offer to someone who loved golf and had a PhD in research methodology and statistics. I needed Beditz more than he realized. The NGF research was not credible. I knew it. The industry knew it. And Beditz would change that opinion in a very short period of time.

However, for me, there was a steep learning curve in developing and implementing a turnaround plan, as well as in learning how to become an effective manager. Being the boss with the ultimate responsibility for the NGF's success or failure required more than I had imagined. It was not long before I realized I was not as capable and experienced a CEO as I had thought. Initially, I wanted to be the kind of boss who challenged employees to the limits of their capabilities and gave them the latitude and support to get the job done. This is what I had learned from Beman. As it turned out, this notion of the ideal boss was naïve. The NGF wasn't the PGA Tour. Many of those who went to work at the NGF did not want to be challenged and were quite happy with their jobs as they were. I soon learned that what motivated me probably didn't motivate the secretary, the shipping clerk, or most managers and staffers at the NGF.

Later, I learned leadership is an acquired taste, seasoned by a few failures. I learned you can't do it all yourself, and you need to hire to your weaknesses, not your strengths. Also, it is very important to create a corporate culture that empowers management to make decisions. Some bad decisions and mistakes will be made, but managers must be allowed to learn by doing, to make and to take responsibility for their decisions; otherwise, with the CEO making all of the decisions, it cripples overall organizational effectiveness; it becomes a one-man show. Last but not least, it is important to associate yourself and the company with leaders and winners. If you (or your company) don't have the ability or credibility to carry it off on your own, borrow or rent it from someone else. It is surprising what people are willing to do and share when they are stakeholders in your success.

At the very onset of this quest, I arranged to meet in Orlando with Mark McCormack, founder of International Management Group (IMG), the world's largest sports management firm, to figure out what could be done to save the NGF. We met in his rented condo during a professional women's tennis event in March of 1984 and brainstormed a variety of ideas. I envisioned that IMG would adopt the NGF as a pro bono project, help us raise some serious money, and then provide us with direction on how to best spend those funds to grow the game.

McCormack expressed some interest and had a few great ideas; however, he was not as magnanimous as I had hoped. He proposed the NGF retain IMG for a nominal retainer of $5,000 per month. That was not much money to IMG, but at the time it was a lot of money for the NGF. I made a counter proposal: $60,000 a year was about the average annual contribution for most of our charter members; I would be pleased to make IMG an NGF charter member in exchange for the consulting services. McCormack said, "David, that's pretty quick on your part. Maybe someday you might like to work for me, but that's not how we work. We need to know that you value our services enough to pay for them, even if it is a token amount. The issue of our contribution or becoming a charter member is a separate matter."

McCormack was more experienced and a better negotiator than I. And I knew that the NGF board would never allow me to pay IMG such a sum to do what they expected me to do as the NGF president. After working for the PGA Tour for a few years, I had met a few important and successful people, but my Rolodex was no match for McCormack's. I wanted and needed IMG's help but could not afford the price; however, I still wanted to make some kind of deal with McCormick. I pleaded poverty (with ample justification), but it didn't make any difference. I was not sure if this was an acid test of my sincerity or if it was just a matter of principle for McCormack.

We parted ways that morning on good terms. I thanked him for his time and consideration, fully knowing that an audience with McCormack wasn't easily granted. Before leaving, I told him that my wife had asked if he would mind signing a copy of his recent national best seller, *What They Don't Teach You at Harvard Business School*. He said he would be pleased to do so, so I pulled a copy of the book out of my briefcase. He then asked me what my wife's name was, and I said, "David."

"That's interesting," he said, smiling. "She has the same first name as you."

***

One quick way to alter an organization's self-image is to move it physically. The NGF had been renting space from the Sporting Goods Manufacturers Association (SGMA) in West Palm Beach, Florida, and to many, it almost appeared we were a part of that trade association. The NGF certainly needed to stand on its own, and a new headquarters would be a step in the right direction. While we didn't have much capital, we were not averse to discussing deals and arrangements with people. To that end, I spent a couple of days with people connected to the Golden Bear organization—namely Bob Whitley, a major commercial and residential developer in south Florida who had built Golden Bear Plaza, an imposing office-building complex in Palm Beach Gardens. He wanted to build a building for the NGF, or at least get us to move from our current offices to Golden Bear Plaza. I also eventually met with Dick Bellinger, president of Golden Bear Golf, and the Golden Bear himself, Jack Nicklaus. It started with a round of golf with Whitley at Grand Cypress Resort near Orlando.

In those days, Golden Bear Golf managed a number of golf courses, including Frenchman's Creek in Palm Beach Gardens. As the NGF president I was given a complimentary membership by the Nicklaus organization to that golf club. I was certainly at home when visiting there, but at Grand Cypress Golf Club, the North and South nines are Jack Nicklaus Signature Designs, known for their difficulty. (Nicklaus also designed the East Nine, which opened two years later.)

Whitley and I went in his car for the roundtrip drive from Palm Beach Gardens to Orlando to play Grand Cypress. At the time, I was not playing very much; I made it a point to let everyone know that fact, trying to lower everyone's expectations— including my own. But when I played golf that day, it was one of those days I hit every shot solidly, and every putt either went in or hit the hole. All of my preplay whining was for naught. I shot a 66 from the back tees. It was one of the dozen or so best rounds of my life.

I had lunch the next day with Nicklaus and Bellinger at Frenchman's Creek. By that time, I was still basking in the afterglow of carving up that demanding track. Needless to say, I was also in awe of the person sitting across the table from me at lunch. I ordered the same thing he ordered and tried to savor the experience and be attentive to every detail. Then Bellinger said to Nicklaus, "Whitley said that David really burned up Grand Cypress yesterday."

This had to be a golfer's dream. There I was, having lunch with golf's greatest all-time player, and someone (not me) tells Nicklaus about one of the best rounds of golf I have ever had. And it happened to be on one of Nicklaus's own Signature Designs. I was ascending into golfer heaven and almost self-actualized right on the spot when Nicklaus said to me, "Really! David, what did you shoot?"

I then stumbled around and humbly muttered, "I had an unusually good day, playing way over my head. . . ."

"He shot a sixty-six," Bellinger interjected.

At this point—with my ego fully inflated—I waited with bated breath for Nicklaus's response. He said nothing and took another bite of his toasted tuna fish sandwich. So I did the same. He seemed to masticate endlessly. I was pretty sure he counted each chew. I had already swallowed my bite, along with a little pride, when he finally said, "What tees did you play?"

While he took another bite of his sandwich, I stammered, "Well, we played the back tees. We probably didn't play it all the way back to the tiger tees [no pun intended, Tiger Woods was only about eleven years old then]." As I waited for Nicklaus to finish chewing, a thousand thoughts went through my mind. Here I was, having lunch with the greatest golfer of all time. I had just finished shooting lights-out on one of his Signature golf course designs. I thought it just does not get any better than this. His chewing and swallowing of the sandwich seemed interminable, but I figured Nicklaus was just lathering me up for the compliment of a lifetime.

He finally swallowed his thoroughly chewed bite of toasted tuna salad sandwich and said, "That can be done from there."

I was crestfallen. Here I was, a complete nobody from a golfing standpoint, not even a remote threat to his greatness as a golfer or as golf course designer, and all he could muster was, "That can be done from there." I would have been delighted with,"Great round David," or thrilled with something like "You must be a really good player, nice round"; or he could have really lubed me with, "I guess that I just can't build them tough enough for you." I would have swallowed it all, hook, line, and sinker; finished both his sandwich and mine; but instead all I got was, That can be done from there.

Needless to say, but I will say it anyway: Nicklaus was not the most magnanimous person I have ever met. I have come to believe that is par for the course among really great achievers. In becoming a great golfer, it is necessary to put your goals and objectives before anything else; that might explain his difficulty in giving even a disingenuous compliment. It is understandable that highly successful people focus on themselves. They could not achieve what they have without such focus. I know I could not withstand the adulation

Nicklaus receives week-in, week-out without thinking I was really something special. As a matter of fact, it wouldn't even take much of a compliment—just say, "David, it looks as if you have lost some weight," and I'll suck in my belly and puff up with self-esteem.

Nicklaus remains an exemplar of everything we admire in great athletic achievement. He is the greatest player of all time. Winner of eighteen professional majors and two amateur majors, his legendary career is defined for posterity in terms of his major tournament wins. He is an honorable man, a person of integrity, and a gracious winner and loser. He approached golf course architecture with a similar fervor, and many, including myself, believe his accomplishments in this field will rival the work of the greatest golf course architects. He has over 235 golf courses open for play worldwide, of which nearly 200 are solo designs; the rest are codesigns. His company, Nicklaus Design, has designed golf courses in twenty-eight countries and thirty-six states. As impressive as these facts are, the myriad of course design architectures is even more impressive, ranging from Muirfield Golf Club in Columbus, Ohio; to Desert Highlands in Scottsdale, Arizona; to Paris International in France; and to Hualālai in Kona, Hawaii. His picturesque designs vary with the topography and equally challenge the duffer and tour pro.

No one really knows Nicklaus, except his family and close friends; however, it is easy to surmise from everything he has accomplished both on and off the golf course that he will be forever known as one of golf's greatest players and course architects. And, most importantly, he is a gentleman in every sense of the word.

In September of 1985, at the World Series of Golf Ambassadors Dinner, I presented Nicklaus with the National Golf Foundation award for exemplifying the values of promoting family golf. Nicklaus and his wife, Barbara, stayed after the dinner presentation for at least forty-five minutes to shake hands with everyone. We named the award after him and called it the Jack Nicklaus Family Golf Award. He, Barbara, and sons Jack, Gary, and Steve were featured in an NGF television PSA promoting family golf. It aired during PGA Tour telecasts.

One sidebar: During the shooting of those television PSAs, Barbara Nicklaus and my wife, Cindy, were sitting in a golf cart between takes, and Cindy asked, "Do you play golf?" And then, realizing what a silly question it was because they were shooting an ad to promote family golf, she suddenly said, "Oh my gosh, I meant . . ."

Barbara kindly saved her from embarrassment, saying, "No, I don't play, but I do have clubs."

Cindy said, "Me too, but I don't play either." So, Barbara and Cindy got along just fine after sharing their common interest in golf.

Remaking the NGF

The NGF was approaching its fiftieth anniversary, and most in the golf industry really didn't see the value in continuing their support unless the NGF could demonstrate its worth. The NGF had to develop its research capability, information products, and membership services. With the hiring of Dr. Joe Beditz in August of 1984, this could now happen. Though it was a first, big step for the NGF, it was what we did with that information that was even more important. Information for information's sake is of little value.

In our preliminary research and analysis, we thought that the demand for golf was largely supply driven. In other words, and quoting the theme from the movie, *Field of Dreams*, "If you build it, they will come." In the late 1970s and early 1980s, golf did not seem to fit the active lifestyle of the boomer generation. This did not bode very well for golf's future. Golf was perceived as a game played by overweight, middle-aged white guys in doubleknit plaid pants. Tennis was hot, and golf just was not very cool. According to the Sporting Goods Manufacturers Association, tennis then had an estimated 35 million-plus participants. Golf had less than half of that. Golf seemed a dying industry. It had the image of an expensive game for the elite, even though there was abundant evidence to the contrary—that it was a game played predominantly by the middle class.

In 1985 the NGF engaged Dr. John Rooney, a geographer from Oklahoma State University, to conduct a nationwide study on golf participation. This study revealed a correlation between the percentage of the population that played golf and the number of public golf courses per capita. Not unexpectedly, Dr. Rooney's research revealed much higher golf-participation rates where there was a greater concentration of golf courses. For example, in Michigan, or just about anywhere on our northern border with Canada, we had very high golf-participation rates—somewhere in the range of 20 percent of the population played golf. These were also the areas that had the greatest number of golf courses per capita. Where there were fewer golf courses per capita, such as in Mississippi, golf participation was much lower, at about 3 percent of the population.

This research, coupled with consumer and demographic research conducted by the NGF with Synovate, Inc., revealed that the huge baby boomer population segment could be a driving force in stimulating the demand and supply for the game and golf business. It was theorized that as boomers aged, they would play golf more often because they would have the time, money, and inclination to do so. In fact, if boomers merely behaved as their predecessors had and played golf only as frequently as the older generation, there would not be enough golf courses (supply) to meet the anticipated demand.

This high correlation between a higher concentration of golfers and more golf courses seemed to imply that the demand for golf was supply driven. While we were aware correlation does not mean causation—in other words, that golf courses don't create golfers—we decided to promote golf course development. This was also consistent with the NGF's historical mission.

However, the questions remained: Did the NGF have the credibility as a research organization and the standing as a golf association to take the golf industry in a new direction? Could the NGF change the golf industry's perception of itself and its future direction? At the time, many considered golf to be a mature industry with little room for growth. The credibility of the NGF research had to be established before any consensus building could begin. New alliances had to be made. The NGF needed to create an industry forum for analysis of the facts, discussion of the issues, and the development of a plan to foster the growth of the game. This was the genesis for the biennial NGF Golf Summits.

***

The first Golf Summit was held in October of 1986 at Westchester Country Club in Rye, New York. By then, President Reagan had met with General Secretary Gorbachev at the first US-USSR Summit in Geneva, Switzerland, so I figured a similar-sounding name would add prestige and pomp to our event. The day before the inaugural event, PGA Tour Commissioner Beman made a promotional appearance on the *Today* show and was interviewed by Bryant Gumbel, who queried him on golf's version of a summit meeting. The tactic to sound impressive had worked. We generated publicity and created high expectations throughout our industry and beyond.

The NGF gathered the golf industry leaders, and we presented the NGF research, as well as that of leading experts in the industry. We defined the issues, challenges, and opportunities for the future of the game and industry of golf. During this time, there were about one hundred golf course openings a year, which was down some 250 per annum from the last boom period in the 1960s; we took heart, however, from the new NGF research about the changing demographics of the US population.

The NGF research revealed a high percentage of the huge baby boomer population segment—those born between 1946 and 1964, some 78 million strong—indicated they were golfers. The hypothesis was that golf stood to benefit. The Pepsi Generation was then playing tennis, but it was expected that in the future they would be looking for more social recreational activities, which boded very well for golf. This theory was a radical departure from the prevailing sentiment regarding golf's future prospects. Most thought that golf was dying, and the pie was not expected to get much larger. We had to change that perception. Such a view was bold and controversial for the time and intended to attract some attention (and investment). Keep in mind that the economic recovery under the Reagan administration was just then revealing itself, and golf was lagging far behind.

The most significant outcome from the 1986 Golf Summit, other than providing a better understanding of the current state of the game among golf's

This Golf Summit 1988 poster illustrates the challenges confronting the future of the game and golf industry at that time. *Courtesy of the National Golf Foundation.*

leadership, was the decision to develop a strategic plan for the golf industry. At this point, the NGF did not have the standing to pull off something of this magnitude on its own. So I decided to rent it. McKinsey & Company (McKinsey), the highly regarded management consulting company, was hired. Along with the NGF, McKinsey developed a *Strategic Plan for the Growth of Golf,* to be unveiled at the next Golf Summit in two years. Linking up with McKinsey provided the NGF with the gravitas to be more than just a research company; it gave the NGF's research and organization the standing to develop a plan with credibility, a plan which would serve as the main topic for discussion and deliberation at the 1988 Golf Summit.

Golf Summit '88 was held at the Sawgrass Marriott, near PGA Tour headquarters in Ponte Vedra Beach, Florida. It was not intended to be an NGF meeting. The NGF only brought the leadership of the game and the golf industry together to discuss the proposed plan and decide what could be done collectively to chart a new course for the growth of golf. It turned out to be an unprecedented gathering at the Sawgrass Marriott: all the movers and shakers from all reaches of the game and business were there. It was a *Who's Who* of golf.

The NGF and McKinsey plan presented seventeen programs—most of them boring but important ideas ranging from golf course insurance programs to having an introduction to golf class in the curriculum at college business schools, free introductory instruction at golf courses, and uniform systems of accounting for courses. However, the centerpiece for this strategic plan was a clarion call to build a *Course a Day* from 1990 to 2000 in order to meet the anticipated demand from the aging baby boomer generation.

I was the person responsible for coining the Course a Day slogan. It not only quickly captured the meaning of the concept, it was easy to remember. Beditz wanted to say we needed 375 new golf courses a year, which just didn't have much sizzle. So, being more of a marketing guy than Beditz and since I was responsible for making the decision, I opted for the catchier Course a Day slogan.

The plan worked beyond our wildest expectations. The promotional campaign had the support of the PGA Tour and the golf media. *Inside Golf*, a nationally syndicated television program featured the NGF in 1988.[1] The PGA Tour even ran PSAs to promote the initiative, which captured considerable attention both within and outside of the golf industry. The Course a Day concept caught fire and led to a change in the public's view of golf as a dying industry to the perception that it was a growth industry. Golf became a great investment opportunity.

The promotional campaign lit a fuse that set off an explosion of growth in the game and business. During the 1990s, more than $20 billion was invested in all facets of the golf industry. Many sectors in the golf industry, such as real estate, travel, media, golf course management companies, golf equipment companies, and the PGA Tour benefited from this investment and the great expectations for golf as a business. Making over an industry's perception of itself was a significant achievement.

We went from pessimism, gloom, and doom to optimism, boom, and explosive economic growth. During the 1990s, more than a golf course a day was built, and the impact was more far reaching than increasing the number of golf courses and golfers. The democratization of the game was also a *fait accompli* as golf—once known as an exclusive game for the elite, with 80 percent of golf courses owned by private clubs—was now a game for the middle class, with 72 percent of golf courses open to the public. This represented a

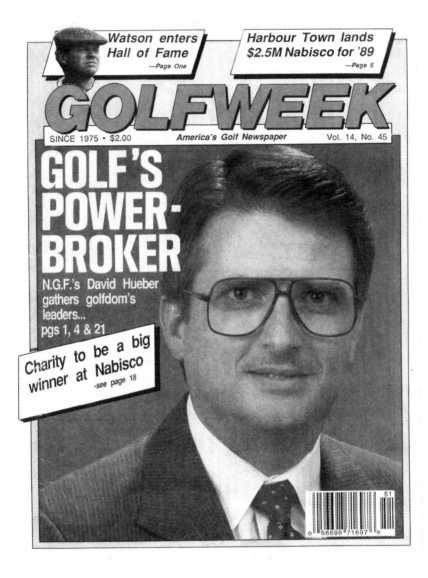

Golfweek magazine did a cover story following Golf Summit 1988 at the Marriott Sawgrass. *Courtesy of* Golfweek *magazine, reprinted with permission.*

complete turnabout from where golf stood at the beginning of the century. By the year 2000, the golf industry had sixteen thousand golf facilities with nearly 30 million golfers playing an estimated 520 million rounds of golf each year.

Retrospective: Unplayable Lies

The March 1988 issue of *Golf Shop Operations*, a *Golf Digest* trade publication, featured the article "David Hueber: Are his Plans for the NGF too Ambitious?" with the subtitle "David Hueber has helped modernize the National Golf Foundation. Can he also triple our course-building rate?" While the article was complimentary, the challenges and opportunities were made perfectly clear for the NGF, the game, and the golf industry.

Later, at the NGF board meeting following the 1988 Golf Summit, I had discussions with board members regarding what we could do to grow the game and golf industry. We all wanted golf to be more like tennis, wistfully hoping someday golf would be cool, with professional athletes and celebrities playing the game. Our dreams were eventually realized when Michael Jordan, Maury Povich, Céline Dion, Emmitt Smith and the like were publicized playing golf. It would happen; golf was at the precipice of its third boom in golf course development and an explosive growth in popularity. The first of these booms was in the 1920s, the second was in the 1960s, and the third would be in the 1990s.

In retrospect, we were wrong in our preliminary analysis that demand for the game is supply driven. While there is a correlation between a higher percentage of the population that plays golf and having more golf courses per capita, the relationship is not what academics would call "causal." We were wrong. Golf courses do not create golfers and vice versa; however, we were right in our assessment that there was a latent demand for golf based upon the behavior of baby boomers who were likely to play more and spend more on golf as they aged. Blissfully ignorant of our misdiagnosis that golf courses create golfers, we embarked upon the Course a Day promotional campaign, and it was successful beyond our wildest expectations.

While a course a day was built during the 1990s, there were unintended consequences. Back when this strategy was conceived in the late 1980s, it was inconceivable that too many golf courses might be built or that they might be built in the wrong places. In our evangelical quest to preach the gospel that golf was on the precipice of becoming a growth industry, we never considered what might happen if that didn't happen or even what might happen if we were too successful.

We couldn't foresee that some real estate developers would spend too much building golf courses relative to market capacity, or that these golf courses would increase the cost of playing the game, or that the golf courses they built would be too difficult and take too long for average golfers to play.

No one anticipated or understood that real estate developers were primarily interested in using these golf courses as an amenity to sell real estate at premium prices. They were not concerned about the economic viability of operating these golf courses. In fact, they subsidized the golf courses, as they did other amenities like tennis courts, swimming pools, fitness facilities, and so on. In the end, the developers created a product its customers didn't want to buy. When the economy and real estate market soured, the golf industry inherited a large inventory of unsustainable golf courses. As one of the people who first studied the demand projections underlying the Course a Day slogan (one of the people who helped create golf's supply problems), I can assure you the road to our present situation was paved with good intentions.

At the time, however, with the turnaround of fortunes at the NGF and prospects for the growth of the game and industry much improved, new opportunities were about to present themselves. I was about to embark upon the opportunity of a lifetime: becoming the president and CEO of the Ben Hogan Company.

THE WEE ICE MON AND THE AMERICAN SAMURAI

How many Japanese whims can you fit into a Texas ten-gallon hat? In the wake of AMF's acquisition by corporate raider Irwin Jacobs (Minstar), the Ben Hogan Company was spun off to the Japanese Cosmo World conglomerate. I suddenly found myself with the opportunity of a lifetime, becoming the CEO of the Ben Hogan Company. However, this giant career step was awash in a sea of uncertainty. I had to discover how to work with this foreign corporate culture and managerial mentality.

Minoru Isutani, president and owner of Cosmo World Corporation, purchased the Ben Hogan Company in 1988. Hogan wasn't real happy about it. When he met with Isutani the first time during lunch at Shady Oaks, he reportedly told him through an interpreter, "Mr. Isutani, you have bought the family jewels. Don't fuck it up." Though Hogan never really warmed to the Japanese, he was pleased with their commitment to excellence and their willingness to make an investment in the company. He was also flattered that an entire professional development golf tour would be named after him.

As far as Hogan was concerned, these aspiring professional golfers were playing for a whole lot of money—more than he ever had. In 1990 Jim Kelly, an ESPN golf commentator, did an interview with Hogan.[1] In it, Hogan said, "Well, I think it is a great thing to give these boys a stepping-stone to playing the major tour. It starts them out early and trains them in how to compete, how to travel, and how to read a golf course, and most importantly, how to improve their game and just enjoy life better. I wish I had the opportunity to do something like this." He then added, "My only advice would be to look out for the buses."

AMF had never spent much on building the Ben Hogan Company, and the short time that Minstar controlled the company was not a time for investment but a time to dispose of the company at a profit. Companies being prepped for sale are managed differently. Inventories and receivables are often overvalued, and management decisions that might lead to an unfavorable financial picture are often deferred.

In the case of the Ben Hogan Company, there was a strike to be settled with the steelworkers before the deal with the Japanese could be consummated. The steelworkers had to take a big cut in pay; as a result, there were significant losses in productivity. Much to his credit, my predecessor, Jerry Austry, who was promoted from within by the interim owner, Minstar, did get the Hogan Company back into the forefront by using Ben Hogan as the spokesman in the introduction and advertising of the new Hogan Edge irons. Unfortunately, the Hogan Company had introduced a product that it seemed incapable of manufacturing.

The Japanese paid about twenty-five times projected earnings for the Ben Hogan Company (at the time, six to seven times earnings was more common). Between the Ben Hogan Tour sponsorship and sponsorship of the newly acquired PGA Tour professional staff, the Ben Hogan Company had a promotional investment in the range of $6.7 million before dollar one could be spent on advertising.

When I accepted the position in December 1988, I knew the level of promotional investment was disproportionate for a company of Hogan's size. I was promised that corporate (meaning Cosmo World) would subsidize these promotional investments, but they never did. That was the beginning of my education in working for the Japanese. I soon learned that we (Americans) viewed the marketing and management of a business entirely differently from the Japanese. The Japanese equated promotional expenditures with advertising expenditures. Japanese golfing consumers were more brand oriented in making golf equipment purchases. Product performance and features were secondary. The Japanese viewed promotional investment (building the brand) as having the same impact as advertising a product's features and benefits.

From an American business standpoint, a company makes a *promotional* investment to position itself in the marketplace and an *advertising* investment in order to leverage its promotional investment to sell products. There was nothing wrong in sponsoring the Ben Hogan Tour or spending millions on PGA Tour players; unfortunately, there was just not much left over to advertise the products or to take advantage of the promotional positioning. By the time I arrived, there wasn't enough money to fund the promotional commitments, let alone sustain the advertising momentum.

The Hogan Edge iron was supposedly the first cavity-back forged iron. It really was not. A couple of years earlier, Wilson had introduced a similar product, but it was a model produced for sale in retail stores rather than pro shops, and no one, except Wilson, really noticed or cared who was first. As far as the marketplace was concerned, the Hogan Edge was a genuine innovation. Sales, however, were well beyond the company's manufacturing capability. Part of the problem was good: we had a hot product. Ironically, our inability to produce the product enabled us to reduce our advertising expenditures.

In retrospect, it is interesting that when I was hired, they wanted a marketing person but probably needed a manufacturing specialist. The manufacturing process was a pretty steep learning curve for me, and by the time I finally climbed it, the demand for the Hogan Edge had decreased to more normal levels.

Compounding the supply problem was a directive from Cosmo to take most of the Hogan Edge irons and send them to Japan. Ben Hogan Japan was launched in February of 1989, and they wanted that product immediately. They didn't seem to be concerned about what might happen to the Ben Hogan Company when it could not supply the hot new Hogan Edge irons for the US market. We had a six-month waiting list for the Edge irons, and this demand from Japan pushed that out even further.

We ran apology ads, advising US consumers we were sorry we could not produce enough product to meet the demand. We did not tell them we did not know how to manufacture the product; or that we launched a major advertising and promotional effort before we knew what our production capabilities might be; or that we sent most of what we did produce to start up a new company in Japan. These were just a few of the minor problems I inherited. I had a great deal to learn about marketing and manufacturing golf equipment. Furthermore, dealing with a foreign culture was an extraordinary educational experience. I began to read as much as I could in order to understand how we each do business.

Around June 1989, we secured a $20 million credit line because Cosmo World did not fund, as promised, the extraordinary promotional expense for the upcoming Ben Hogan Tour and the greatly expanded PGA Tour professional staff. Unfortunately, $6 million of the credit line went immediately to fund real estate options in Hawaii for Cosmo World—the site of the future Four Seasons Hualālai resort. Unforseen by me was that another $3 million would later be demanded. That meant there really wasn't enough left over in the credit line for the Hogan Company, given the limitations imposed by the loan covenants.

It is interesting that with the Japanese there were always other deals in the works. I was asked to make recommendations regarding the acquisition of both Aldila and Cobra Golf companies. Cosmo World already owned a graphite shaft company in Japan and was frustrated in their attempts to enter the US market. With Aldila, I recommended they not acquire the company. It was too expensive, and I believed they could achieve their goal without that extraordinary expenditure. I remember Isutani turning to his US point

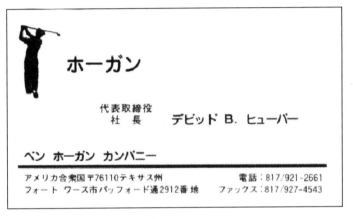

These business cards say the same thing, but have a different meaning depending upon which side of the Pacific is your point of origin. *The Ben Hogan logos are courtesy of the Ben Hogan Company, Perry Ellis International, all rights reserved. Hogan® is a registered trademark of PEI Licensing, Inc. (PEI). This book was written and published without verification or approval by PEI.*

man, Ted Honda, and saying, "Okay let's not buy it. Offer them $80 million. They will never accept it," which ended up being the case. Isutani didn't just decline to make an offer. He felt that he had to save face by making an offer they would refuse.

The Japanese do not like to say no. They avoid confrontations, especially if there is a prospect of litigation. The word for "no" in Japanese is *iie*, which you don't hear very often. They view saying a direct no as impolite. Instead, they prefer to suggest an alternative course of action.

Honda pushed for the acquisition of Cobra Golf Company. The asking price was something in the range of $60 million. Cobra had just signed Greg Norman to a long-term contract, which made the purchase more attractive. Honda, unbeknownst to me, had previously been negotiating with International Management Group (IMG) for Norman to represent the Ben Hogan Company on the PGA Tour. The price was $5 million a year. A ten-year deal would have cost us $50 million to sign Norman. Honda's logic was simple: for another $10 million, Cosmo World could have not just Norman, but an entire company, Cobra Golf, along with its star representative, Greg Norman.

Rub of the Green
Unfortunately, the Ben Hogan Company at that time could not get out of its own way. Our fill rate (the percentage of orders filled completely) on the Hogan Edge irons was too low. While the order backlog might have stimulated demand, causing golfers to want what was perceived as rare, the unintended consequence was that we probably alienated customers quicker than we created them. It is one thing to understand your problems; it is entirely another matter to fix those problems, given limited resources and constantly changing business objectives. The Japanese did not seem to understand how important it was to stay focused on one thing at a time and keep the main thing, the main thing.

In those days, product life cycles for golf club models in the United States and Japan were very different. The Japanese wanted new products before the current ones were even introduced. The typical US product life cycle for a new model set of irons at Hogan was three years. It was like clockwork. For example, with the Hogan blade iron model, the Apex, we knew that in the first year, we would sell 20,000 sets. In year two, we would sell 15,000 sets, and in year three, we would sell 10,000 sets. Following the third year, we would introduce a new Apex model and would once again sell 20,000 sets.

What we tried to do was have the new game-improvement model, such as the Edge, peak at the times when the demand for Apex was less in order to optimize our manufacturing capabilities. Edge sales peaked at 65,000 sets in the first year, went to 40,000 sets in the second, and the Japanese were already demanding new models for both the Apex and Edge. We were not in the position to meet their expectations and service our market.

Marketing, distribution, and retail sales strategies and tactics in Japan were very different and reflected the shorter product life cycles. At any one time, the leading golf companies like Mizuno or Bridgestone might have fifteen to twenty models of irons, and they would cycle out the slowest moving models every six months or so to be replaced by new designs. There was obviously a real collision of US and Japanese business cultures, marketing, and product development cycles. Unfortunately, we were not in the position to meet the expectations of the Japanese. There was no profitable way for us to advertise

A typical Japanese businessman shops for a set of irons at a retail golf store in Tokyo. Japanese golfers are more brand oriented in their purchase decisions, so golf equipment companies offer many models within a brand. *Author's collection.*

and service our market and meet their expectations at the same time.

In the United States, the advertising for golf clubs was more model oriented. American consumers went to a golf retailer looking for a particular model they had seen advertised. In Japan, advertising and promotion are considered to be the same, and tend to be focused more on the brand than the product. Because Japanese consumers are also more brand oriented in making their purchase decisions, they will make that selection among a large number of models within a popular brand.

Golf product distribution and retail sales in the United States and Japan have very different distribution channels. At the time, US golf equipment was sold predominantly off-course (golf retail stores), and about 20 percent was sold on-course (at golf courses). In Japan, there is very little golf equipment sold on course; most golf equipment is sold at high-end department stores like Macy's or at off-course retail outlets.

The Japanese golf club models tended to tag along with the latest US design trends but with seemingly endless variations. Ironically, the US golf equipment market today is becoming more like the Japanese market. Consumers are more brand-oriented and product-line life cycles are getting shorter.

By August 1990, Ben Hogan Japan was perplexed that we could not just keep introducing new models for them to sell in Japan under the Hogan brand. They did not understand that our market was our chief priority. Whatever we could produce for Japan was less profitable, and they, in turn, were impossible to please. For example, it wasn't unusual for the Japanese to return clubs they claimed had a "rattle." They sent them back for repair, but there was nothing to fix. We could not find anything wrong. We had a representative from Ben Hogan Japan come to the factory in Fort Worth to inspect and test every club before shipping the order to Japan, but the clubs that passed inspection in Fort Worth curiously failed once they arrived in Japan. We asked them how this could be, and the Japanese inspector said that our factory was too noisy; he could not hear the rattles.

Finally, it was necessary for me to head over to Japan to see and hear the rattles for myself. I watched "inspectors" swing the iron clubs upside down. They held the clubhead in their hands and struck the ground with the grip side. It was a violent strike of the handle to the ground. A golf club is not designed for this type of "testing," and still it was almost impossible to hear anything resembling a rattle. My conclusion was they had ordered more clubs than they needed. Evidently, this was a face-saving exercise.

They were playing games with us, and it was costing us money and distracting us from our primary mission—selling golf clubs in the United States. We were in a battle for the hearts and minds of the consumer against formidable foes, and trying to please the disingenuous Japanese affiliate company was not helping matters. Our chief competition in the US was Ping. Ping had the number-one iron with its Ping Eye model. Also, Tommy Armour, with its 845 model, was edging the Hogan Edge out of second place.

The Ben Hogan Company was the number one forged-iron clubmaker in the world at the time with the largest number of players on the PGA Tour using Hogan irons. Forged irons have been around for a long time. They require considerable handwork and craftsmanship. They cost much more to manufacture. Forged clubs feel better when hitting a golf shot, because there is more shock absorption within the clubhead. Most golfers can't really appreciate the difference, but that was the sizzle that was selling the steak for the Hogan Company, which also sold these clubs at a time when hardly anyone was selling anything but cast clubs.

The only way to have multiple models—as demanded by the Japanese— was to start making investment-cast irons like all of our competitors. But the Hogan Company had built its reputation on craftsmanship and excellence by making forged clubs. Since we had very limited advertising dollars, we could not afford to further dilute our message with a multitude of iron models.

We did not oppose having cast models. We could have game-improvement clubs that were cast, not forged. The Hogan Company had done so successfully in the past, but it wasn't our strongest play in the marketplace. The problem

Behind the smiles was genuine angst over whether the Japanese ownership would allow us to do what we needed to be successful on both sides of the Pacific. *Published in* Golf Shop Operations, *April 1990, used with permission of* Golf Digest *magazine, copyright 1990.*

was the cost of marketing multiple models. The Japanese, however, saw how much we were spending on promotion (Ben Hogan Tour and Hogan Company PGA Tour staff players) and did not understand that we did not have enough advertising dollars left over to adequately market the existing line of Apex and Edge irons, much less a myriad of investment-cast models.

For a US golf equipment manufacturer, the longer you can stretch out a model, the more profitable it is. For example, the most profitable model for Ping had to be the Ping Eye model, which stretched out over seven years in production due to the grooves controversy with the USGA and the PGA Tour. Golfers thought they had a genuine advantage with the Ping grooves, and the media frenzy over this issue did nothing but sell more Ping Eye irons. Tommy Armour had a five-year run with its popular 845 model, which was essentially a better-looking Ping iron. Bob MacNally, the president of Tommy Armour and a close personal friend, understood this very well, and even commented to me that they were going to "milk it" as long as they could.

Fortunately, the Ben Hogan Company started making a substantial profit in my second year as president, and this gave us more credibility and more autonomy with the Japanese. The Ben Hogan Tour was in full swing. We had top players on television with the Hogan visors and bags. The Hogan Edge television and print advertising started to positively impact sales as our production levels increased. We were making money and still funding the high promotional expenses for the Ben Hogan Tour and the Hogan Company PGA

Tour pro players. And we were doing it without any of the promised financial support from Cosmo World.

There were many who doubted we could do this, especially since the Ben Hogan Company was so steeped in the craft of traditional clubmaking. *Golf Digest's* trade publication, *Golf Shop Operations*, had Lorin Anderson do a feature story in the April 1990 issue titled "Can Hogan Survive a Big Schism Between Tradition and High-tech?" In the article, Anderson noted that "Hogan is healthier than ever, according to its officials, despite the doubts surrounding its ability to deliver its products and its new strategy to sell high-tech equipment to a tradition-steeped customer base." Given the fact we had a six-month waiting list for the Hogan Edge irons, and ownership was demanding we ship our hottest club in history to launch Ben Hogan Japan, we came away from that criticism relatively unscathed.

HOGAN'S COURSE MANAGEMENT

Ben Hogan was known as one of the greatest ball-strikers of all time. His swing had the grace and beauty of a ballet dancer and the power and force of a steaming locomotive. When Hogan played the PGA Tour, the other players watched him practice in awe. Even toward the end of his playing career, it was not unusual to see a number of tour pros following "Mr. Hogan" in the gallery.

Everything about Hogan was controlled, exacting, and near perfect. With his signature Hogan cap, he was always impeccably dressed. His pants were pressed, and his shoes were always shined. Hogan paid attention to detail; he even had an extra spike in each of his golf shoes for better traction during his swing. His swing was honed and grooved, and his balance and follow-through were perfect. He struck the ball with precision. When you examined his irons, you could see a small, dull spot, about the size of a dime, just left of dead center on the iron clubface where he had worn away the chrome with his golf shots.

When Hogan hit an iron shot, it made a distinctive sound. It was a clean, crisp click, a sound I have never heard since. It was audible with every shot that he struck with an iron or wood. And the golf ball sang as it soared into the air. He could control the trajectory of his shot like no other golfer, then or now, and therefore he could control the distance with precise accuracy. It was not unusual for Hogan to occasionally hit a practice shot into the shag bag positioned in front of the caddie. He also practiced like no other golfer of his generation or before and is credited with inspiring the work ethic that has become the standard for the generations of golfing greats that followed.

So it was most interesting to me that Hogan always stated that his biggest competitive advantage in tournament golf was his "course management," not his shotmaking. He said repeatedly that playing golf was 70 percent course management and 30 percent shotmaking. Sometimes the percentages changed, but his emphasis was that course management and judgment were more important than the skill it took to hit a golf shot. If he told me that once, he told me at least twenty times, but I didn't grasp or really understand it until very late in our relationship. I always thought if I could ever hit the ball as well as Hogan, *then* I could also manage my way around the golf course.

It took me a couple of years to finally understand what he was talking about. It was a classic object lesson from the master, and I remember the incident as if it were yesterday. At the time, we were having our annual Hogan Company sales meeting, and a large group of salesmen was huddled around Hogan at a cocktail party one evening at Shady Oaks Country Club. Never one to say more than necessary, Hogan only pontificated on a subject if so moved by the moment—and a stout drink or two. This time, Hogan was once again talking about course management. Being the insightful and stimulating conversationalist that I am, I thought I would ask him a question to drown the drone of the mantra on course management I had heard so many times before.

As a bit of background, I should note there is a very famous photograph, taken by photojournalist Hy Peskin, of Hogan hitting a 1-iron shot to the final hole of the 1950 U.S. Open at Merion Golf Club, in Ardmore, Pennsylvania. This is probably one of the most extraordinary golf photographs ever taken because it captures an epic competitive moment in golf. The rights fee for this photo's usage is still quite high. The photograph focuses on Hogan's follow-through. His form and balance are perfect. The gallery in the foreground provides a corridor to the stage of green, where that famous 1-iron shot played. It was a singularly difficult shot under the circumstances, played with the most difficult club in the bag. Hogan executed the shot perfectly, leading to a tie with Lloyd Mangrum and George Fazio. The next day, he beat them both in an 18-hole playoff. Adding to the drama, this was just a little less than a year after the head-on collision with the bus near Van Horn, Texas, where Hogan almost met his Maker. To paraphrase famed sportswriter Grantland Rice describing Hogan's determination and comeback: Hogan played on legs just barely strong enough to carry his heart.

In this one picture, Hogan embodies the competitive calm, the resilience through adversity and poise under pressure that we all admire in our heroes. With this picture in mind and with this situation as the backdrop, my question to Hogan at the cocktail party was a simple one. I asked him why he happened to play a 1-iron for that shot, since he normally did not carry a 1-iron and usually played a fairway wood for that particular distance. (In 1938, the USGA adopted a rule now known as Rule 4-4 that limits the number of golf

This painting by Don Adair (copyright Judy Adair 2010) is an artistic rendering of Hy Peskin's photograph. Peskin was positioned behind Hogan when his famous photo captured Hogan's extraordinary 1-iron shot to the 72nd hole of the 1950 U.S. Open at Merion. *Credit Don Adair, reprinted with permission of Judy Adair, copyright 2010.*

clubs a player can use to fourteen during a round of golf; therefore Hogan had to drop a club when he added the 1-iron.)

Hogan curtly replied, "Because I didn't have a seven-iron."

My response was glib and ignorant, "What happened to your seven-iron, did you lose it, or did someone steal it?"

With some disdain in his tone, he said, "No . . . no one stole it, and I didn't misplace it. There was just nowhere on that golf course where I needed to play a seven-iron. And I needed to use that one-iron at least once or possibly twice on that golf course that day."

I was dumbfounded. It is hard to imagine that someone could know his game so well, and be so clear in his strategy and the tactics he would use to play a particular golf course, that he could know he would not need to use a 7-iron over the course of 18 holes. And at the same time, it is equally revealing to know that he knew he would need to use a 1-iron at least once or maybe twice. As I thought about my own game, I could think of a number of clubs I would discard before my 7-iron. I then asked Hogan the logical follow-up question: "What did you do when you had a seven-iron shot?"

"I just told you that I didn't need the seven-iron," he said. "If I did have a seven-iron distance shot, then I just backed off of my six-iron [hit it easier]. It is much easier to adjust your swing speed with a shorter club versus a longer one." In other words, it is easier to reduce and control the distance with a short-iron shot by swinging easier versus swinging easier with a long iron or fairway wood.

My questions were, at best, cavalier and ill-conceived. His answers were succinct and illuminating. And, taking this course-management concept one step further, it's evident this philosophy was applied in how he managed his life and business affairs.

Logo Development

A silhouette of Hogan's follow-through next to the Hogan name created the new Hogan brand logo. The intent in using the silhouette was to recapture that extraordinary moment in time (Hogan's 1-iron shot) because it revealed Hogan's poise, character, determination in overcoming extraordinary adversity, passion, and the unrelenting quest for excellence that made Hogan such an icon. The Hogan Company could be nothing less than the man. We envisioned using the silhouette separately (without the brand name) as time pro-

A silhouette of Hogan's swing was used as the logo for the Ben Hogan Company and the Ben Hogan Tour. A 1990 PGA Tour promotional video about the Ben Hogan Company and the Ben Hogan Tour may be viewed at: www.mindseyegolf.com. *Ben Hogan logos are courtesy of the Ben Hogan Company, Perry Ellis International, all rights reserved. Ben Hogan® is a registered trademark of PEI Licensing, Inc. (PEI). This book was written and published without verification or approval by PEI.*

Ben Hogan and I at Shady Oaks Country Club, Fort Worth, Texas, during the 1989 Hogan sales meeting. *Author's collection.*

gressed, much like the alligator was used to identify Lacoste or the polo player for the Ralph Lauren brand.

When I described the logo concept to Beman, he urged me to have a white background instead of a dark background, like they did with the original PGA Tour logos. He noted that the new PGA Tour logo was designed by Disney, and though it was a big improvement over the old logo—a shield with PGA Tour insignia—the PGA Tour image and lettering were reversed in white. This meant that various applications were limited. The new PGA Tour logo looked like a patch, and if the logo image and lettering were reversed and colored, the logo looked entirely different. That was great advice. The new Hogan logo had the silhouette in dark red and the lettering in black. The black and white versions or any other one-color versions looked the same as the color logo.

Hy Peskin's Photo Postscript
You might find this novel tidbit of history interesting regarding Hogan's 1-iron shot on the 72nd hole at Merion in 1950. Back when I was CEO of the Ben Hogan Company, I received a package from a Hogan fan. He claimed to be in the gallery watching that 1-iron shot. In the letter, he said he had collected the divot after Hogan's shot, and had saved it in wax paper because "that was the best way to preserve things in those days." He then put it into his freezer for some thirty years, changing the packaging to a ziplock bag once they came into use.

At the time, we were using Hy Peskin's classic photo for the promotion of the new Ben Hogan Tour. Our promotional slogan was: The Next Generation of Champions. The promotion and famous photo appeared in *Golf Digest*, and this fan had circled the divot in that picture. What he had sent me in the Ziplock bag looked like what might have been called a "nickel bag" when I was in college—nothing but grass shreds. I took the nickel bag to Hogan, whose office was next to mine, and shared the story with him. Hogan looked at the dried grass in the Ziplock bag and said, "Yes, that's the divot." He smiled.

I put the nickel bag in one of the trophies in the Hogan room at Colonial Country Club. It is probably still in a trophy at the Hogan room in the USGA museum.

AN UNRELENTING PURSUIT OF EXCELLENCE

Mikimoto pearls, the leading brand around the world, was founded in Japan in the late 1890s by Kokichi Mikimoto. Part artist, part businessman, he wanted to be associated only with the finest quality cultured pearls. However, as the twentieth century wore on, the Japanese pearl industry had grown beyond its ability to control quality. In 1932, Mikimoto threw a basket of pearls into the fire because they were not good enough to bear the name Mikimoto. As they disappeared into the flames, what had been merely a reputation for high quality grew into bona fide legend.

Hogan had a similar sensibility. He was always particular and precise about his golf equipment. He had been affiliated with the MacGregor Company since the mid-1930s and by the early 1950s had become increasingly displeased with the performance of the MacGregor golf ball. It also irked him that the golf clubs bearing his name were of middling quality and marketed through retail stores rather than pro shops. By 1953, Hogan refused to use the MacGregor ball, opting instead for either a Titleist or Spalding Dot golf ball. He continued to play his MacGregor Tommy Armour Silver Scot irons, but it was an exacting, custom-made set and only earned his approval after lengthy and painstaking alterations.

Typically, this meant Hogan spent several days with the craftsmen at the MacGregor factory in Cincinnati. They loved to see him and discuss club design but dreaded his visits because of his uncompromising demand for perfection. Eventually, Hogan would get the set he wanted, but he wondered why MacGregor couldn't make a set of golf clubs for all golfers that were as good as the ones they made for him.

In 1953, Hogan split with his longtime golf equipment sponsor and formed the Ben Hogan Golf Company. The business concept was simple: Make perfect golf clubs. Make golf clubs of the same high quality as those made for the tour professional. When the company's first production run of golf clubs was finally completed, the clubs didn't meet Hogan's high standards. The cost of that first run was more than $150,000, which was a lot of money in those days, and Hogan's business partners were not pleased when he ordered that the whole lot be destroyed. He was unyielding: the clubs simply weren't good enough to bear the Ben Hogan name. Like Mikimoto, Hogan had an uncompromising commitment to quality. Another legend was born when those golf clubs, like the pearls, were figuratively thrown into the fire.

Something else occurred in 1953 that got far more attention—the culmination of his own uncompromising commitment to golfing excellence. Hogan won a sort of Triple Crown of golf—the Masters, the U.S. Open, and the British Open. He didn't play in the PGA Championship because it was match play, and he simply could not play that many rounds on legs that had been irreparably damaged in that near-fatal 1949 accident. Also, travel to Scotland back then—by boat—made it very difficult to make the round trip to the British Open and then play in the PGA Championship.

Hogan played in six tournaments in 1953 and won five times. He swept the majors that he entered, a feat that wasn't duplicated until Tiger Woods matched it in 2000 when he won three majors. Hogan also won the Pan American Open and the Colonial National Invitation Tournament. The only professional event that he entered and did not win was the Greenbrier Pro-Am in White Sulphur Springs, West Virginia—Sam Snead's stomping grounds. Hogan shot 67-68-68-69 for 272, and finished third to "the Slammer" on his home course—not a bad year for Hogan and as close as any golfer would ever come to a perfect season.

Hogan was the heart and soul of the Ben Hogan Company. When I came on board as CEO in 1988, I found it ludicrous that the previous owner, AMF, had been so blind to his value for the twenty-plus years they owned the company. AMF had never spent much on building the Ben Hogan Company business, and Hogan was "chairman" in name only. AMF didn't pay him much money or confer with him. They viewed Hogan as a garden-variety brand-name manufacturer of golf equipment.

My job was to take the founder's legacy, the Ben Hogan Company (his pride and joy), to the next level, such that his namesake company could begin selling far more product than Hogan could have ever imagined. I wanted to involve Hogan in the business. I wanted him to take pride in his golf company, because it was his name on the clubs, and it was his legacy that made it such a premium brand. I was just beginning to earn his confidence.

Early on, I am not sure he expected much from me or even felt it would be possible to trust me. There had been a revolving door of presidents in recent

BEN HOGAN
Born: 1912 in Dublin, Texas
Joined Professional
Golfers Tour: 1931
Married: 1935 to Valerie Fox
Founded Ben Hogan
Company: 1953
Residence: Fort Worth, Texas

CAREER HIGHLIGHTS

MAJORS:
Masters Champion—1951, 1953*
U.S. Open Champion—1948, 1950, 1951, 1953*
British Open Champion—1953*
PGA Champion—1946, 1948

One of only four players in history to win all four major championships

The only time in the history of golf a player has won these three tournaments in the same year.

Winner of 60 other P.G.A. Tournaments
Leading Money Winner—1940, 1941, 1942, 1946, 1948
Vardon Trophy Winner—1940, 1941, 1948
PGA Golfer of the Year—1948, 1950, 1951, 1953
Professional Male Athlete of the Year—1953

While at the PGA Tour, I made a deal with Donruss to produce and market bubble gum trading cards of the leading PGA Tour players to raise interest in golf among kids. Unfortunately, this left out the great players who came before, so the Ben Hogan Company produced its own trading card. *Courtesy of the Ben Hogan Company, Perry Ellis International, all rights reserved. Ben Hogan® is a registered trademark of PEI Licensing, Inc. (PEI). This book was written without verification or approval by PEI.*

years, and he seemed hesitant to share much at first, especially since I represented the new Japanese owners. I moved files and furniture from an office across the building—where my predecessor had been—into Hogan's office suite. We had coffee together at least two or three times a week when I was in town. I always asked him questions about everything related to golf and the business.

When I reviewed his contract, I was appalled at what the company was paying him, and quadrupled his compensation to about the level of the leading staff players representing the Ben Hogan Company on the PGA Tour. It seemed crazy to me that this eminent figure who had founded the company and established its principles and commitment to excellence would be paid at the salary level provided in his 1960 sales agreement with AMF. I also bought an insurance policy for the benefit of his wife, Valerie, which I know Hogan appreciated.

This was not some magnanimous gesture on my part, and I wasn't trying to buy his trust. It was simply the right thing to do. Hogan did not need the money. He had made more money with his friends in the oil business than he ever did in golf, but this was more a matter of principle and a recognition of his contributions. We needed to do the right thing for the company's founder. And if we were going to ask him to get more involved in the company, not just as a spokesman, but really ask him for his advice and direction, then I felt we ought to compensate him fairly for it.

I found myself easily caught up in the company's impressive culture—for which Hogan set the tone, despite AMF's penchant for marginalizing him. The Hogan persona permeated every aspect of the Ben Hogan Company. Every detail had to be right. Salesmen were required to wear jackets and ties on every sales call even though their customers all dressed casually in golf wear. They had to be well groomed and well-spoken because that was part of the company culture. Hogan insisted on it. Back in the days when longer hair was fashionable, it would not be unusual for a salesman to be sent to the barber at Shady Oaks before he could attend the sales meeting. If the salesman refused, he could find a job elsewhere.

We had a number of things going in our favor. We had a great brand. When someone said the word, *Hogan*, it conveyed a notion of quality, which is an attribute that cannot be easily created. The Ben Hogan Company was the best in the world in making forged irons. We had a hot golf club; we had the Ben Hogan Tour and a stable of professional staff tour players that would win, place, or show in just about every event. We were all over the TV screen during PGA Tour golf telecasts. We appeared to be a more formidable company from a revenue- and market-share standpoint than we really were. Most importantly, we had Ben Hogan and the greatest brand in golf.

Two Balls in Play at Once

At the time of the Pebble Beach acquisition in September 1990, what had been working for the Ben Hogan Company was our focus on the golf-equipment business. We persevered in our quest for uncompromised excellence in the manufacture and sale of golf clubs. We were making money, even with the disproportionate investment into promotion for a company of our size. We were balancing the sale of Apex and Edge irons and were efficiently managing production levels. The Hogan Edge became the most successful club in the company's history. I saw the use of Hogan, himself, in television and print ads as critical to maintaining that momentum.

When the bubble burst in Japan just a few months later, it would eventually overwhelm the Ben Hogan Company and its affiliated companies. Any resources available to the Ben Hogan Company were designated, claimed, and diverted to the more immediate and pressing needs of the Japanese owner, Cosmo World.

Meanwhile, in November 1991, we decided to invest what limited resources remained into a series of television ads featuring Mr. Hogan. We knew we needed to piggyback on the highly successful commercials previously made for the Hogan Edge irons. We called those original television commercials the "yellow sweater" ads, because Hogan wore a yellow sweater. Those ads were shot back in 1988 at Riviera Country Club in Los Angeles. The problem was that Hogan had stopped hitting balls, so we could not reshoot any of the ads showcasing his golf swing. I rehired our advertising agency, TracyLocke. This agency had done the original work on the Hogan Edge ads but was fired by Cosmo World's interim consultant, Dick Babbit. I wanted to recapture the excitement and appeal of the original ads.

It was decided to use the original swing footage as background for the interviews, with Hogan dressed in a suit and at his desk. We set it up to shoot the ad in his office. I would sit across from Hogan (out of camera view) and interview Hogan. Our plan was to ask him a series of questions and hopefully get some comments we could use in a series of thirty-second spots.

I spoke with Hogan about this plan several times, and finally he agreed to do it. Then, on the appointed day, after we had the camera and sound crew all set up in his office, he refused. His secretary, Doxie Williams, just looked at me, shrugged her shoulders and said, "Mr. Hueber, this isn't a good day. Let's try it again next week. I think all of these people and this equipment just put him off. He had forgotten that this was the day."

So we rescheduled the shoot for about ten days later. This time, I reminded him every day of the upcoming camera shoot and promised him we would not run any of the television commercials if he wasn't pleased with the results of the filming. He agreed to do it once again. When the day finally arrived, we had the cameras, lighting, and sound systems set up, but it was turned off, and there were no people in his office when he arrived. When Hogan came through the back door of his office, I was waiting for him. I reminded him that this was the day. He looked around his office and seemed surprised to see all of the equipment. I sat down and had a cup of coffee with him and told him we would be ready when he was. He paused, looked me in the eye and said, "You are going to ask me some questions and you are going to make some commercials from what I say?"

I responded, "Yes, we are going to make some great commercials, and when we are finished, you will have the say on whether or not we can use them."

Hogan replied, "Okay, bring them in. Let's get started."

I sat across the desk with my two pages of questions, asked the first question, and then could not shut him up. He pontificated on every subject presented and was simply marvelous. At one point, I asked him, "Mr. Hogan, what is the difference between a forged and a cast club?"

His answer was a classic: "With a cast club, you can make a beautiful golf club. But it's just no good. No good for hitting a golf ball. With a forged golf club you get the feeling of a well-hit shot that goes up the shaft into your hands and right into your heart."

I turned around to the commercial's director standing behind me and said, "Did you get that?"

And he said, "Oh, yeah!"

That comment was used in one of the seven 30-second ads that all had the tagline "No one makes golf clubs like we do." We had enough material for a dozen more ads of what we called "The Mr. Hogan Ads." When the first ads were completed, I took Hogan over to the conference room so he could review them, and so we could get his approval as I had promised. I knew the ads were good, but I was uncertain he would approve. Hogan was never one to put his golf game on display if it wasn't up to his standards. I did not know if Hogan would like seeing himself on film now that he was older.

When we got to the conference room, I asked him to sit down and he said, "No thanks," which I did not interpret as a good sign. I darkened the room and then started the VCR. We ran through all seven 30-second commercials. Hogan said nothing.

I then asked him, "Would you like to see them again?"

He then pulled out a chair and sat down and said, "Yes."

After that showing, I said, "One more time?" He nodded, and I noticed a tear in his eye.

After the last ad was played for the third time, he stood up and simply said, "Thank you, David. That will be just fine." He then turned around and walked back to his office.

The television ads were a tremendous success and can be seen at www.mindseyegolf.com. Viewers could sense sincerity and genuine emotion from Hogan in the ads. We were offering them more than just great golf clubs from a company with an uncompromising commitment to excellence; we were inspiring them to improve their game and to appreciate the feeling that only a forged club can give—a feeling that any golfer can enjoy, which "goes up the shaft into your hands and right into your heart."[1]

15

"W'S" VISIT

Occasionally, famous people visited the factory. Earlier, I had given fellow Hoosier Vice President Dan Quayle a set of golf clubs along with a red, white, and blue Hogan golf bag with the presidential seal embroidered on the belly of the bag. Later, in May 1992 I had an opportunity to play Burning Tree Club, in Bethesda, Maryland, with the vice president. It was great fun. The Secret Service had everyone step aside while we played through. It took us less than three hours to play 18 holes, and we never lost a ball in the woods. Quayle is a pretty good player. He shot something in the low eighties, and could easily be a mid-seventies shooter with a little practice. After the round, he went over to the practice range and hit some more balls with his new clubs.

You can tell a lot about a person after playing a round of golf with him. While it was clear the vice president's game was rusty due to lack of play, he was a serious golfer. Quayle used a long putter but still struggled on the greens. Interestingly, he didn't ask for, nor did he give, any putts. The same was true for mulligans: there were no mulligans. Quayle played by the rules. Lastly, I would like to note that the vice president was a genuinely nice person and very smart—not at all the buffoon *Saturday Night Live* and the media portrayed him to be.

It was cool to hang around the Burning Tree clubhouse, soak up the atmosphere, and see famous politicians relax outside the glare of the Washington media. While I was putting on my golf shoes in the locker room, I spotted Senator Sam Nunn out of the corner of my eye. He was having what I assumed was an adult beverage. I introduced myself. Reportedly, Nunn was a single-digit handicap player, and he was very gracious in our brief conversation. I asked him if he had already played that day, and he replied that he hadn't. Then I told him that I had given the vice president some Hogan golf clubs and was going to play a round with him.

He said, "Great, maybe now we will see him out here a little more often."

Later, when I shared that story with Max Elbin, the longtime head professional

Vice President Quayle and I playing golf at Burning Tree Club, Bethesda, Maryland. *Author's collection.*

at Burning Tree and a former PGA president, he reminded me that Burning Tree was a unique club because it served as a refuge away from the limelight for many of its members. Elbin, however, was used to the celebrity climate at the club. Having personally coached some eight US presidents, he was cognizant of what his members wanted and expected.

***

Word was that Vice President Quayle really liked the golf clubs and told the president's son about them. Not too long after that, Lanny Wadkins brought George W. Bush by the Hogan plant for a visit. At the time, the younger George Bush was the managing general partner of the ownership group that had acquired the Texas Rangers. We made him the same golf bag and custom set of graphite-shafted golf clubs we had made for the vice president. Bush was very appreciative. He then started pitching me that a local company, like the Ben Hogan Company, really ought to have box seats at the Rangers games.

I said, "That sounds great to me."

Bush then said he would have someone from the ticket office give me a call. I replied, "Okay. I'll pay the same thing for those tickets that you paid for the golf clubs."

Bush looked at me, smiled and said, "You got me there. Let me first thank you for the golf clubs and bag, and please let me know if you would ever like to come to a Rangers game as my guest." He then said, "David, would you mind if I took a tour of the factory to meet some of your employees?"

I said, "That would be great. We would love to have you visit and take an official tour."

So Bush, along with his Secret Service entourage, went on the tour. He wasn't running for office, but you would never have known it by watching him work the different areas of the factory. He went out of his way to say hello to and shake hands with everyone within reach as he introduced himself and said, "Hello, I am George Bush. It's nice to meet you."

It seemed to be going very well until he ran into the foreman, or should I say the forewoman, of the Custom Fit Department. As he walked into the room with his entourage, Bush walked straight over to the person wearing the different colored manager's smock, the one who wasn't working on the assembly of a set of custom built irons and said, "You must be the boss around here. My name is George Bush, how are you doing?"

She didn't recognize him and was bemused by his statement. She looked him *up and down*, as they say in Texas, and knew this was not the president of the United States standing in front of her. He was much too young. And she was busy. She raised her right hand to shake his and sarcastically said, "So, glad to meet you, Mr. President. My name is Jackie Collins." Evidently, the successful novelist was her equivalent to president of the United States.

George Bush smiled. Everyone around started laughing as he said, "No, my name really is George Bush. My dad is the president."

"Yeah, right," she responded. "Who let you in here anyway? You need to leave; we have a lot of work to do."

The future governor of Texas and president of the United States left with a smile on his face and a dose of down-to-earth Texas humility.

TORA! TORA! TORA! THE JAPANESE SURPRISE ATTACK ON PEBBLE BEACH

n Japanese, Tora means tiger. The code word that the Japanese used for signaling their attack on Pearl Harbor was, "Tora, Tora, Tora." To American golfers, the acquisition of Pebble Beach by the Japanese caused equal surprise and indignation. However, to the Japanese, it was just another business transaction, like the purchase of Rockefeller Center, dumping steel at below-market prices in the United States, or acquiring a major market share of the US auto market.

The real fight was a clash of cultures, buoyed by nationalist pride and prejudice. Eventually, it resolved unfavorably for the Japanese due to mitigating economic circumstances at home and America's home-court advantage in the political, legal, and public-relations battle. In the final analysis, it is evident that ethnocentric-driven business initiatives fail for a number of reasons, with the foremost simply being that sometimes a great notion is a bad idea. In other words, just because you can do something doesn't mean that you should.

In the early summer of 1990, I was called to Los Angeles for a meeting with billionaire maverick-entrepreneur Marvin Davis regarding Cosmo World's impending purchase of the Pebble Beach Company. Minoru Isutani, head of Cosmo World, had never been shy about making acquisitions and would seldom go a long stretch without contemplating one. In the past, he had called me in from the get-go to evaluate such targets as Cobra Golf and Aldila. But the Pebble Beach deal was a different story. I had no clue it was even being considered. And yet, had I somehow been shown the management roster of Ben Hogan Property Companies—the subsidiary they had formed to absorb

Pebble Beach—I would have seen my own name, right up there at the top.

By the time I made my trip west, the conveyance of Pebble Beach from Davis's group to Cosmo World had been thoroughly discussed by the parties. Valuations, terms, the timetable—all this information had been circulating on a need-to-know basis. Since I would be president of the company that would own Pebble Beach, they decided I finally needed to know about it. A driver was waiting for me at Los Angeles International Airport (LAX) when I arrived. He took me straight to Cosmo World headquarters on Robertson Boulevard in Beverly Hills, where I was greeted by Isutani's chief US liaison, Ted Honda.

The two of us walked downstairs to Robata's, a Japanese restaurant Cosmo World owned, to have lunch and talk about what would take place later that day. Honda had a warped sense of humor and decided this was the proper time for me to become better acquainted with Japanese cuisine. He ordered sushi for both of us, and when it arrived, he pointed out the green stuff on the side of the plate and told me it was delicious. With my chopsticks I scooped up a nice portion of what I later learned was wasabi, a horseradish paste that is hotter than a three-alarm fire. As I ingested it, I felt as if I were losing control of my senses. Fiery pain seared through my head. Honda laughed. I gripped the edge of the table, trying to extinguish the flow of lava burning through my brain, as tears flowed uncontrollably. In hindsight, this dining mishap proved a fitting prelude to my experience as president of Ben Hogan Property Companies—nearly every aspect would be unforeseen, wickedly painful, and beyond my control.

Once I recovered, Honda laid out the agenda for the meeting that afternoon. We were headed over to the 20th Century Fox Plaza in Century City to meet with Marvin Davis's group and discuss our purchase of Pebble Beach. Isutani, bank officials from Mitsubishi Trust and Banking Corporation (MTBC), as well as other Cosmo World consultants and lawyers would be there.

Colossal as this deal was to me, to the seller it was probably just business as usual. A fixture on the Forbes richest-people list, billionaire Davis made his initial fortune in oil and gas. Known as "Mr. Wildcatter," Davis expanded into real estate and show business, buying the Beverly Hills Hotel, Pebble Beach, and 20th Century Fox. He also built and twice sold the Fox Plaza in Century City, where our meeting was scheduled. As the cars pulled up to let us out in front of the building, I recalled with some amusement that it had been known by a fictitious Japanese name, Nakatomi Plaza, when it was used as a location in the original *Die Hard* movie.

We entered the lobby and rode a special express elevator up to the top floor. In the group were Isutani, MTBC bank officials, our investment banker, a Cosmo World consultant named Dick Babbitt, a few Baker & McKenzie lawyers representing our side, Honda, and some other Japanese who were part of our team in an undetermined capacity. Greg Davis, Davis's son, ushered us into a conference room. It was a vast, lavish space containing the largest circular conference table I have ever seen. The hole in the middle of the table looked big enough for a small orchestra. On the walls were massive murals—paintings of oil wells, the Pebble Beach Golf Links (as the course is properly called), the Beverly Hills Hotel, movie scenes from 20th Century Fox pictures—all of it a Technicolor testimony to Marvin Davis's worldly achievements. Greg Davis, who was understandably proud of his tycoon father, explained the significance of the murals to the "humble" Japanese who had been herded into the room.

Ironically, he had no clue how offensive this life-size display of braggadocio was to the Japanese. They simply bowed and nodded as the son nodded back, beaming with pride. We then took our seats and waited for the sellers to arrive. First came Myron Miller, and I believe it was Donald Spiegleman and Ronald Kravet representing the partnership selling Pebble Beach. Their attorneys were also present. We all sat looking at one another for what seemed an uncomfortably long time. Finally, Marvin Davis, the great one, arrived.

As he ambled into the room and settled into his chair, I found it difficult not to gape. The man was huge. He had to weigh over 400 pounds. From the moment Davis entered the room, he assumed complete control of the proceedings, and he maintained it throughout, even though he didn't say all that much. I couldn't help comparing him to Jabba the Hutt, the crime-lord character from the *Star Wars* series 20th Century Fox had produced. It was rumored the success of the *Star Wars* movies helped fund the purchase of Pebble Beach, which added to the irony. I sank into my seat and watched the action unfold. At the time, I was uncertain why I was even there, although my status as the only "round-eye" officer in the Cosmo World group was surely significant. The question as to why I was there hung over me, providing yet another harbinger of the nature of my role in the management of Pebble Beach—as mysterious as my role in this meeting.

There was a formal exchange of greetings, and Miller opened up the proceedings. Looking across at the Japanese contingent, he said, "Are you aware of the asking price?"

Our side was more than aware of it. "There will be no negotiation," stated Babbitt, speaking on behalf of Cosmo World. He rose from his chair, scanned the room once, and said: "The asking price is acceptable."

Miller asked if we could provide evidence of our ability to pay the agreed-upon price. At that point, an MTBC official presented a letter stating the bank would provide up to $760 million on behalf of either Cosmo World Corporation or Ben Hogan Corporation to make the purchase. Isutani would provide the balance of the amount in cash.

Then, one of the attorneys from our side introduced a potential sticking point: "We would like a short period of time to undertake some due diligence," he said.

Davis leaned over to confer with Miller, who listened a moment, said something back, and nodded. Miller responded to the lawyer's request with a rather stern proviso: "You may have forty-five days. But we want a ten million, nonrefundable deposit for that time period. We have other suitors for this property. If you go forward, that deposit will be applied to the purchase price."

Years later, I read a *Sports Illustrated* article quoting Davis as saying he could have sold Pebble Beach for more money to another Japanese buyer, but did not do so because he had made a commitment to Isutani. That statement wasn't entirely accurate, given that Isutani *paid* for Davis's commitment. I was sitting right there when Isutani signed the Cosmo World check for $10 million that won him the right to take a close-up look at what he was buying.

The due-diligence period was never more than a formality. They could have found Jimmy Hoffa under the 18th green at Pebble Beach, and it would not have mattered. The purchase price for Pebble Beach (including its sister properties: the Lodge at Pebble Beach, the Links and Inn at Spanish Bay, Del Monte and Spyglass Hill golf courses, along with other developable property) was $828,853,145.69. I'm not certain how they came up with the sixty-nine cents. You would think they could have rounded it off to an even seventy cents, even with the uncertain exchange rate.

The closing of the Pebble Beach acquisition took place on September 4 and 5, 1990, at the offices of Cosmo World's attorneys, Baker & McKenzie. The loan closing took place at the offices of Gibson, Dunn & Crutcher, attorneys for MTBC. As president of Ben Hogan Property Companies, the newly created partnership entity, I signed all of the closing documents on behalf of the purchaser, Cosmo World Corporation. Miller signed many a document alongside me. Other documents were signed by the various partners coming in and out of the room. In the two-volume set of closing documents, of which each ran 1,000 pages or more, I certainly did see Davis's signature, but I never witnessed him sign anything. I can't say I blame the great one for not being there. After several hours of signing your name over and over, your hand and wrist develop cramps. I got to the point where I had to think about the letters in my name after signing it mindlessly so many times.

Following the closing, Davis hosted all the parties to a celebration dinner at Spagos in Beverly Hills. There were innumerable attorneys and accountants on hand, as well as representatives of the principals. Tom Oliver, president of the Pebble Beach Company and a former restaurateur, was visibly dismayed at Davis's menu selections, which were not what you would call nouvelle cuisine. Starting the menu off was an appetizer of hearty chili; salad was served, followed by steak, lobster, French fries, and a few sundry items. It didn't matter to me. I would have been happy in a ghetto soup kitchen as long as I didn't have to look at any more legal documents.

There was some clinking of glasses, many polite words passed back and forth, and when we were finished, the amazing deal was sealed. A Japanese

DAVID B. HUEBER
PRESIDENT

BEN HOGAN PROPERTY CO. I
BEN HOGAN PROPERTY CO. II
2912 WEST PAFFORD   TELEPHONE (817) 927-4539
FORT WORTH, TX 76110   FACSIMILE (817) 927-4543

Because Pebble Beach was a partnership, two companies were actually formed for the acquisition: Ben Hogan Property Company I and II. For convenience sake, we referred to it as Ben Hogan Property Companies. *Author's collection.*

company now held title to the "Sistine Chapel of golf," as former USGA President Sandy Tatum once called it. This was no minor real estate transaction. News of it was not well received by an America that had witnessed such a rapid rise in Japanese economic and manufacturing strength. It didn't help matters that MTBC bankers had also provided backing for the acquisition of New York City's iconic Rockefeller Center by Mitsubishi Estates.

Out in California, echoes of "Tora, Tora, Tora" could be heard along the Monterey Peninsula. The controversy brewed, and there I was, an American, with no reputation outside the golf industry, nominally in charge of it all—a front man in other words, with nobody to watch my back.

At this point, I still wasn't aware what my role would be at Pebble Beach. Soon after the closing, I was fingerprinted for the resort's alcohol and pharmacy licenses. I must have passed since those businesses continued operating. But the charade had begun, and even a blind man could see that the Ben Hogan Company and its Indiana-bred president were mere props in a clumsy diversion. Culturally trained to make false displays of deference, the Japanese, at least some of them, behaved toward me as though I were indeed the key guy. Unfortunately, communication from further up the chain of command was nonexistent. No one told me I was in charge; no one told me I wasn't.

If there was a game plan for day-to-day management or long-range policy at Pebble Beach, no one discussed it with me. I was the president of the Ben Hogan Company and the president of Ben Hogan Property Companies, the parent company of the Pebble Beach Company. Throughout the fall of 1990 and the winter, spring, and early summer of 1991, I split my time between Fort Worth and Monterey. Basically, I spent a week or so at Pebble Beach and then spent ten days or so in Fort Worth. I was running the Hogan Company, and Cosmo World even gave me a nice bump in pay with respect to my new responsibilities (if I indeed had any) in the management of Pebble Beach.

In time, I saw that this was not a workable situation. I was forever stuck in catch-up mode. If I'd had stronger support, some of that work could have been handled without my attention. Or if there had been Internet technology at the time, I could have stayed in closer touch, and fewer issues would have fallen through the cracks. Instead, by the time I caught up on work at one place, it was time to shuttle back to the other. I was no longer a proactive CEO; I was in a reactive mode. I had to make a choice, so I focused more on the Ben Hogan Company.

Working at Pebble Beach was never what you'd call a chore. My office was usually a suite at the Lodge at Pebble Beach or at the Inn at Spanish Bay. Actually, the Inn was a much better place to stay. The rooms were much nicer, and I usually got the governor's suite. I had my run of the place, but never took advantage of it the way I could have. When you are in the midst of a job like that—even when things aren't going so well—you think it will never end and that you will always have unfettered access to the greatest place in golfdom.

From time to time, I tried to get away and play a few holes in the late afternoon. Sometimes I played Spyglass Hill, which is the toughest course on the peninsula and has a little bit of everything. The first few holes play like the seaside links of Turnberry, and then you feel like you are at Shinnecock, only to finish the last half of your round on Pinehurst No. 2. At one point, I entered into preliminary discussions with the PGA of America about hosting the PGA Championship at Spyglass. It is a very challenging golf course. Only on rare occasions did I play Spanish Bay. I did not consider it much of a golf course. It is scenic and fun to play, but not on par with the others on the peninsula.

My favorite course was the Pebble Beach Golf Links. In the late afternoon, I would take a golf cart out and play a few balls on every hole until I caught up to groups with the late-afternoon tee times. That usually happened on about the ninth or tenth hole. It was fun hitting shots until I was on the picturesque, par-3 seventh hole. I suppose I have played that hole with almost every iron in the bag. The most I ever hit into a strong ocean breeze was a punch, four iron; I've also hit as little as a sand wedge.

Late one November day, I was playing by myself and arrived at the eighth tee. I had hit a good enough tee shot, and when I arrived at my second shot, I was just enraptured with the beauty of the place. It was a clear, blustery afternoon, almost chilly. I peered out over the cliffs and looked at the Pacific whitecaps. I could see the afternoon play was just ahead on the ninth green, meaning this was as far as I could venture. I really did not even want to hit my next shot; I just sat in the golf cart and enjoyed the serenity of the moment. Everything was perfect. I thought to myself, *It just does not get any better than this.*

Finally, I forced myself out of the golf cart to play the next shot. It was a good lie, about 185 yards out, with a slight breeze into me. I selected a three

At the top left side of this aerial photo, the eighth tee is just a short walk from the famous par-3 seventh green. A good drive for a single-digit golfer will take a longer route to the fairway to avoid the oceanside cliffs. From the plateau above, the next shot to the green below requires a utility wood or long iron. (Pebble Beach, Pebble Beach Golf Links, its holes and individual hole designs are trademarks, service marks, and trade dress of Pebble Beach Company.) *Used with permission. Copyright Joann Dost.*

iron and took dead aim at the flag. The ball flew like a rifle shot and struck the flagstick almost halfway up, then dropped straight down into the hole.

I looked to see if anyone was around to witness what I had just done. No one was around, except some deer off in the distance, and the seals off the cliffs of the beach below. They did not care, and neither did I. With no one to revel with me in my seemingly celestial feat, I turned my golf cart around and drove back to the clubhouse, leaving my Hogan 392 LS golf ball in the cup. After I dropped off my clubs at the bag storage room, I walked over to the 19th hole at the Lodge and had a Chivas on the rocks with a splash of water. I was alone in my celebration of this extraordinary experience at Pebble Beach.

***

Tom Oliver, the Pebble Beach president, justifiably believed that he was the man in charge, since Cosmo World consultant Babbitt had just renegotiated and renewed his contract. Oliver hated me, mostly because he couldn't figure out whether or not I was his boss. His thinly veiled hostility was of little consequence. I considered the man a nitwit, and beyond that, I was concerned about certain allegations I had heard. Several years later, Oliver was charged and convicted of racketeering in connection with his role in a local savings and loan—although those convictions were reversed on appeal.

I had breakfast with Oliver one November morning in 1990 at the Lodge, Pebble Beach Resort's beloved hotel. We had set aside the morning for a goodwill mission to meet with some of the county commissioners. Oliver sat at the table grilling me on how many people reported to me at the Ben Hogan Company, what the Hogan Company revenues were, and how that compared to his responsibilities. I tried to allay his fear that I was trying to usurp his authority, but the more he talked, the more it struck me how little he knew. Perhaps I was out of my pay grade, but this guy seemed to know absolutely nothing about golf resort operations or the golf business, and here he was the president of the premier golf resort in the world.

From that point on, I tried to get a better understanding of what Oliver actually did. I remained unimpressed by his managerial abilities. The personal and professional conflict between us only intensified over time. I held a series of conversations about this with Harry White, Cosmo World's chief financial officer (CFO). White and I both felt it would be wise to make a change in management. We approached Honda, told him about our concerns, and proposed that Oliver be relieved of his duties.

In his inimitable way, Honda said: "Okay, but what does he do?"

Speaking for White and me, I said, "Not much, from what we can tell. The Lodge and the Inn at Spanish Bay both have solid general managers. Paul Spengler, the director of golf, takes up the slack on the golf side, where Oliver is the weakest. We've studied the operation pretty thoroughly, and our conclusion is that life would be a lot easier for us without him." Honda thought for a few moments.

"Okay," Honda said without a shred of irony, "I can do that job. Go ahead and let him go."

More bold decision-making from Honda. I then had to explain to him that it would not be so simple a task, given that Oliver had just signed a new five-year contract. He told us to study the situation further, which the two of us did, as time permitted. Eventually, White and I even spoke with Oliver about terminating his employment contract, but it never got any further than that, in part because of the prospect of litigation but mainly because far bigger problems were looming.

As sometimes happens in dysfunctional organizations, the right hand learns what the left hand is doing through a phone call from an investigative reporter. I found myself on the receiving end of one of these journalistic grenades one afternoon about a month later, in December. The phrase "privatization of Pebble Beach" sat me up straight in my chair. Was it true, the reporter asked, that Pebble Beach was about to become a private club and that golf memberships would be sold in Japan? Naturally, I denied this. Then I went looking for Honda to ask him from where a rumor like that might come. Though he spoke excellent English and understood my question fully, he said nothing. The two of us stood there, Honda locked in a long, embarrassed silence and me ascending toward a profound and stunning consciousness. "If this is true," I demanded of him, "why was I not told about it?"

Honda regained his composure. Speaking matter-of-factly, he said the company was indeed planning to sell Pebble Beach golf memberships[1] on the Japanese Membership Exchange for about $475,000 apiece. The grand plan was to sell at least 1,500 to 2,000 memberships on the exchange, a bold tactic that would summarily erase the entire debt incurred by the acquisition. There was a certain elegance to the whole thing, if you ignored the obvious flaws. The Japanese golfers who bought the memberships would not all come over at the same time, which would allow the world's most famous and beloved public-access golf course to remain open for play just as it had in the past. Cosmo World would, from time to time, charter jumbo jets out of Tokyo International to accommodate the new members, and everyone would be happy.

The infuriating haze that had surrounded the Japanese acquisition of Pebble Beach was dissipating somewhat as this issue—dubious and more contentious—now confronted us. The secret had been leaked; there was no opportunity to strategize privately about how to counter the inevitable protest and resistance. It fell to me to put a positive spin on the membership concept, an impossible task in light of the anti-Japanese sentiment on the peninsula and elsewhere in the United States. Not long after the plan became known, I found myself in a meeting hall at the Inn at Spanish Bay hotel making a presentation to the Pebble Beach Property Owners Association. I stressed to them we were investing in the peninsula, doing all we could to make it an even better place to live. Our efforts included building a new water-treatment facility (which would provide irrigation water during any future droughts) as well as further improvements to the Pebble Beach golf course in anticipation of the 1992 U.S. Open. Also, I advised the assembly that Jack Nicklaus had agreed to consult on the course design in preparation for the tournament. When my presentation ended, I opened up the floor for questions.

A gentleman (I later learned he was the president of the property owners association) got to his feet and said, "Mr. Hueber, I like much of what you have said this morning. You reportedly have a good reputation in the golf industry, and I believe that you are sincere. But I have to tell you this . . . I fought against those bastards in the Pacific and I'll be damned if they are going to take over after losing the war!"

There was a muffled cheer, light applause, and then quiet. I was caught off guard by this display of such longstanding bitterness. I strung a few thoughts together and said, "I am sorry to hear that you feel that way. Obviously, I am too young to really appreciate and understand your point of view. Isutani was a child as well during World War II. He acquired Pebble Beach because he loves it here, believes that it will be a good investment, and is willing to do whatever he can to make it a better place." I asked if there were other questions or comments, and no hands were raised. I ended the meeting and walked out of the room.

I returned to the Lodge and waited for Honda to come in from his round of golf with Mr. Tsuchiya, one of Isutani's chief advisers in Japan. Honda needed to know in detail about the backlash we already faced. I told him what had been said at the meeting, which prompted him to ask, "What can we do about it? Can they cause us problems?"

I responded, "There is nothing you can do, not unless you can change the perception of who owns this place and promise never to make Pebble Beach an exclusive private club for the Japanese."

He shook his head. "There is no way that we can pay for this acquisition without selling memberships," he said. "Also, selling memberships in Japan will not change how Pebble Beach operates. It will still be open to the public."

"In a case like this," I replied, "perception is more important than reality. There is an entire tourism industry here that relies on the perception that this place is open to the public. If you change that perception, then everyone will be working against us."

Honda then said, "Marvin Davis said that we could do what we are planning."

"Marvin Davis does not control the permitting process in California. Furthermore," I continued, "Pebble Beach is considered to be a public landmark. We have security guards at the gates dressed up like park rangers, and tourists who pay a fee to drive their cars down Seventeen-Mile Drive, which we own. They think the Monterey Peninsula is a state park. Selling memberships disrupts that whole mind-set. It is an uphill fight that we are very likely to lose."

Trouble on one Pacific coastline was soon echoed by calamity on the far distant shore. The great bubble burst in Japan, and real estate values plummeted—a bad situation indeed for Isutani. The assets securing the short-term loans for the purchase of Pebble Beach were Isutani's real estate holdings in Japan, which were primarily golf courses. He had borrowed a total of $575 million from MTBC and Japan Leasing Incorporated (JLI). Even though the interest rates were relatively low, the fact that the loans were short term put Isutani in a precarious financial position. It was unclear whether he could hang on long enough to implement the membership plan for Pebble Beach, a plan that was in need of regulatory approval and was already unpopular with the public. Politics and public relations now became our top priorities, and this new reality posed some formidable obstacles in the development of an appropriate strategic response. Unfortunately, the decision-making process for the Japanese is slow, which is quite a handicap when you find yourself in a volatile public-relations climate. And so our difficulties multiplied. By the time the Japanese responded to some new piece of misinformation, that misinformation was already accepted as gospel truth by the American public.

That's how things went on the PR side; then the politicians got involved. US Representatives Duncan Hunter of California and Helen Bentley of Maryland asked, without any evidence or justification, that the Justice Department look into the possibility that Japanese organized crime, the *yakuza*, was involved in the Pebble Beach purchase. Similar accusations were made by NBC. Meanwhile, the California Coastal Commission claimed that preferential tee times violated the public's right to coastal access. They declared that if the Japanese went ahead and sold memberships, it would constitute a "change in use" of the property. As such, Cosmo World's plan would require approval from the Coastal Commission, which the famously hands-on agency was not inclined to provide. Isutani's plan began to disintegrate before our eyes.

Most efforts by communities and citizens to rein in a highly capitalized investor don't get past the bumper-sticker stage. A majority of citizens—and even a few sincere public officials—will want to "stop the tunnel" or "save the bay," only to find themselves outspent and outmaneuvered. But Cosmo World's initiative to partly privatize Pebble Beach Golf Links was not your typical case. The resistance came together as if a brilliant war council had planned it long in advance. The media, local and national, pounded on the story like a birthday piñata and didn't stop until all the candy and treats had fallen to the floor. While all this was going on, Isutani retreated to Japan— only to be more vigorously pursued.

NBC tracked Isutani to Tokyo for a 1991 news program, *Expose*, hosted by Tom Brokaw, and a camera crew parked outside his home. They then followed his limousine to work. As he exited his vehicle to go into his office building, they shouted questions in English such as, "Are you part of the Japanese yakuza?" Isutani finally agreed to appear on camera and made the mistake of speaking candidly. The interviewer tried to build the case that he was part of the yakuza by first asking whether he had ever had dealings with them. Isutani replied, "Yes, every businessman in Japan, especially those who develop golf courses, must deal with the yakuza at some point. In our situation, the yakuza sometimes helps in securing the permits to build golf courses."

The NBC correspondent then said, "So, you admit that you work with the yakuza?" Isutani replied, "No more than any businessman in the US works with the Mafia." This caught the interviewer by surprise. He seemed to think he had unearthed another scintillating story angle because he next demanded: "Are you saying that all US businessmen are in league with the Mafia?"

Isutani replied, "It is a fact that the Teamsters and the Mafia have business relations [involving union pension funds]. Most every business sends its product by truck, so you could say the same about them that you do about me.

I have no choice in my business, which is how this business is done in Japan."

By the time NBC finished the story, there was no doubt in anyone's mind that Isutani was indeed part of the yakuza. Isutani should have never spoken with them. I received a dose of this same medicine myself, and I speak English better than Isutani. I was playing in the 1991 AT&T Pebble Beach Pro-Am. My professional golf partner was Kenny Perry, and we had played well enough to give ourselves a chance at making the cut. We were just coming off the 18th hole at Spyglass Hill (where part of the AT&T tournament is played) when a news crew approached our group. I assumed they wanted to talk with Kenny, since he finished second in the previous year's event. Instead, a microphone with the NBC peacock logo appeared in front of my face, and someone said, "Are you David Hueber, president of Ben Hogan Properties, which owns Pebble Beach?"

I said, "Yes, I am. Can I help you?" Out of the corner of my eye, I saw Perry looking at me with a wry smile. When our eyes met, he gave me a wink and a nod, as he escaped the media that now had me cornered. I swung into my PR posture and presented the talking points on what our company was doing to improve Pebble Beach and how much money we had donated to worthy charities out of tournament revenues.

The reporter paused while my statements went in one of his ears and out the other. He said he had a couple of questions to ask. The first was, "Mr. Hueber, how familiar are you with Mr. Isutani? How long have you known him?"

I said, "I have known Mr. Isutani for several years. I have been to his home in Japan. He is a very successful businessman and is making a big investment in Pebble Beach for the local community, for this tournament, and for the upcoming U.S. Open in 1992." And, if public relations were an infallible science, he then would have asked me how many greens and bunkers we expected to rebuild.

Instead, the next question was, "Are you aware or do you have any knowledge of the yakuza—that is, Japanese organized crime—being involved in funding the purchase of Pebble Beach?"

By now, I knew that Kenny Perry was long gone. I could picture him sitting in the scorer's tent, rechecking our scorecard. If it weren't for this unpleasant reporter, I would have been sitting alongside him, reveling in the day's fine shots and mourning the unlucky breaks that kept us from posting an even better score. The spell of a wondrous golf day was certainly broken. In a flat voice I said: "I take it that this is not NBC Sports asking these questions, so let me say only this. It is a matter of public record that MTBC and its affiliate companies provided the loan for the purchase of Pebble Beach." I continued, "And I don't believe that you would want to go on record saying the same bank that financed the purchase of the building that houses NBC headquarters, Rockefeller Center, is involved with organized crime, do you?"

The interviewer kept his bearings, then asked, "Well then, as far as you know, Mr. Isutani has no ties to the yakuza, and organized crime had nothing to do with the financing of the acquisition?"

"That is correct," I responded.

He continued. "Then, as far as you know, Mr. Isutani is not part of the Japanese Mafia?"

By this time, I was desperate to get away from this slimeball, so I just said, "That is correct. And beyond that I really don't have anything more to say." I walked away, feeling a chill run down my back. Answering questions about your employer's connections to mobsters on national TV will do that to you.

I took a long, hot shower, got dressed and walked over to Honda's hotel room. Vinny Giles, the sports agent for many of the players on the Hogan Company professional tour staff, was just leaving. He had stopped by to give his buddy, Honda, an expensive silk tie and a smart-looking cashmere sweater vest, which was hardly out of the ordinary. Giles knew that giving gifts was a Japanese custom, and he knew how much Honda loved to receive them.

I sat down in an armchair and told Honda what had happened to me out at Spyglass—how aggressive the reporter had been in trying to link Cosmo World with Japanese organized crime. I then confronted him in the same way the reporter had confronted me: "Ted, is there any truth to these rumors? Is Mr. Isutani involved with the yakuza?"

He replied, "No, Mr. Isutani is not involved with the yakuza. . . . But I am. My family is involved. I grew up with it. My family owns some sports arenas in Tokyo. Mr. Isutani only deals with them when he has to, like any business-man in Japan. Sometimes I help."

This admission by Honda scared the hell out of me.

***

A memorable duty fell to me—coordinating some of the preparations for Pebble's hosting of the 1992 U.S. Open. Much of what we had to do concerned the golf course itself, and for help with that, we enlisted the services of Jack Nicklaus. We went over to the Monterey County airport for his scheduled arrival. He and his son, Steve, had just finished a hunting trip in the mountains somewhere. Steve decided to stay on their private Gulfstream IV jet and take a nap while we took Nicklaus over to Pebble Beach for the golf course tour.

When we arrived at the first tee at Pebble Beach, Nicklaus's chief designer was there with a notebook in hand. Paul Spengler, the Pebble Beach director of golf, had some old course blueprints, but they would not be needed because Nicklaus was noted for his memory, according to everyone in his entourage. As we stood on the first tee, Nicklaus noted there used to be two trees on the left side of the fairway.

Spengler said, "Do you want us to put them back?"

Nicklaus said, "No, I just remember them being there."

When we got to the first green, he then gave us a detailed description of the changing shape of the green and greenside bunkers over the years. He explained how golfers hitting shots out of the bunker raised the height of the berm between the bunker and green and how mowing patterns changed the shape and size of the green. This primer was repeated, again and again, hole after hole, with references to tournaments and events which added color and credibility to his comments and recommendations.

Spengler then asked, "How do you remember all of this?"

Nicklaus responded, "I don't know. I just do. I can remember every important shot in every important tournament that I have ever played."

By this time, we were at the tee of the sixth hole, an uphill par 5 with a fairway bunker on the left side where a tee shot might land, and a forest of trees along the right with a cliff that towered over the ocean below.

Nicklaus then declared, "Back at the PGA in 1977, that bunker on the left was closer to the fairway. Evidently, you've allowed the fairway and rough to encroach into the bunker."

Spengler wrote down what he had just said and asked him, "Should we expand the bunker, or just cut the fairway and contour-mow it more along the left side?"

Nicklaus replied, "You probably should enlarge the bunker and keep the fairway in the same place. Over time, the fairway and rough area just enlarged and encroached into the bunker area. Also, I noticed that the trees on the right-hand side are much taller."

At this point, I was becoming increasingly uncomfortable with what seemed like our obsequious patronizing of Nicklaus's every utterance and the attendance to his pontification on every detail. I said under my breath, "Do you want us to cut the tops of the trees down as well?" I did not mean for him to hear me, but the guy has supersonic hearing.

However, he did not take offense at my snide remark and actually said, "No-o-o, that won't be necessary," and he went on to say with aplomb, "You need to understand that golf courses are dynamic organisms—they are always changing. Sometimes you let change take its course, and sometimes you scale it back."

Nicklaus knocked me right off of my self-righteous pedestal. Either he ignored my sarcasm and chose to answer the question as he did the others, or he did grasp my sarcasm and was classy enough to ignore it and answer the question. My suspicion is that my comment was not any more stupid than the others he had been fielding, so he just let it ride. Regardless, I felt like a jerk, because I was. We were paying him $100,000 plus jet fuel for this exercise in futility. The least I could do was listen and not let my ego get in the way, which is exactly what had happened.

***

One day in the springtime of 1991, I received an invitation that I took as a positive sign. Isutani summoned all his senior executives to Japan and even invited them to bring along their wives. I saw this as a vital opportunity to pick up some unequivocal direction from Isutani himself; unfortunately, it was not to be. The trip turned out to be little more than a boondoggle. I was at least able to avoid additional discomfort because I decided to travel solo. I had been to Japan many times by then, and I knew better than to bring my wife on this trip. Not only would she hate it, but Isutani really didn't *want* the wives there.

He told me one evening when he and I were sitting at a hostess bar (all of the wives were seated at a separate table with their spouses) that I was smart not to bring my wife.

"I see that you do not bring your wife to business meetings," I told him, "so I figured I should not bring mine." Isutani smiled and nodded. In his Japanese way, he had wanted the pleasure of extending the invitations, and he had likewise wanted them to be politely declined.

The Japanese are able to function in their organizations with no clear lines of authority, and they assume we Americans can do so as well. In the greater organization known as Cosmo World, Isutani was the ultimate authority and beyond that, the ebb and flow of authority was unknown and unknowable. On paper, I was head of the parent company that owned Pebble Beach, yet I took my direction from Honda because he was Isutani's chief adviser in the States. Regrettably, Honda was not the swiftest pony in the race and was surprisingly cavalier in his decision making, especially for a Japanese national.

My gut had told me that everything was on the up-and-up as far as Isutani was concerned, but I had never really trusted Honda. Whatever allure this Pebble Beach assignment had held for me was fading fast, and I began to long for the full-time normalcy of Fort Worth, Texas. Over the next few months, it became clear Honda and Oliver were vying for control of the Pebble Beach Company. Cosmo World CFO Harry White called me one afternoon when I was back in my office at the Hogan Company to tell me Honda and Oliver were in Japan meeting with Isutani. He thought I should be concerned, but I was past caring. I had never asked for the Pebble Beach assignment, nor was I ever formally given it. I wanted to run the Ben Hogan Company, and as it happened, things were beginning to go quite well with that business.

For any American raised on golf, Pebble Beach exerts a magnetic attraction. To have even a close brush with the top management position there should have thrilled me, and in many ways it did. But I could never be comfortable trying to exert authority there, for obvious reasons. Perhaps I should have done as Honda and Oliver did and tried to engineer a power play, but the situation and managerial circumstances were too foggy to even consider it. By this time, Honda was a total disaster. There was not a small-size cashmere sweater or expensive golf shirt in the Pebble Beach golf shop that Honda had not purloined. The pro shop employees joked openly about it, and White sent me a memo one day saying Honda had run up personal charges in excess of $100,000.

Between what I knew about Honda and what I suspected about Pebble Beach president Oliver, I was in a moral and managerial quandary. Each had cobbled together his own plan to secure the permit we needed from the Coastal Commission, and they were off on their separate goose chases trying to make it happen. I was becoming increasingly concerned about my personal legal liability. In theory, I was protected by the corporate structure, but the situation was dicey, and I could picture myself enmeshed in litigation that might crush me financially. At one point I checked into getting some directors-and-officers coverage and was quoted a $40,000 annual premium. Evidently, the insurers saw some of the same risk I had detected on my own. Isutani said that, in the event of a lawsuit, he would cover my costs, but that came as faint reassurance. Too much was happening that was beyond my influence or control.

Honda and Oliver came back from Japan with each thinking Isutani had put him in charge. During one of our meetings with the attorneys and consultants at the Inn at Spanish Bay, the two of them got into a shouting match on the patio right outside the meeting room. I was inside, leading a discussion on how we might turn things around with the Coastal Commission, and these two clowns were out there stomping their feet and saying, quite audibly, "Mr. Isutani put *me* in charge!" "No he didn't, he put *me* in charge." It was humiliating for all concerned. It was also the moment when I knew that I would have to resign my titular post. When I eventually submited my resignation of the Pebble Beach title to Isutani, he told me he understood, but I do not think he really did. I was not Japanese. I was not willing to fall on my sword for this job.

Eventually, the vote of the Coastal Commission went against Cosmo World. Isutani was denied the right to sell memberships on the Japanese exchange because it was determined to be a change in use and required a permit by the commission. Obviously, none would be forthcoming. Honda suggested we file suit against the commission, which despite the source was not a bad idea; what we had proposed was not truly a change in use. Right or wrong on that point, we would have lost based upon the strength of the anti-Japanese sentiment at the time. The party we really should have sued was Baker & McKenzie, whose shoddy legal advice had fouled things up from the start. Interestingly, a couple of attorneys from that firm actually suggested we bring action.

The final blow was the sudden evaporation of any market in Japan for Pebble Beach golf memberships. Japan's economy had slid to the point where the golf membership exchange had been forced to shut down, which meant that even if we somehow attained that elusive permit, it would have been worthless. The game plan failed before we could run the first play from scrimmage;

nor was it in the Japanese playbook to plot a quick Plan B to handle the new circumstances. An alternative course of action should have been in place from the beginning. And, even though contingency plans have always been a specialty of mine, it had not occurred to me to formulate one because I was never aware of the original plan until told about it by reporters. Now the whole affair had gone awry. The Japanese were in spin mode and weren't very good at it. They had no idea what to do next.

***

Officially relinquishing my Pebble Beach title had the effect of clearing my thoughts. Before long, an alternative course of action on Pebble Beach occurred to me. It was a simple plan, but it seemed to cover the essentials. The gist of it, as I explained in a letter and proposal to Isutani, was to sell off all the assets except the Pebble Beach golf course and the Lodge at Pebble Beach, which could generate $350 million in revenue. Then, having set up the course and the Lodge as a separate entity, we would sell 49 percent of it. This could be in the form of shares or it could be a limited partnership. I felt pretty confident there were 2,000 investors out there who would be willing to pay $250,000 for part ownership of Pebble Beach. Some of them might even do so out of a patriotic desire to return this famous site to American ownership.

From the perspective of the potential investor, it would be a lot cooler to be an owner than a member, since an owner would pay no club dues and could expect to receive a return on his investment. The owners, under my plan, would also enjoy privileged access to the Pebble Beach Golf Links and the Lodge. Pebble Beach would continue to be open to the public. There would be no change of use. It would simply have 2,001 owners rather than just one Japanese guy. If all this could be put in motion reasonably soon, the debt to the banks would be paid off, and Isutani would still control the Pebble Beach Company.

It seemed like a very do-able deal to me. I presented it all in a detailed plan, bound in book form with a translation into Japanese. Months passed, however, and I heard nothing from Japan. In the late summer of 1991, I met with Isutani in Tokyo regarding the new $3 million loan Cosmo World had exacted from the Ben Hogan Company. I brought up my Pebble Beach recapitalization idea, but he showed no interest in discussing it.

Just before Christmas that year I was over in Japan again to discuss Ben Hogan Company business. After we had gone through our agenda of Hogan Company issues, Isutani pulled me aside and walked me back to his office with a translator. "Hueber-san," he said, "I have decided to implement your plan."

"That's great," I said, "But isn't it too late? It is my understanding that the transfer of ownership is already underway to someone else within the *keiretsu* [a group of like Japanese businesses using the same financial institutions]."

Isutani replied, "It isn't too late, and I want you to implement the plan."

I expressed a desire to go forward, but in the same breath told him, "Mr. Isutani, one of the reasons that I resigned was that I was concerned about my personal liability in being associated with Mr. Honda and Mr. Oliver. I do not want to work with them."

Isutani then said, "You will be in charge and can do what you need to do. After the holidays, I will send you a letter with instructions and the formal authorization."

I was ecstatic. After all that had transpired—the ordeal and chaos—I was going to be put in charge of Pebble Beach with full authority to do what needed to be done.

The first part of the year for Japanese businessmen is a time for unofficial vacations. The Japanese always claim to never take holidays, but they never work during this time of the year. This is why it made sense for Isutani to tell me to wait for further instructions until after the fifteenth of January. When that date arrived, I received the promised letter from Isutani, but its contents were anything but what I expected. He wrote to send his regrets that he could not proceed with the plans as we discussed regarding Pebble Beach; he then instructed me to contact Mr. Takahiko Suzuki, general manager, and Mr. Atsuo Igarashi, senior vice president at MTBC's New York Branch, regarding the disposition of the Ben Hogan Company. Time had indeed run out, and the mega-million loss on the sale of Pebble Beach had to be paid from the sales of a number of assets, one of them being, of course, the Ben Hogan Company.

Every business career has its ups and downs, but that letter took me from the penthouse straight down an elevator shaft into some dark corner of the subbasement. I was devastated. I spent a whole day in stunned disarray, not able to focus on my job. By the close of the afternoon, I headed over to Shady Oaks to have a drink in solitude at the men's grill—something I never did. I was by myself, like I was not so long ago at the 19th hole at Pebble Beach, celebrating my solo eagle on the eighth hole. I ordered another Chivas on the rocks with a splash of water. This time I needed the splash for a refreshed outlook. I regrouped and came up with my own contingency plan: I would put together an investor group and become a major shareholder in—and continue as president of—the Ben Hogan Company.

KNOWING WHEN TO HOLD 'EM AND WHEN TO FOLD 'EM

T he demise of the Ben Hogan Company was becoming a certainty in late 1991 with the looming sale of Pebble Beach. The relatively modest amount of money allocated to Ben Hogan Company advertising was reduced further. We began to lose ground to Ping and Tommy Armour, and we were still paying the big bucks for the Hogan Company tour staff professionals, as well as funding the Ben Hogan Tour. Something had to give.

We had started to build a club inventory in anticipation of upcoming labor negotiations, thinking we could better stem the tide of a prolonged strike if we had something to ship. But inventory at this time was an expensive luxury, especially when our parent company (Cosmo World) required another $3 million from our credit line. With the loss of that $3 million, the Hogan Company did not have the ability to issue Letters of Credit (LOCs) to purchase product overseas, so we were confronted with the possibility of shutting down our apparel business or licensing that business to a third party.

Looking back on everything that transpired, my biggest mistake was giving up that last $3 million to Cosmo World. At that point, the Ben Hogan Company was paying interest on $6 million in borrowings that were not related to our business. More importantly, those funds were not available for the needs of the Hogan Company. The decision to lend the last $3 million to Cosmo World (for a total of $9 million in loans) started the fall of the financial dominos. It eventually stymied the funding of Ben Hogan Company operations. I did not feel I had any choice at the time, but one always has choices. I made what I thought was the right decision because I believed the parent company when they said they only needed the money for a month or two. One of my most trusted Japanese advisers, Mr. Nakahara, told me I would never see that money again, and he advised me to refuse to lend them the money. He was right, and I was naïve to trust them. I unwittingly put the financial health of the company at risk with that last financial accommodation to the parent company.

The last two years of my presidency at the Hogan Company were probably my best work as a CEO. Almost any competent manager can manage a business with the required financial resources at his disposal. It is a more difficult matter to do so without those resources. The company mind-set had gone from building momentum and ascending to the next level among the leading golf companies in the industry to figuring out how we were going to survive. It was a rude awakening.

Fortunately, we not only managed to survive, but also remarketed the Hogan Edge and recaptured our market share. And most of this was done with mirrors and sleight of hand, because we certainly did not have the financial resources. It was necessary to cut expenses drastically to run the new Hogan television and print campaign to spur sales. I advised our tour players we could not renew all of our endorsement contracts for the following year, and it would be in our mutual best interests if they could find another golf company affiliation. If they had a multi-year agreement, we provided a release from their contracts.

Davis Love was the first to go. He went to Tommy Armour. Most of them, except for Tom Kite, who had a long-term contract, left of their own accord. Vinny Giles was the agent for many of the Hogan Company tour players, and I suspect this was the beginning of the philosophical discord between Vinny and me. My decision created a lot of work for him as he tried to find new deals for his clients. We went from having one of the larger tour staffs to a much smaller cadre of golf pros representing the Hogan Company on the PGA Tour.

Other facets of the business were also affected. Since we could no longer issue LOCs, we were out of the apparel business unless we could find a licensee. While apparel was never a very profitable business for the Hogan Company, we were doing about $20 million in sales, and our sales force relied upon those commissions to maintain their incomes. The Ben Hogan Company had one of the best sales forces in the industry, and our competition would cherry-pick them if their incomes were reduced; I had to do whatever I could to stay in the apparel business. Alan Owens, director of Hogan Apparel, eventually found a licensee for us. As part of the deal, we had to sell our inventory at cost to the new licensee. This really hurt our bottom line, but it could not be helped. At this point, business decisions were driven by our cash position.

When I presented my business plan to the bank in late November of 1991, I was hoping to get some relief from the covenants so I could draw the remaining $5 million of our credit line. They liked our business plan, but said no to the release of any of the loan covenants. There was a credit crunch in the banking industry at the time, and they were trying to reduce their number of smaller customers. In fact, they demanded that Cosmo World return the $3 million they had taken from our line. At the time, Cosmo World had $9 million of the available $15 million borrowed by the Ben Hogan Company. We were heading into the winter, when golf equipment companies have little cash inflow. But that was not the worst part. The bank wanted us to take our borrowing down by $5 million, or they would call the loan.

Cosmo World eventually returned the $3 million to the Hogan Company before year end, but we had to return it shortly after the first of the year. We now had to secure new financing for Hogan Company business. These were desperate times calling for desperate measures, which explains why we took such draconian steps like cutting major promotional costs and licensing out the Hogan apparel business. In spite of this, the Ben Hogan Company managed to survive somewhat unscathed from a market-share and corporate-valuation standpoint. We went from making money and carrying a substantial promotional overhead to losing a modest amount of money without the burden of the promotional overhead. In total, these financial ramifications represented about a $10 million swing on sales that had dropped 15 percent; it was quite an achievement to continue operating with these complications. Unfortunately, it would look less brilliant to the future new owner.

Fortunately, from a company-reputation standpoint, no one in the media took great notice of the cutbacks. We still had our name on the Ben Hogan Tour, and Tom Kite would win the U.S. Open at Pebble Beach in June of 1992. We were lucky. The value of the company could have dropped substantially, but it did not, which is illustrated by the fact that the Ben Hogan Company was soon sold for the equivalent of about $20 million (adjusting for the assumption of debt) more than Isutani paid for it.

I had spent some time with MTBC in Japan regarding the financing of Pebble Beach. Its world headquarters building in Tokyo was some sixty stories or more and very impressive from the outside, but inside it was a different story. I was struck by how modest the interiors were as we were escorted to the executive-level conference rooms. Most banks impress you with their lobby, offices, and furnishings, but MTBC's Tokyo headquarters was unimpressive and sterile looking, except for the paintings on the walls. I suspect they were purchases from the Sotheby auctions in New York, where MTBC was known for making substantial investments in art. It was an interesting dichotomy to see multi-million dollar paintings on the walls and have such modest furnishings.

When Bob Drury, the Ben Hogan Company CFO, and I arrived at the MTBC branch office in New York in 1992, I expected to see the same spartan interiors I had seen in Tokyo, and I advised Drury of the same. But, as they say, "when in Rome...." The MTBC New York offices looked like any other bank office in the United States. Mr. Suzuki, the MTBC general manager, greeted us upon our arrival. He was very polite and exceedingly cordial, but his manner struck me as insincere and perfunctory. It caused me some concern. It almost seemed as if he didn't want to meet with us. He wanted us to feed him information in order to prepare the company for sale. I told him I already had received about forty inquiries from various qualified sources who were interested in acquiring the Ben Hogan Company. He said fine, but never asked me for a copy of the list.

Mr. Igarashi, the MTBC senior vice president, then asked that we prepare a prospectus they could use to sell the company. Bob and I already had one prepared, but we wanted to wait a couple of weeks in order to get a better sense of the process and an expected timeline for the sale. We were uncertain what they wanted, and we wanted to play some role in the disposition of the company. Furthermore, it was my experience with the Japanese that the decision-making process would take some time; there was no rush to accelerate the process. Then, Suzuki said that I should not speak with Isutani, which seemed very odd to me. I still worked for Isutani, and my employment contract with the Ben Hogan Company was signed by him. However, it was now clear the bank was in control of the situation.

About two weeks later, I submitted the first draft of the Ben Hogan Company prospectus, along with a list of about forty companies and individuals who had expressed an interest in acquiring the Hogan Company. My name was on that list, and I had some financial backers who had already agreed to bid as high as $45 million for the company, which I believed was a generous and fair offer, given the current circumstances. We express-mailed the report on Thursday, and on Friday evening around 10:00 p.m. I received a phone call from Suzuki.

By this time, I was well accustomed to receiving late evening calls from Japan, or in this case, from New York and Igarashi. I did not think much of it, so after exchanging greetings, I asked Igarashi how he liked the report and if he had any comments or questions.

Igarashi then replied, "Thank you for the list and the report. The report was excellent—very good work, but it is not necessary."

I replied, "What do you mean that it is not necessary?"

"It is not necessary, because we have received a preemptive offer for the Ben Hogan Company that we have agreed to accept," he said.

I was stunned and didn't know what to say.

Igarashi continued, "We will execute a sales agreement in March. There will be a due-diligence period, with the deal closing to be in late May or early June."

By then, I had gathered myself enough to ask who was buying the company, to which he replied, "Mr. Bill Goodwin is buying the company. He is a qualified purchaser and owns the AMF Bowling concern. However, you are not to communicate with him. Any direct discussions between yourself and Mr. Goodwin or any of his representatives is forbidden. Any information requests must be coordinated through our offices. Do you understand?"

I replied, "*Hai* [yes], Igarashi-san. Let's discuss this some more on Monday." I needed a couple of days to sort this out.

The next few months were filled with anxiety and apprehension, mostly because I was forbidden to speak with Isutani and the prospective new owner, Goodwin. I soon learned that Vinny Giles was a close associate of Goodwin. Both lived in Richmond, Virginia. I suspected that Giles didn't much care for me, since I had released some of his players and created a lot of work for Pros Incorporated, his sports agency. Goodwin successfully leap-frogged the entire bidding process with the preemptive bid, and I hoped if the sale closed, they would understand what I did, and why I did it.

Eventually, the sale did close. It was difficult to find out much about Goodwin. There was not any way to Google in those days. I only knew he had made a lot of money in the computer leasing business and then purchased AMF Bowling and a couple of smaller AMF companies a few years earlier from Irwin Jacobs. I prepared a briefing book for Goodwin that provided some history and a comprehensive analysis of the Hogan Company situation. Our first meeting was outside Ben Hogan Company headquarters in Fort Worth in June of 1992. We were going to have breakfast at his hotel, the Marriott Courtyard, situated across the Trinity River from Colonial Country Club.

His greeting to me was cordial, but terse: "Hello, David. Good to meet you."

So far so good, I thought, and then said, "Mr. Goodwin . . ."

"Call me Bill."

"Bill, I have prepared a comprehensive analysis of the Ben Hogan Company for your review, which should be helpful during this initial period of your ownership."

Then, Goodwin looked at me almost with contempt and said, "David, I've seen your books and already know more about this company than you do. I understand better than you what the AMF culture is and what needs to be done to fix it." He then sat back in his chair and said out loud to himself and I guess to me, "I swore that I would never do this again; I wish that I hadn't bought this company." Then, he turned and looked at me with a sigh and said, "David, I don't know if you are willing or are able to do what you will have to do if you think that you are going to survive as the company's president."

That statement was chilling on this hot and humid June morning in Fort Worth. I found myself at a loss for words once again and then finally said, "I would certainly like to give it a shot, but I need to have some notion of what you are talking about."

"Fair enough." He then proceeded with a speculative litany of the numerous shortcomings of the Ben Hogan Company, such as spending too much time and money on R&D. He said the sales force was lazy and needed to be cut in half (and have their pay reduced, so they would have to work harder for the same amount of money); we didn't know how to market our products;

we didn't know how to manufacture golf clubs and fill orders; we needed to get rid of the Ben Hogan Tour obligation; and, generally speaking, we didn't do anything right.

After that diatribe, I wondered why he bought the company. He paid the equivalent of $18 to $20 million more for the Ben Hogan Company than Isutani had paid a few years earlier. Certainly, he must have seen some value in it. Obviously, he felt that he could fix the problems as he saw them, but I was beginning to wonder if he really understood what he was talking about. He seemed to assume we still had the AMF culture, even though it was almost ten years since AMF had owned the company. That was troubling because he seemed very fixed in this opinion.

We then went over to the factory, and I took him on a tour of the company and introduced him to the key management. He seemed impressed with the manufacturing operations. All of the factory employees had new Hogan base-ball-style hats with an American flag on them, signifying the change from the Japanese ownership. Everyone was excited and had smiles on their faces for the new American owner. I was proud to tell him we had recently converted to "quality circles" and productivity had increased almost 80 percent, and our scrap rate had been reduced by 50 percent.

When the tour was finished, Goodwin asked me if I was an engineer and seemed quite disappointed to learn that I was not and that I only had an MBA. Later, when we were meeting in the conference room, he told me he wanted the Ben Hogan Company to become a "world-class manufacturer" with a 95 percent or better fill rate on all orders. We then talked about marketing and new-product planning. He told me the Hogan Company did not know how to market products. He described a very successful marketing campaign AMF Bowling had done with their new Sumo bowling ball. The campaign featured a Sumo wrestler. In the television ad, his hand got stuck in the bowling ball as he slung it. The Sumo wrestler, along with the bowling ball, slid down the al-ley and knocked down all of the pins. Frankly, I had never heard of the Sumo bowling ball or seen the ad.

The next story he told me was to illustrate that the Hogan Company need-ed to quit inventing things and spending so much on R&D. This was the "gaff hook" fishing company story about how one of his businesses had spent over $100,000 trying to design a new gaff hook. He said he was so fed up with them he finally said, "Just copy the best one out there," which they did. Evidently, it was a big seller. His point was that the Hogan Company was always making new gaff hooks and ought to just copy or make their version of the top-selling iron, which in this case was the Ping Eye model (enjoying a surge in sales related to the grooves controversy and litigation with the USGA and PGA Tour).

Our chief competition in the iron set category included a company that had done just that: Tommy Armour. We were competing effectively in that category because we had remarketed forged golf clubs in the game-improvement category. We were the number one forged clubmaker in the world, a distinctive niche that any golf company would like to have. My presumption was this niche was one of the reasons Goodwin had paid a premium price for the company. I was wrong.

Goodwin definitely had insight as to some of our shortcomings, but he didn't seem to recognize the changing business environment of the golf equipment segment of the golf industry. There were only a few golf equipment manufacturers at this point. The manufacture of clubheads was largely done in the Far East, and the trend was for that to continue. Eventually, golf club assembly would also move across the Pacific simply because the cost was so much less, and the quality was still very good. For example, the cost to assemble a driver might be four dollars in Carlsbad while it could be seventy cents in mainland China.

This was the beginning of the shift in golf equipment companies moving away from manufacturing their products and toward becoming product development and marketing companies. The golf industry was always a business that relied upon innovation, or at least the perception of it, to stimulate sales. This change to outsourcing product lines would not alter that reality. Golf equipment companies would spend less on making their products (through surrogate companies in the Far East) and more on the R&D and marketing of their products.

The Hogan Company was one of the last true manufacturers of golf clubs (as was Ping) and we were also transitioning to become more of an R&D and marketing company. While we were a maker of forged clubheads, we outsourced many of our other products such as golf bags, golf gloves, apparel, and other soft goods through licensees. It would not be too long before we would need to outsource the manufacture of golf clubheads as well. We already outsourced putters, metal woods, investment-cast irons, and some wedge-iron heads.

Goodwin's declaration that we would become a world-class manufacturer of golf equipment ignored the reality of what we needed to be in order to compete in the marketplace. He was obviously a very bright, capable, and successful businessman. He now owned the Hogan Company and could run it any way he wanted. Unfortunately, there seemed to be a lot of ego and not enough open-mindedness in his plans for the direction of the company.

He was right earlier that morning when he said that I might not be willing to do what I would have to do if I was going to continue as the Hogan CEO. At this point, I still wanted to comply with his wishes and told him, "We could have a cast club like the Ping or Tommy Armour in a very short time. That is not the problem. We have had cast iron sets in the past and have sold them successfully."

Then I added that while we certainly could introduce a major new cast iron line, we had already made a significant investment in marketing and promoting the new forged club technology. It was working. It was our market niche. The Hogan Edge iron was the most successful product in the company's history. Furthermore, we did not have the financial resources to effectively advertise both forged and cast clubs—to tell both stories. That was a strategic marketing decision that had to be made, given the existing financial parameters.

"If the financial situation and circumstances are now different," I continued, "and there are sources for more advertising dollars, then we can consider it. But I would not recommend walking away from the forged club franchise."

Goodwin looked at me with some disdain and then rebuked me with the Nike slogan: "Then just do it! I don't know what your problem is." He then proceeded to outline a game plan to downsize the Hogan company. He used AMF Bowling as an example once again to illustrate how they took that sales force down from fifty-plus salesmen to twenty-two, reiterating that all salesmen were lazy. He said we needed to cut the number of Hogan salesmen by half, cut their commissions, and increase the size of their territories. He then said we should take the factory workforce and management down by two-thirds and told me to put a plan together showing him how I would orchestrate it.

Goodwin then changed the subject to say, "Next week or the following week, let's go see the PGA Tour about the Ben Hogan Tour commitment."

At this point, I felt like one of the pins in the AMF Bowling television commercial. I had just been knocked over by a sixteen-pound bowling ball with a Sumo wrestler trailing behind. Never one to know when to shut up, I then asked Goodwin if he would like our sales force to sell Bag Boy (pull) golf carts, a small golf company he had recently acquired. Bag Boy Company did not have a sales force, and even with a reduced Hogan sales force, it would represent better distribution than he already had.

Goodwin's response reflected his low regard for me and the Hogan Company's sales force when he said, "No, I don't want you to fuck that up too."

It was the end of a perfect day.

***

Over the next few weeks, I did just what he asked. I put together a reorganization plan, and we visited PGA Tour headquarters. We met with Commissioner Beman and then deputy commissioner Finchem, a fellow University of Virginia graduate with Goodwin. I prevailed upon my longtime relationship with Beman to obtain a release and settlement from the Ben Hogan Tour contractual commitment. Some back payments would be made, and Goodwin could extricate himself from the deal.

My guess is the PGA Tour made a calculated business decision, knowing that pursuing damages from a company having financial difficulties wouldn't look good. Even if the tour prevailed in any litigation, they would probably not get anything more than liquidated damages. In this case, I suspect they had Nike in the wings ready to take our place, so it wouldn't be worth the cost. Later, Beman told me the only reason he did it was for me, and if he had known what Goodwin would do later, he would have never done it. That was probably a factor as well, but I knew Beman always made pragmatic business decisions. He probably did not want to get into any more lawsuits while the Ping litigation regarding the grooves controversy was still contested.

Goodwin used me to resolve the business issues as he saw them. We quickly moved forward on the development of the new cast irons. He then started sending his bowling marketing people to the Hogan Company to show us how we should market golf clubs. One of my first visitors was an AMF Bowling marketing director who came into my office unannounced and started to explain how we could improve our marketing.

His first declaration was: "We are going to take the 'Ben' out of Ben Hogan." He then said, "Bill [Goodwin] doesn't like your new handles."

I looked at him, somewhat bemused and said, "You don't play golf do you?"

He replied, "No, I don't golf [by the way, I wanted to tell him, golf is a noun, not a verb], but what has that got to do with the handles?"

I then explained that the handles on the golf clubs are called grips and asked him, "What is it that he doesn't like about the new grip design?" He said he didn't know, but promised to check with Bill or Vinny.

Vinny Giles, I thought. I wondered if he was behind some of these initiatives.

I understood what the AMF marketing executive meant when he said, "We are going to take the 'Ben' out of Ben Hogan." He meant we should deemphasize Ben Hogan, the man, and do more Hogan-brand advertising and promotion. But after working so hard to get Hogan back into the company, it seemed stupid to walk away from such a unique promotional and advertising asset. Golf equipment companies invest millions into building a brand without any guarantee they will ever attain what the Hogan Company already had.

Clearly, the new ownership did not have a clue as to the innate value of the Ben Hogan Company brand or how to leverage it. It was a unique brand with a loyal following; it epitomized the life, character, and mystique of Ben Hogan. Over the course of thirty years, Hogan golf equipment was synonymous with an unrelenting pursuit of excellence in the making of the highest-quality golf equipment.

At the time, I figured they must have a game plan. Eventually, I would learn they did not. Goodwin and his acolytes were confident that what they knew about business in general, and what they knew about the sporting goods business specifically, were directly applicable to the golf equipment business. It would turn out their arrogance would be very costly as they wantonly walked away from the Hogan forged clubmaking franchise without any notion of what they would do instead.

Next, the marketing wonder from AMF Bowling said their advertising agency had a great idea for what we should name the new line of cast irons and how we should market them. I answered that we had not told our ad agency about the new product, but it was probably time to involve them. The ad agency had been doing a great job, and the Mr. Hogan television and print ads had been quite successful. The Hogan Edge irons had just passed Tommy Armour for the number two spot, just behind Ping. The advertising campaign, "No one makes clubs like we do," was working very well.

Then I was told we would have an advertising agency review. I was to have various agencies bid on our work, including AMF's agency, QL4. We were to have each prospective agency prepare an advertising campaign for the new cast-model irons. Eventually, four advertising agencies made presentations. I can only remember a couple of them. The first, TracyLocke, our agency, was clearly the best. Their campaign described the birth of a new kind of cast club, Genesis.

Next, QL4 made their presentation. They wanted to call the new iron the Panzer after the WWII German tank. On the back of the iron clubhead, they had a Panzer tank stamped into the cavity. Their television ad storyboard had a tank appearing on the television screen, with the gun turret turning toward the golf green and blowing up the green. The person making the presentation for QL4 then said triumphantly, "What we are trying to do is bring the tank commander out of every golfer." My guess was this was the same guy who did the Sumo ad for the AMF bowling ball—same template, different application: bad ad.

After the agencies departed, we had a discussion with the Hogan and AMF marketing people. I was surprised I had to explain how bad the Panzer ad idea really was. They thought it was a great idea, and I quote, it was a "powerful and memorable" ad. At first, I tried to explain that tanks were slow-moving, low-tech vehicles as compared to an F-16 fighter, and it did not convey the right image for a golf club. But they didn't get it.

Next, I tried to explain the more obvious notion that there were a lot of people who had fought and suffered greatly during WWII. Those golfers probably wouldn't appreciate the reference to a German Panzer tank. They still didn't get it, so I said, "The QL4 presentation was the worst of the four that we saw. We are going to stay with TracyLocke as our agency; they are clearly the best and made the best proposal." I was then told it was not decided yet, and they would have to confer with Richmond. Several weeks passed by, and nothing more was said.

Meanwhile, I moved forward on downsizing the company. It was the most difficult thing I have ever done. I tried to do it with compassion and with the best judgment I could exercise. A couple of confidants asked me how I could do this, and I said, "Would you rather I do it, or would you prefer that someone from Richmond come here and do it?" I personally met with all of the executive-level management employees who were being terminated. It was an excruciatingly painful personal experience for me but more so, of course, for them. Some reacted professionally, with class and dignity. Some surprised me with vitriolic, personal rebukes. I tried not to take it personally.

The sales force was reduced from forty-seven to thirty-two. Territories were enlarged and commission rates reduced. If they worked harder, they could make as much money as before. The question was whether or not we could keep those who remained. We had a good sales force, one of the best in the industry. This action did not make any sense to me, and I was beginning to doubt whether or not I could continue to orchestrate the dismemberment of the Ben Hogan Company.

By September of 1992, I was beginning to feel like a whore doing whatever I could to keep my job. Even though I still had four years left on my contract, I didn't feel secure in my position and generally did what Goodwin wanted. I knew my contract wasn't going to keep me from being fired because we had another Hogan employee who also had a contract. I remember what Goodwin said when he told me to let him go: "Just give him whatever he is entitled per company policies," he told me.

I said, "He could sue us, and he would win."

Goodwin replied, "His contract doesn't provide for liquidated damages. He has a duty to mitigate any damages and get a new job. It will take at least eighteen months before his case is heard, and by then the damages will be less. The damages are always less over time. Go fire him."

As I heard this, I knew it foreshadowed my own demise, but I must have been delusional at the time. I was a capable CEO and doing a very good job; sooner or later, I thought, Goodwin will recognize my capabilities and see the good job I am doing. I failed to see the obvious signs. During one visit to Richmond, I was even introduced to my replacement. I dismissed it because his only tie to the sporting goods business was that Goodwin had bought his bowling alley services business. Evidently, he had made a machine that smoothed and polished bowling lanes. I had a perverse thought that perhaps Goodwin might have a higher regard for my professional experience if he knew that as a teenager I once had worked setting pins in my grandfather's bowling alley.

Late one October morning, I was speaking with Goodwin on the phone, when he complimented me on the analysis and recommendation I had made relative to our golf ball business. He said, "David, that was a very good report; I am accepting your recommendations. You really ought to go back to school and get an MBA. The University of Virginia has the Darden business school, which is excellent."

I replied, "Bill, I already have one of those degrees, but not from Darden."

About a week or so later, on a Friday morning, I received another phone call from Goodwin. It started out very congenially, with Goodwin complimenting me on what a good job I had done in downsizing the company, and how good next year's product line looked. Then he said, "David, you will forget more than I will ever know about the golf business. I really appreciate the job that you have done under some very difficult circumstances." He paused, and I said nothing.

Next he said, "What I wanted to tell you is that we have decided to relocate the company to Richmond."

So I asked him, "Why do you want to do that?"

"I really don't want to discuss it with you."

"Why not? I am the president of the company."

"David, you have done a good job, and have taken a lot of heat and criticism in downsizing the company. I know that it was very hard for you, and I really do appreciate your effort in that regard. That is why I just don't think it would be fair for you now to take all of the heat for relocating the company to Richmond, and then not have a job when you got here."

Again, I was at a loss for words. I felt like I had just been punched in the gut and had the wind knocked out of me.

Finally, his words sank in. I responded with, "Well, Bill, I would have to agree with you that it wouldn't be fair for me to take the heat for relocating the company and then to lose my job. I have two questions for you. First, why didn't you wait until next Monday to discuss this in person when I will be in your Richmond office? And, second, you do realize that I have four years left on my employment contract?"

Goodwin replied, "David, I wanted to give you the weekend to think about it. Who knows, maybe you can talk me out of this decision. I don't know. Look, David, you need to understand something if you don't already. Do you really think that I bought this company because I wanted you to run it?"

I didn't respond. There was another pregnant pause.

"Regarding your contract, David, you have every right to sue me if you like, or we can work out a settlement. It is up to you."

For the ensuing months, I watched with great dismay the continued dismantling of the Ben Hogan Company. In spite of my failure to thwart Goodwin's misguided redirection of the company, I still wanted the company to prosper. I loved the Ben Hogan Company and everything it represented.

Unfortunately, about five hundred people lost their jobs for no reason other than the move from Fort Worth to Richmond. Presumably, they wanted to get rid of the steelworkers union and reduce manufacturing costs, but that economy was never realized. Their ill-conceived notion of becoming a world-class manufacturer also never materialized. When the Ben Hogan Company later turned to the Far East for their forgings, and the company only assembled golf clubs in Richmond, their component costs, reportedly, actually increased. They also had difficulty assembling the clubs with Richmond's new, smaller, and inexperienced workforce. They eventually had to outsource some of the golf club assembly.

The justifications for moving the company clearly were not valid and made no business sense. If the new owner had done his homework, he'd have realized that moving the assembly as well as the manufacture of golf clubs to the Far East was inevitable. Ironically, with the introduction of the new cast irons to supplant the Hogan Edge, the company was already headed in that direction. I viewed moving the company to Richmond as egotistical, costly, and nonsensical.

The costs were more than financial. People lost their livelihoods. They cut out the company's heart and soul. Ben Hogan was devastated. He was never the same after the move. I witnessed many factory workers stopping by Hogan's office just to say good-bye and to thank him. Some had worked for him since the beginning. Many had worked for him for twenty years or longer. There was no anger in their demeanor, only kindness and respect. The class and dignity of these people was amazing.

I had a conversation with one person waiting his turn to see Mr. Hogan. He said, "Look, this has been a great job. It paid the bills, and I raised a family. I was part of something special. I just wanted to stop by and thank Mr. Hogan. This job enabled me to buy a pecan farm, and I still have an income and can afford to retire early, but I wonder how the younger ones are going to manage. There aren't many good jobs like this around Fort Worth."

The Hogan Company was still a great brand with a stellar, but smaller, sales force. Hogan was the number one maker of forged golf clubs in the world. It was a mistake to abandon that market niche and focus instead on investment-cast clubs.

18

GOOD-BYE BEN HOGAN

t's July 29, 1997, and a solemn occasion. The last person I wanted to see when I entered the church vestibule (the gathering place for the pallbearers) was Bill Goodwin. We made eye contact, and he waved me over. I obliged and politely said, "Bill, I hope that you are well. It is a sad occasion that brings us together." Goodwin, the owner of the Ben Hogan Company, was a fellow pallbearer for Ben Hogan. I was accorded the honor to serve as a pallbearer (the only former Ben Hogan Company president), along with such luminaries as PGA CEO Jim Awtrey; PGA Tour Commissioner Tim Finchem; Tommy Bolt; Sam Snead; Ken Venturi; famous sports writers Dan Jenkins and Jim Murray; Mr. Hogan's personal club designer, Gene Sheeley; Mike Wright, the director of golf at Shady Oaks Country Club; and a number of personal friends.

Goodwin responded in a voice loud enough for everyone in the room to hear, "Yes, Mr. Hogan hasn't been well for some time now."

I nodded, and said in a hushed voice (hoping to not turn heads with our conversation), "Yes, I have kept up with things, mostly through Valerie."

Then Goodwin said in a quieter but still resounding voice, "David, I would like to ask your advice on something."

"Are you sure about that, Bill? Don't you remember that you fired me about five years ago?"

Somewhat oblivious to the setting and circumstances, he responded, "David, that wasn't anything personal." [It certainly was to me.] "You did your best to turn things around. We've tried to turn it around, and it just hasn't worked out. Take a guess how much money I have lost since I acquired the Hogan Company?"

His voice could still be overheard by everyone in the room, and at that point, a few of our fellow pallbearers turned in our direction, so I replied in what then felt like a whisper: "Bill, I would really rather not even make a guess."

"No, go ahead and guess."

I thought for a moment, and having some notion that the Hogan Company was bleeding pretty badly I estimated, probably about $10 million a year, which would be about $50 million over the past five years. So, I said, "Well, I hate to say this, but I would guess that you lost at least fifty million dollars so far."

"Nope, you are not even close. I have lost twice that amount, over one hundred million."

"Well it's a good thing that you sold AMF Bowling to Goldman Sachs." He sold AMF for $500-plus million and made a lot of money.

"No one can afford to lose that kind of money; it has to stop." He continued, "What I wanted to ask you, or get your advice on, is whether you think I should just license out the Hogan brand or if I should try to sell the company?"

The irony of this question was lost on him. Before me was the man who had single-handedly orchestrated the demise of the Ben Hogan Company and broke Hogan's heart, and now he was asking me, the person he fired, for advice—*at Mr. Hogan's funeral!* I resisted my first inclination which was to tell him what I really thought. I really wanted to tell him to be fruitful and multiply, but not exactly in those words.

What I did say was, "Bill, obviously you need to stop the bleeding, but I would hate to see you license out the Hogan brand. Even if you were able to secure a high minimum royalty guarantee, you would never recoup even a small part of your losses. The Hogan name is iconic; it is too strong of a brand and has too much value to go that route. More than likely, if you license the brand to one of the bigger golf companies, they will take the brand and pigeonhole it, somewhat as Wilson Sporting Goods did with the Walter Hagen brand. Why don't you just sell the company? When you bought the company, I had over forty companies that expressed an interest. Surely, some of these companies still have an interest."

"You are probably right," Goodwin said, "about licensing out the brand, and I wouldn't get much for it. So far, no one has expressed an interest in buying the company."

"That is really surprising to me," I said. "Have you spoken with Spalding? I would think that they would have an interest."

"No, Spalding really doesn't have their act together and really isn't in the position to do something like this." The irony of that statement, particularly after admitting that he had lost over $100 million to date, could not be overlooked. We all then filed into the church pews for the funeral service.

Four months later, Goodwin sold the Ben Hogan Company to Spalding Sports Worldwide.

19

THE USGA TAKES ITS EYES OFF THE BALL

One of the best-known admonitions in golf is to keep your eye on the ball. A generation ago, while the golf industry focused on a controversy concerning the width of grooves on iron clubfaces—spending millions of dollars litigating over a matter of no great importance—an issue of far greater consequence emerged, and not a penny was spent in defense of the game. No punches are pulled here in telling the real inside story of the grooves debacle, why it happened, and how it led to the transformation of golf from a game of strategy, course management, and skilled shotmaking to a power game.

Sometimes controversies are accidental. At least that was the case with the grooves controversy that plagued golf during the latter half of the 1980s and into the early 1990s. These were chapters in the annals of USGA, PGA Tour, and Ping company history which everyone would prefer to forget. The origins of the controversy were quite innocent and revolved around conflicting notions of what would be in the best interest of the game. The premise was that the square or U-shaped grooves on Ping Eye2 golf clubs were purportedly too far apart, thereby enabling golfers who used Ping golf clubs to have an unfair advantage in stopping the ball on the green.

Prima fascia evidence of this presumed advantage was none other than Mark Calcavecchia, who appeared out of nowhere to win on the PGA Tour without the prerequisite pedigree of a professional golfer. He notoriously used the Ping L-Wedge that had 60 degrees of loft, which enabled him to extricate the ball from the deep rough and stop it atop the roof of a Volkswagen Bug. In particular, at the 1987 Honda Classic at TPC Eagle Trace in Coral Springs, Florida, Calcavecchia made lofted shots settle obediently on hard and wind-swept greens while everyone else bounced their shots off the firm greens and into trouble. It had to be the grooves, golf writers and fellow pros said, and not the fact that he launched his irons with an unusual vertical climb that enabled the ball to descend steeply and land softly onto the putting surfaces—all thanks to a more pronounced loft angle on his wedge. Soon, the magical qualities of the L-Wedge and the Ping Eye2 irons were legendary. Tongues wagged, demanding that something had to be done quickly to protect the integrity of the game.

The origins of this controversy go back to inventor Dave Pelz's ill-fated Featherlite golf clubs. It seemed golfers could hit those Featherlite irons farther than normal weight clubs. Calvin Peete won a PGA Tour event with them, saying he could hit his featherweights at least a club farther than his old irons (for example, a shot requiring a seven iron for distance could be reached with an eight iron).

Other golf equipment manufacturers jumped into the fray. Even Karsten Manufacturing, makers of the Ping brand and seldom a trend follower, was tempted and developed its version of the super-lightweight clubs. The company tooled up to manufacture them but delayed production and release of the new line. While Karsten stayed on the sidelines, the featherweight phenomenon faded as quickly as it had arrived. The pros complained they could not control their distance with featherweights, and everyone soon stopped selling them.

The Ping brain trust took a look at the tooling it had developed to enter the now defunct featherweight category and figured out a way to salvage the featherweight molds for a new set of iron clubheads. Their trick was simply to use a heavier and denser metal, beryllium copper, as opposed to stainless steel. This would yield iron clubheads in the same weight range as their other steel-headed irons, which also had a lighter swingweight than their competitors, but not as light as the Pelz Featherlite clubs.

There were a couple of unusual factors about producing beryllium copper irons. First, the edges on the grooves were so sharp they easily cut the soft, synthetic balata covers of that era's tour-preferred golf balls. It was almost like a potato peeler shaving off the golf ball's skin. PGA Tour players found they were using a dozen or so balls during the course of a competitive round. Second, the clubs were a different color. Ping's regular irons were a dull silver or monolithic gray. They were not chrome plated because they were made of stainless steel and did not rust. The new beryllium irons were a fairly bright copper color when new, but quickly faded to a muted, dark brown, somewhat like a new penny changes in color and luster with age. I remember talking on the phone with Allan Solheim about the color change, and he said, "If it bothers you, clean them with Coca-Cola, and they will return to their original color . . . both old Coke and new Coke work just fine."

No matter how well-liked a golf club is by tour pros, the continued scuffing and defacing of golf ball covers was not desirable. The golf ball manufacturers, particularly those who made balata-covered golf balls that were softer and easier to cut than the tougher Surlyn-covered balls used by most amateurs, could not fix the problem.

There was an unofficial meeting during the 1984 U.S. Open Championship between Karsten Solheim and the leading golf ball manufacturers. I was not there, but Bill Davis, cofounder of *Golf Digest* magazine, was. He told me how it all played out. Davis was a member of the National Golf Foundation (NGF) Executive Committee back when I was the NGF president and CEO. As he told it, the golf ball guys were all commiserating about the problem they were having with the sharp edges of the grooves on the Ping beryllium irons. I suspect that Solheim was somewhat enjoying the situation, particularly because he had tried and failed to develop a commercially viable Ping golf ball.

When the golf ball makers were through complaining, they asked him what he could do to help. Davis said Solheim's response was classic—he turned to his competitors and looked them straight in the eyes one-by-one, and said, "Gentlemen, you really have a big problem don't you?"

Eventually, Solheim simply rolled the edges of the grooves. He actually put a radius on the edge of each groove, so the golf balls would not be so easily damaged. It worked. The pros quit cutting their golf balls. Karsten and Ping then put rolled edges on the grooves of their very popular Ping Eye2 irons, even though the steel-headed irons were not cutting the golf balls. The issue was never an issue of U (Square) versus V grooves. The USGA had officially allowed the use of square grooves back in 1981; however, Ping was one of the few companies that used them in the early 1980s.

Regardless of the shape of the grooves in cross-section, the distance between grooves—according to the USGA, the rules-making body of golf—could not be less than a certain specified minimum at the surface of the clubface. By rounding the groove edges, Karsten Manufacturing widened that distance to an unacceptable width as measured by the USGA. How far short of acceptable was the gap between the Ping Eye2 grooves? It was five-thousandths of an inch—about the width of a human hair. Seeing the discrepancy as materially insignificant, Ping did not bother to submit its modified Ping Eye2 iron to the USGA for approval.

Ping's U-shaped grooves—with their radii edges—were measured by the USGA and determined to be wider apart than what the USGA Rules permitted. From that determination, a fair amount of chaos and mayhem ensued.

The leading players on the PGA Tour, primarily the non-Ping players, believed square grooves (which became the new descriptive label for this controversy), provided players of lesser skill with a competitive advantage. Commissioner Beman carried the banner for the leading players by publicly asserting that square grooves provided an unfair advantage. He commissioned scientific testing by Joe Braly, a former business associate before Beman became the PGA Tour Commissioner. Braly was best known as the inventor of the Con-Sole wedge and frequency matched (FM) golf shafts. Ironically, his coinvestigator, Dave Pelz, was the inventor of the Featherlites (indirectly responsible for the development of the controversy in the first place).

Their charge was to thoroughly test the performance of U- versus V-shaped grooves using both mechanical and PGA Tour player testing. The USGA also undertook tests using its guru for golf equipment, Frank Thomas, once known as the Father of Graphite Shafts. Thomas invented them while head of R&D at Shakespeare when that fishing tackle company had a brief foray into the golf equipment business. In the USGA's golf club performance tests, there was no advantage that could be observed.

The PGA Tour, on the other hand, found that under certain conditions, like hitting a golf shot out of a wet rough, U-grooved irons performed better. Ironically, V grooves performed better out of the fairway in dry conditions. There was considerable anecdotal evidence from the pros to support the claims, but none of it was really clear cut. Tom Kite, then a Hogan Company PGA Tour staff pro and leading money winner on the PGA Tour, told me when I was president of the Hogan Company that he did not want to play square grooves because he could not predict how much spin he would impart to the ball with them. Kite said, "When I am in the rough, I know how much of a flier lie I have; and when I am in the rough with V grooves, I know how far it is going to go. But with square grooves, I never know for sure how far it will go, and it may go short or long of where I want it to go."

Beman panned the USGA study. He told me flatly: "You can't expect an amateur body like the USGA to understand and comprehend the difference and advantage for golfers who play at this level." The PGA Tour then acted unilaterally, forbidding the use of square grooves at their events, claiming they "changed the character and nature of the game."

The issue between Ping and the USGA was in how the square grooves were measured. The USGA did not rule square grooves as nonconforming. They believed the distance between the grooves was wider than what they allowed in the rules because they measured it at the surface of the clubface. Solheim felt the differences in performance were immaterial and that the measurement should be from the interior, vertical wall of the groove. Further, he told me at the 1989 Open at Troon (Calcavecchia won in a three-way playoff with Australians Greg Norman and Wayne Grady) that the primary utility of the groove was in channeling moisture off the face in wet conditions, like tire treads do when the roadway is wet. The U groove could disperse more moisture because it had more volume than the V groove, but in his opinion the amount of moisture that was channeled or displaced was not material.

The only previous definitive research conducted on the benefit of having grooves was *Search for the Perfect Swing*, by Alastair Cochran and John Stobbs, published in 1968, as well as some work conducted for the USGA by the Arthur D. Little consulting company. Both reported that smooth clubfaces (no grooves) could impart as much backspin as ordinary grooved faces, but smooth surfaces were less consistent in doing so. Their tests showed that very shallow grooves consistently imparted as much backspin as normal or extra-deep grooves did.

The USGA and the PGA Tour were unwitting bedfellows in what Ping believed was a conspiracy to undermine its reputation and commercial interests. Ping was the leading iron and putter maker in the golf equipment business and had a great deal at stake when the USGA ruled its irons nonconforming. The PGA Tour then announced its own rule forbidding square grooves. With its commercial interests at stake, Ping sued the USGA for $100 million and the PGA Tour for $100 million.

The USGA and Ping, neither of them in search of a pyrrhic victory, reached an agreement in late 1990 on this dispute. The gist of the settlement was that the USGA would clarify its rules to provide for the measurement of grooves with rounded edges—the so-called 30-degree method. Ping agreed to modify its tooling to conform to this new measurement method. Meanwhile, Ping irons that had been deemed nonconforming as of 1985, as well as clubs produced and sold over the ensuing few years, would be allowed. Both Karsten and the USGA stated this was a technical issue, and there was no unfair advantage in the use of U or square grooves. The battle would continue, however, between Ping and the PGA Tour.

The effect of the USGA-Ping settlement was to catch the PGA Tour with its pants down. The PGA Tour persisted in fighting the $100 million lawsuit. From the PGA Tour's standpoint, it was a matter of whether or not the organization could make its own rules for the conduct of its competitions. A court ordered an injunction regarding the PGA Tour's ban on square grooves. At this point, I became entangled in the litigation process. I was the president and CEO of the Ben Hogan Company at the time, and according to court documents, an unindicted coconspirator with the PGA Tour.

There were subpoenas for Ben Hogan Company documents trying to link my close ties with Beman and the Hogan Company's title sponsorship of the Ben Hogan Tour. We had nothing to hide and cooperated. In the spring of 1992, I was deposed for two days by Ping's legal counsel, who tried to prove there was some unsavory alliance between the PGA Tour and its prohibition of square grooves that might give the Ben Hogan Company some competitive advantage over Ping.

The deposition itself was an interesting experience. The PGA Tour and Ping had their attorneys there. I had my attorney at Kelly Hart and two, three-ring binders of notes. The first thing the opposing attorney asked when we were all seated in my attorney's conference room was, "Are those binders for us to review?" I said, "No, they are just my notes and reference materials."

My attorney whispered to me, "Put them back into your briefcase and remember what I told you: Only answer the question asked; say nothing more." I did as he asked and put the binders in my briefcase, but did not heed his warning about saying no more than asked during the deposition.

I knew I had nothing to hide and thus thought the truth would win out. What I did not realize was they were not looking for the truth. They were trying to build their case for a conspiracy. So, comforted by my ignorance, I went on to say too much while I was deposed. My attorney became so exasperated by my ramblings that he asked for a ten-minute break in the proceedings. I thought I was doing great; the truth would prevail, or so I thought.

My attorney said, "David, what in the hell are you trying to do? They are leading you like a lamb to slaughter. You need to shut the fuck up!"

I was stunned by this rebuke. I considered firing him but had second thoughts. Maybe he is right, I thought to myself, and I did not really understand what was going on.

Jim Triola, the PGA Tour's attorney was more kind in his criticism and said, "David, if you can answer their questions with a simple yes or no, it is better to do that. So far, you haven't said anything that might hurt us, but you might say something that seems innocent to you, but could be misconstrued—particularly if they are probing or looking for something." Having been taken to the woodshed by both counsels for our side, I then only answered the questions asked. As the interview continued, I realized they were right, and I had been naïve.

At one point, the Ping attorney pulled out a copy of a *Golfweek* magazine article written by Joe Much, a professional colleague and longtime personal friend who once served as the NGF executive director when I was its president. The article, "A Match Made in Heaven," was about me becoming president of the Ben Hogan Company. It went on to say how close Commissioner Beman and I were and how Beman was stretching his tentacles throughout the golf world. It concluded with something along the lines of, *While it might look like a match made in heaven, don't turn up too many rocks because you might not like what you see underneath.*

As I quickly read those last words, I chuckled to myself thinking that Much was always a little edgy in his writing style and had a unique way with words. I had seen the article before, but had forgotten about it. He had a knack for seeing the underside on most matters and was still a little mad at me for asking him to retire before he wanted. Still, I had a very high personal and professional regard for Much. If you knew him as I did, you would understand why this article would not affect our friendship. So, after skimming the article I said, "Okay, I have read it. I remember reading this article a few years ago."

The opposing counsel said, "Do you know the author of this article?"

I said, "Yes, Joe Much worked for me at the NGF and is a close friend."

The Ping attorney said, "Did you read what he said about you and your relationship with Deane Beman?"

Sticking to my instructions to keep my answers short I simply said, "Yes."

The Ping attorney then followed with, "Did he have any basis in making those allegations?"

I said, "No."

He then asked, "What kind of friend would say those things?"

My response was succinct, "He had no basis to say what he said. It was his opinion at the time. And, I would say that Joe is still a good friend. Sometimes the test of a true friendship is in being able to overlook such things."

The Ping counsel dropped that line of questioning.

At the time of the deposition, the Hogan Company was the number two iron clubmaker in terms of market share, just behind Ping. And we were the number one forged clubmaker in the world. Because we made forged clubs, it was a simple matter to stamp square or U grooves into our clubs. We made V grooves until the market indicated we should produce square grooves. The Ping Eye2 model was introduced in 1983 and was by far the top-selling iron model of all time. It was in its seventh year and would continue in production for another two years. It was a record run for an iron-club model.

If that product life cycle could be extended another year or two before a design change was needed, most companies would be delighted because it would be more profitable for them. Interestingly, Ping probably received an unexpected boost in sales because golfers believed the grooves on the Ping irons provided some advantage. Ping would have preferred not to have this public legal battle to provide that sales stimulus, but it had that effect regardless. The Ping Eye2 mystique was born out of this controversy.

Ironically, I was one of the few people in the golf industry who enjoyed a good relationship with both Ping and the PGA Tour. In the fall of 1992, Allan Solheim and I both attended the NGF Golf Summit in Orlando, which was followed by the Sporting Goods Manufacturers Association meeting in Ponte Vedra Beach. I rented a car, and we rode together from Orlando to Ponte Vedra Beach, home of the PGA Tour. It was only a two-and-one-half-hour drive, and we talked about the grooves controversy the entire way. I argued the PGA Tour had the right to make its own rules and, surprisingly, Solheim agreed. The more we talked, the more it seemed there was not an insurmountable breach between the Ping and PGA Tour positions. While I knew Beman sincerely believed there was some advantage with square grooves, the stakes were unreasonably high for both Ping and the PGA Tour over a technical matter of no great consequence.

If Ping prevailed in its lawsuit, it could bankrupt and end the PGA Tour. In the process, Ping would lose one of its key avenues of promotion and suffer public relations wounds in the marketplace that might never heal. If the PGA Tour prevailed, Ping's reputation and commercial interests would be irreparably damaged. It was a no-win scenario for both parties.

It seemed to me there had to be some solution, especially if Ping was agreeable to a settlement that preserved the PGA Tour's right to make its own rules. Ping was agreeable to abiding by those rules, just so those rules were not arbitrary and didn't single out Ping as a violator. Also, I knew that lately there was a lot of pressure on the commissioner to dispose of this matter. Too much was at risk over a matter based upon disputable evidence and contrary to the USGA's settlement with Ping and its revised ruling on square grooves. If the PGA Tour pushed this matter any further, it would be all alone; the other governing bodies of golf had already capitulated.

By the time we reached the Sawgrass Marriott where we were both staying, I had convinced Solheim that a personal meeting between him and Beman might be just the opening both parties needed to break the impasse. I called Beman that night at his home to see if he would be willing to meet with Solheim privately. Beman said somewhat condescendingly, "I would be happy to meet with Allan. He always seemed like a nice young man," to which I replied, "Deane, I think Allan is older than you are." We then agreed to meet at 8:00 a.m. the next day in Beman's office at PGA Tour headquarters, which was about a drive and a 5-iron from the Sawgrass Marriott. I told Solheim about the meeting, and he and I agreed to meet the next morning at 7:00 a.m. for breakfast at the Marriott. I did not plan to attend the meeting between Beman and Solheim. I would just take him over and wait outside until they were finished.

At the appointed time the next morning, Solheim came down to the restaurant wearing what looked like the same white golf shirt he had worn the day before. He was unshaven. His clothing was wrinkled, and his shirt partially untucked. I took this all in and said: "Allan, it looks like you had a tough night."

"I did. I spent the night talking with our attorneys and my family. It was decided that I should not meet with the commissioner at this time. Can you explain that to him?"

"Sure. It won't be a problem, but I think that this might be a missed opportunity for both sides to resolve this matter without the cost and risk of further litigation." He nodded his head, but did not say anything. I then told him that I would call the commissioner at home before he left for the office.

Beman was matter-of-fact when I called to let him know, only saying, "That's fine; I really didn't expect much to come of it anyway."

**

An out-of-court settlement was reached in April of 1993 in the $100 million lawsuit filed by Ping against the PGA Tour and for the tour's countersuit. While no admission of fault or wrong was made by either party, the result was that golf club irons with U-shaped or square grooves would remain legal on the PGA Tour. PGA Tour Deputy Commissioner Tim Finchem did confirm that as part of the settlement, the PGA Tour would pay Ping's legal fees. It was widely speculated Ping had spent something in the range of $10 million, which was disputed by Ping's legal counsel, Leonard Decof, as being exaggerated.

Finchem said the tour's legal fees were approximately $8 million, of which insurance covered $4.5 million. The PGA Tour also agreed to drop its countersuit—wise when one considers that Ping's case was an antitrust matter, which meant damages could be trebled. *Golf Digest* described it more colorfully: "Deane blinked and Karsten winked." Of course, Karsten Manufacturing did not want the PGA Tour dismantled. It was its primary promotional and marketing vehicle. The settlement seemed to say that Ping had made its point.

Collateral Damages of the Grooves Controversy

The real casualty of the grooves imbroglio was that the USGA was reduced to being the rules-making eunuch and silent watchdog of the golf world. Many pundits, including myself, speculate that the fear of litigation with golf equipment companies has been a big factor in the USGA's abrogation of its critical role to preserve the nature, character, and integrity of the game. Somewhat emasculated, the USGA took its eye off the ball during the 1990s. It failed to develop rules to limit technological advances in golf equipment. This has changed how the game is played and has adversely impacted the economic viability of many golf courses.

The technical evolution in golf balls and the implements used to propel them has outdistanced the USGA's ability to monitor and rein in these innovations to reasonable standards. As a result, there has been a negative impact on the demand and supply for golf. Course footprints have increased as golf courses have become longer and more difficult to play. It now costs more and takes longer to play golf. Consequently, the preservation and sustainability of the game is at risk.

20

REQUIEM FOR THE GREATEST GAME

U nless you're blessed with an extraordinary presence of mind and foresight, you probably won't know what you've got until it's gone. Most golfers who played in the 1960s, 1970s, and 1980s sense a difference between how the game was played then and how it is played today. They also see the changes in the golf courses built since the 1990s. Most golfers remember when playing golf was less expensive, when golf courses were more fun to play and required a different variety of golf shots, and importantly, when a round of golf didn't seem like it took five hours to play.

During the 1990s, two major issues emerged that transformed the design (and therefore the degree of challenge) of golf courses. First, real estate developers had a profound impact on the nature and type of golf courses built. Second, the USGA and R&A (Royal and Ancient) allowed technological advances in golf equipment performance to change how the game is played, which indirectly influenced the length, design, and sustainability of golf courses.

***

Back when the NGF and PGA Tour were promoting building a Course a Day to meet the anticipated demand from aging baby boomers, it was inconceivable that the supply of golf courses might exceed demand or that the wrong kind of golf courses might be built. Because more than 40 percent of golf courses built during the 1990s were tied to master-planned communities, real estate developers played an influential role in the development of high-end golf courses that were used in selling premium-priced real estate.

The conventional wisdom among developers was that golf courses designed by big-name architects and known for their difficulty led to higher property values. From the perspective of real estate developers, it made business sense to build longer golf courses. They could squeeze in more premium-priced golf course frontage lots. For example, by adding seventy yards to a hole, a developer could theoretically add four 100-foot-wide lots (two on each side) of the fairway, green, or tee. At $250,000 per lot, those extra seventy yards could represent one million dollars—on just one hole.

Developers spent too much building these more challenging golf courses; typically, their footprint was bigger, and they were more costly to maintain. As a result, the cost of playing golf increased, and it took longer to play a round of golf. Ironically, this business model that called for building bigger and more expensive golf courses had a greater impact on more than just the golf courses that were built. My dissertation research at Clemson University revealed that developers renovating existing courses in the 1990s and even building new golf courses that did not have a real estate tie made golf courses longer and more difficult because they believed they needed this type of golf course design to compete with what the real estate developers were offering. So the real estate developers' idea snowballed.

Since the real estate development golf course was an amenity of a master-planned community, just like tennis courts, sidewalks, or swimming pools, operational costs for the golf course were subsidized. Typically, the developers' exit strategy (after selling the real estate) was to sell the golf course to a third party or to the club members; however, beginning in the late 1990s that strategy began to disappear as an option because there were signs that the US economy and the real estate market were changing. It soon became evident that the developer golf courses were not financially viable. In economics, the value of a business is either a multiple of its projected earnings or its replacement value, whichever is higher. However, if a golf course loses money, it has little value to anyone except those people who purchased property around it. These homeowners had an interest in maintaining the value of the golf course. But for the real estate developer, the course quickly moved from the asset to the liability column on the balance sheet.

The result was golfers were left with courses that were designed for pros in order to sell real estate. These courses were ill-suited to the skills of the average golfer, who plays a different game. This disparity between the pros and amateurs was noted by Phil Mickelson prior to the 2011 PGA Championship at the Atlanta Athletic Club. The two-time Masters champion was critical of the design changes made to the club's 7,467-yard, par-70 Highlands course. He felt some holes had become unplayable for the members. "It's a good reason why the number of rounds is down on this golf course amongst the membership," Mickelson said. "And it's a good reason why, in my opinion, this is a great example again of how modern architecture is killing the participation of the sport, because the average guy just can't play it."

Unfortunately, the 1990s boom in golf course development created a product that its customers didn't want to buy. Playing golf was perceived as being costly, difficult, and time consuming, which over time, along with the slowdown in the US economy, contributed to the downturn in the US golf economy.

Since 2001, the golf industry has experienced declines in the key barometers of economic well-being as defined and measured by the number of golfers, the number of golf rounds, and the net increase (or decrease) in the number of golf courses. In 1990, the percentage of people playing golf was 12.1 percent; by 2000 it was 11.1 percent; and by 2010 it was down to 10.2 percent. Rounds played were down 5.7 percent, from an estimated 520 million in 2001 to 460 million rounds today, which translates to a decrease of about 4,000 rounds per 18-hole equivalent golf course.

Over the past decade, the golf industry has endured two major economic downturns: (1) the real estate meltdown that began in 2006 and (2) the Great Recession, which most believe started in 2008. The golf industry is in the midst of a crisis in the economic viability of many golf courses. The demand and supply for the game is positively or negatively impacted by the changing economic conditions, as well as changing societal and cultural conditions.

The US golf economy has been adjusting and right-sizing to the new norms. It could be that the golf industry's new normal might be 24 to 25 million golfers, 14,000 to 15,000 golf courses, and 460 to 490 million rounds played, but no one really knows. How long this malaise will continue is anyone's guess; however, most estimates focus on the theory that the reduction in supply will afford those remaining golf courses more customers. In other words, fewer slices of the pie means each slice will be larger. However, this theory assumes that the pie will stay the same size and that demand for golf will stay the same even as the number of golf courses decreases. This is illogical because the golf industry will continue to have a decrease in supply in the near term. The premise underlying their prognostication is uncertain at best.

The ramifications of these changes in the supply and demand for golf are unknown. The adverse impact that real estate developers had upon the game, golf participation, and the golf industry is evident. The current contraction in the number of golf courses is estimated to be a net loss of 140 golf courses per year (golf course closures versus new golf course openings), and this will probably continue for a number of years.

How Technology Changed the Game
In winning the 1986 Masters, Nicklaus used a MacGregor 945W driver (a real wood-headed driver with a 43.5-inch steel shaft). With that golf club, a mis-hit tee shot struck a half inch off-center would land shorter in distance and might be in the rough. That same mis-hit shot would go much farther and straighter with today's oversized, metal-headed driver with a longer and lighter graphite shaft. Today's technology offers a perimeter-weighted clubhead

that enables golfers to hit better shots with off-center hits. Today's drivers have very thin clubfaces that have a trampoline effect which increases the velocity of the golf ball upon impact with the clubhead. The result is a golf club that weighs less, can be swung faster, and can hit a golf ball that flies farther and straighter.

The improved performance of the golf ball during the 1990s is of particular note. The evolution started in the mid to late 1980s when the golf ball manufacturers focused on producing golf balls with better aerodynamics. Known as the dimple wars, this series of innovations led to the development of golf balls that spun less, curved less, and went farther. In the mid-1990s, multi-layered golf balls replaced the traditional three-piece synthetic balata-covered ball that had a small rubber liquid center with rubber bands wound tightly around the core. The significance of this change was that the new generation of golf balls could be manufactured more consistently; historically, the USGA allowed for manufacturing tolerances for the old style wound balls, but these tolerances were no longer needed with the multi-layered golf ball. Golfers playing in the 1980s and the early 1990s will remember that out of a dozen, two or three golf balls were "hot." When a golfer buys a dozen golf balls today, they are all hot because they are all manufactured within the USGA limits, plus the allowance for manufacturing variances. Today's golf balls are simply better. They spin less, fly farther, go straighter, and are easier to control.

Golf equipment companies developed clubs and balls that made the game easier for the pros. These golfers learned how to take advantage of the new technology to optimize the combination of clubhead, shaft, and ball to attain the ideal launch angle with minimum ball spin. This maximized their clubhead speed, the distance they could hit the golf ball, and their ability to control its direction. Unfortunately, average golfers are just as bad as they have always been and do not have the skills to take advantage of this technology like the pros. Consequently, the handicaps of average golfers have not improved dramatically over the past fifty years, even with the new technology, and those golfers who pay to play the game are confronted with golf courses that are too long and difficult.

The art of golf is gone. Golf has become a power game for the pros. The facts are unequivocal. The game and the golf courses have changed.

How did we get to this point? If the top players in the world were not hitting the golf ball so far (and straight), would a 7,000-yard golf course still be a relevant challenge? Will many of golf's historic championship venues become obsolete or need to be lengthened and redesigned? Interestingly, in an Associated Press news story, Jack Nicklaus joked that if Augusta National kept expanding its golf course, "pretty soon we'll be teeing off downtown somewhere." As it turned out, Nicklaus's quip wasn't that far out of bounds. *Golfweek* magazine reported on March 2, 2016, that Augusta National approached Augusta Country Club about acquiring some adjacent property so that Augusta's 13th hole, a 510-yard par 5 could be lengthened to challenge the likes of long-hitting Bubba Watson, who had reached the green in two shots (a drive and a sand wedge).

About a year or so ago, I was watching the South African Open Championship on the Golf Channel. The Jack Nicklaus Signature Design course at Serengeti Golf and Wildlife Estate in Johannesburg, South Africa, was heralded by the golf commentators for its challenging design. They noted the length and difficulty of the course, the meticulously maintained conditions, and the challenging tournament setup. From the vantage point of my home in Ponte Vedra Beach, I could see the perfectly manicured fairways and the high roughs. The lush fairways had a checkerboard mowing pattern, revealing they had been double-cut in a crisscross pattern with triplex mowers. On the third hole, a 619-meter (677 yard) par 5, one of the tournament leaders, Merrick Bremner, hit a 359-meter (393-yard) drive and reached the green in two with a four iron. This single moment in the tournament competition revealed what is wrong with golf today and what it portends for the future of the global game of golf. It wasn't that long ago that a par-5 hole approaching 600 yards was considered unreachable in two shots, and now the pros can do it with a perfunctory drive with a hybrid wood or a long iron.

Some facts: In 1980, the PGA Tour started its Official Statistics program. Back then, two holes were picked where most of the tour players would be hitting drives. Ideally, one hole was to be into the wind and one against it. Only drives that landed in the fairway were counted. Dan Pohl led the average driving distance category at 274.3 yards, and Nicklaus was tenth at 260 yards. Of course, these golfers were using wood-headed drivers with steel shafts and playing wound balata-covered golf balls.

In 2015, Dustin Johnson led the PGA Tour driving distance category with an average of 317.7 yards; way back at tenth place was Keegan Bradley at 306.1 yards. These days, the PGA Tour measures the distance of all drives on par-4 and par-5 holes, including layup shots with fairway woods, hybrids, and irons; this means the average distance that a PGA Tour player hits his driver is actually farther than the statistics reveal because he wasn't always using his driver.

Here's one last statistic taken from the *PGA Tour Book* (media guide) that is quite revealing. In 1989, twenty-five-year-old Davis Love III, who had a reputation for being a long hitter, finished eleventh on the PGA Tour with an average driving distance of 274.2 yards. Thirty years later, Love finished forty-eighth on the PGA Tour Champions circuit with an average driving distance of 299.2 yards. And, notably, it's not just the drives that are going farther and straighter. That length advantage extends throughout the set, which is probably more attributable to the performance of the golf ball. For example, it's not uncommon for PGA Tour professionals to hit long irons some 250-plus yards and hit wedges and nine irons 150-plus yards.

Golf has become a power game. There are those among golf industry leadership who actually support how far the pros are hitting the golf ball. At the November 2015 HSBC Golf Business Forum in China, PGA Tour Commissioner Tim Finchem and the R&A's chief executive, Martin Slumbers, both went on the record stating they are not interested in doing anything about the "distance controversy." One could speculate that the rationale for the tour commissioner's position is because the PGA Tour is in the entertainment business. Their foremost interests are television viewership and ratings, and it's a better show with the pros hitting the golf ball such prodigious distances.

What's difficult to fathom is what the R&A's rationale might be. Slumbers might have just fallen asleep, but his comments seemed to imply that the distance controversy had been contained when he said, "The average [increase in distance] has only moved three to four yards in the last ten years. There is no burning desire on our part to make any changes." This rationale from the R&A, as well as similar statements from the USGA, presumes that the ruling bodies can get ahead of the R&D teams at golf equipment companies (which they have failed to do in the past). It is unlikely the USGA and the R&A can wrest control of this runaway issue, especially when so much damage has already been done to the game and golf's built environment.

Further, there has been no published research regarding how and why today's golf balls go so much farther and straighter. How can this not be a critical issue for the USGA and R&A? Imagine if Major League Baseball allowed hot baseballs and lightweight alloy bats. They would have to build new ballfields to contain the game. Second basemen would be breaking Babe Ruth's homerun record; pitchers would be wearing catchers' masks to keep from getting killed by a batter's line drive.

In a personal meeting during the 2014 PGA Show, Frank Thomas, the former USGA technical director, admitted the current standard for clubface flexibility (trampoline effect) was set specifically to avoid litigation. The USGA and the R&A have taken a similar public relations stance as it pertains to the distance controversy. Clearly, both governing bodies are in a state of denial. They justify their inaction with misleading statistics. It's easy to mislead with statistics. It's simply a matter of defining the research parameters and how the statistics will be analyzed. The USGA and the R&A would have you believe that the pros' ability to hit the ball greater distances has been contained (defining the research parameters), and furthermore, the average increase in distance over time (statistics) has only been a yard or two per year. However, the critical measure of consequence is in the *cumulative* difference or increase in the distance golf balls go now compared to then. It is not the average annual increase over a span of time.

This research can be done. The USGA has the equipment and the in-house professional capability to measure the performance of the golf equipment used in the mid-1980s compared to the golf equipment used today. If the difference is not statistically significant, then there is no problem.

Sometimes research isn't undertaken, however, because the results might require actions that the investigators don't want to take. The problem may reside in the fact that it is not just one technological advance; it may be the combination of an array of innovations collectively creating the distance controversy. The damage to the integrity of the game was done slowly and incrementally over decades; unfortunately, no one really took notice until it seemed too late to do anything about it.

The conundrum for the USGA and the R&A is how to limit the adverse impact of technology upon the game without inviting the risk of costly litigation. Unfortunately, it is very likely that if the USGA and R&A develop new rules regarding how golf balls and clubs perform, they will be sued by the golf equipment companies. The golf companies have played by the existing rules and have invested millions into R&D to develop the technology that enables them to compete in the marketplace.

It's a very difficult decision, because it will be an unpopular decision. The case needs to be made with the golfing public and golf course owners and operators that for the sake of golf's future, advances in golf equipment should not be allowed to undermine the play of the game, the integrity of golf's built environment, or the sustainability of the game. Many leaders, including many former PGA presidents, strongly disagree with this idea. They say average golfers need the help that technology provides, And most golfers want to have that technology, regardless of whether or not they can really utilize it.

Theoretically, it would be great if the USGA and the R&A could revise golf equipment performance standards to preserve the integrity of the game. The problem is that while new golf equipment performance standards could be developed, there would be considerable disagreement as to whether or not those same technological limits should be applied to all golfers. Ironically, the obvious sentiment is that amateurs need the help *because* golf courses have become too long and difficult. Do we really want the game played by the pros to be different from the game that the amateurs play? Philosophically, I am opposed to the idea that PGA Tour players could play with clubs and balls that are different from what amateurs use; however, we may not have a choice.

It seemed at one point, the USGA and R&A were laying the groundwork for cooperation in rules changes as they worked with golf equipment companies to find common ground on other issues: re-addressing the old grooves controversy and the development of the new anchored-putting-method rule. Unfortunately, that doesn't seem to be the case when it comes to the distance controversy. I am not so sure there is even a plan.

Golf purists, and I include myself in this group, believe that the game should only have one set of rules; this includes equipment rules. However, the ruling bodies have lost control, and the game has changed, much to the detriment of the game and the golf industry. As much as I hate to say so, I believe it may be time for a bifurcation of the rules as they apply to golf equipment. Golfers playing at the highest level (international, national, state, and collegiate competitions) could use golf clubs and balls that perform more like the golf equipment played in the pre-1990s era. Amateurs and recreational golfers could use the modern clubs and balls currently allowed by the USGA and R&A. Average golfers need the help technology affords but cannot take advantage of it as the pros do. Who knows, golf equipment companies may sell more clubs and balls because there may be some amateurs who play in national and state competitions that want to have the other pro-level clubs and balls.

The golf equipment manufacturers will object, of couse, because their usual promotional pitch is to claim their clubs or balls are the most popular on the tour. However, major golf equipment companies could still market the technical superiority of their PGA-Tour-inspired designs, and they will continue to enjoy the advantages their market share and brand dominance provide. Further, litigation damages will be minimized, because they will still be able to sell the current, technologically superior version of golf equipment to the golfers who actually purchase their products and pay for their green fees.

There are a number of possible ways new golf equipment standards for pros could be orchestrated. For example, graphite shafts could still be allowed to the maximum length already permitted by the rules; oversized drivers and fairway woods could be allowed (at the USGA and R&A's maximum size). However, new USGA and R&A performance specifications could be introduced to make oversized drivers and fairway woods perform more like real wood-headed drivers without the rebound or trampoline effect. This might be as simple as thickening the clubface to change the clubhead's weight distribution, center of gravity (CG), COR, and MOI in order to make these clubheads less forgiving on mis-hit shots.

The multi-layered golf ball construction could stay the same. However, this could be a more challenging task. Former PGA Tour Commissioner Beman believes that the golf ball issue can be fixed for the tour pros with the addition of a "minimum spin rule," meaning that under specific and controlled launch conditions, the spin imparted by the driver clubhead would impart no less than X miles per hour in golf ball backspin. The fact is, golf balls that spin more don't go as far and curve more. The USGA made similar rulings in the past, when they introduced the Spherical Symmetry rule in response to the Polaris litigation because they claimed the dimple configuration created an anti-slice or self-correcting golf ball.

Amateur and recreational golfers would not be impacted by these changes. They will simply continue to play as well or badly as before. Golfers playing at the highest level, however, will be challenged to play the same game that Ben Hogan and Jack Nicklaus played. Championship golf courses won't need to be "Tiger proofed." U.S. Open courses won't need to have twenty-yard fairways, deep roughs, and greens as slick as skating rinks. The footprint of golf courses could be reduced, thereby using less water and chemicals, preserving our natural resources for future generations.

The Endgame of Golf

Golf has to be difficult, and it has to be fun—that's a fragile equilibrium. The challenge of the game is different for the professional golfer versus the amateur; yet the pros and the average golfers play the same golf course. Golf's answer to that disparity has been to have different sets of tees suitable for the length that golfers hit the ball. This approach, however, does not always work.

An analogy with snow skiing might be useful in explaining this point. Imagine a ski resort charging $100 for a single-day lift ticket and requiring all skiers, regardless of their abilities, to ski on the most difficult, black-diamond run. And the only accommodation for the less skillful skiers is they are allowed to start farther down the mountain. This is how many golf courses built since the 1990s accommodate the majority of their golfing customers.

For example, if the design of a golf hole has a landing area that is 160 yards from each set of tees, it could pose an unreasonable challenge to most golfers who have lesser shotmaking skills—that is, 99 percent of the people who pay to play the game. From 160 yards, the pro may be able to hit a towering, eight or nine iron onto a shallow green while the typical male golfer might need a five or six iron to carry a golf ball that distance. That golfer may or may not be able to hit the ball high enough to stop it on a green that does not have much depth (room for a shot to land and stay on the green). Older, younger, and shorter- hitting golfers can't carry the golf ball that far and must *navigate* their way over, around, or between the hazards in order to reach the green.

The length of a golf hole is not the only consideration. In the "good old days," golf courses were firmer to play and not so perfectly manicured. Golfers had the option to bounce a ball along the ground because the greens and approach areas were not wet sponges, and the golf holes did not have hazards which leave golfers no choice but to fly the ball to the green like a lawn dart. Golf today can be best described as target golf, a version of the game totally foreign to the way golf originated and continues to be played in Scotland (bump and roll).

Many American golf courses now have maintenance budgets exceeding $1 million annually. They use oceans of water to irrigate courses so real estate developers can sell fairway lots. The roughs are so thick, golfers can't find their golf balls, let alone play the next shot toward the green. The standards of excellence defined on television each week have golf commentators praising the length and difficulty of golf courses. Meanwhile, average golfers still bounce their balls along a soggy fairway over water and sand bunkers and onto the green, hoping the next great innovation in golf equipment will enable them to enjoy this increasingly expensive game.

The maintenance and set-up of the golf course also impact the playability of the game. How wide are the fairways? How deep are the roughs? How fast are the greens? Are there forced carries over water hazards or sand bunkers that make some of the holes unplayable for the majority of golfers? Are the roughs around the green so tall and thick only a skilled player can execute play to the green?

A few years ago in June, I played the Tom-Fazio-designed Thornblade Country Club course in Greer, South Carolina, as the guest of the late real estate developer, Howard "Champ" Covington. Thornblade annually hosts the PGA Tour's (Web.com Tour) BMW Charity Pro-Am in April. The greens were firm and fast, the fairways were narrow and mown very low, and the roughs were thick and cut very high. By the time we reached the 11th tee, we had spent about three hours on the golf course looking for golf balls in the roughs and slashing our way around.

Since I was Covington's guest, I did not want to criticize the course's setup and maintenance, but I did ask why the course was still being maintained for the play of a PGA Tour event. Covington's reply was that in two weeks, Thornblade hosted an American Junior Golf Association tournament. In order to make the golf course a severe test for the junior golfers, the membership at Thornblade had to endure playing conditions that made the course too difficult, not much fun, and too time-consuming to play.

There is no reason to maintain a golf course like they do for a PGA Tour event. The pros play a different game, and it costs too much to maintain those playing conditions. Most golfers want to be able to find their golf ball in the rough and be able to hit the next shot toward the green. They do not want to chop it sideways back to the fairway. Most golfers don't want to hit a shot from a tight lie in a fairway groomed for the pros; they want a little "fluff" under the ball. And most golfers don't want to putt on green linoleum; they want a smooth surface, but they want the greens to be a reasonable speed.

In actuality, it is less expensive to give golfers the kind of golf course they enjoy playing than to maintain a course suited for pros, and doing so will reduce the time it takes to play a round of golf. As a business, the golf industry needs to encourage golf course owners and operators to offer a product their customers want to buy. While we don't mind paying $500 once or twice in our lives to play Pebble Beach or to try our luck on the 17th hole of the TPC, sojourns to such golf meccas do not constitute the regular diet for, or satiate the everyday appetite of, most golfers.

Recently, I watched a 1994 episode of *Shell's Wonderful World of Golf* on the Golf Channel. It featured Jack Nicklaus versus Arnold Palmer playing Pinehurst No. 2. Palmer, then 64, used a real wood driver; Nicklaus, 52, used a smaller-sized metal driver. Both used wound, balata-covered balls. Palmer started out well, but the younger Nicklaus finished strong and easily won the match. The final scores didn't matter. It was just fun to watch. What I found most interesting was the distance they both hit the ball and the types of shots they attempted to play. There were a number of occasions when the longer-hitting Nicklaus played a six or seven iron from around 155 to 165 yards out. It was a cool day in April, but tour players today would hit those same shots with a nine iron or wedge. Palmer hit a few great shots out of the rough, curving the ball to get back into play. The way championship golf courses are maintained today, Palmer wouldn't be able to play the same shot out of the deep rough.

Fond memories of what golf used to be are fading away. Golfers and non-golfers alike are choosing to pursue other recreational interests for a variety of economic and sociocultural reasons, in addition to the time constraints. The golf economy is changing and contracting. There are fewer golfers playing less often. Golf courses have fewer rounds played and financially, they suffer. The golf industry has inherited a large inventory of courses that are unsustainable in their current forms. So where do we go from here?

Sustainability is often misunderstood to be synonymous with environmentalism. While sustainability has become a ubiquitous term, it is not in the lexicon of the business professionals in the golf industry. At this point, there is little understanding among golfers and golf course operators as to what a sustainable golf course is and what it would mean for the enjoyment of the game. In addition, there is no understanding of what it could mean for the economic well-being of the golf business.

To many in golf, sustainability means that "the greens will become the browns," which is what USGA President Jim Hyler was quoted as saying at the USGA 2010 annual meeting. While I agree with the sentiment of Hyler's remarks, I disagree with the syntax because it is misleading as to what a sustainable golf course is, what it will look like, and how it will play. The golf course will not be brown; what we are really talking about are different shades of green. The underlying premise for sustainable golf courses is based upon ecological concerns and the associated environmental cost savings; however, the primary drive for sustainable golf course development is the creation of golf courses and a golf experience that better meet the needs of golfing customers—a golfing experience that is reasonably priced, economically viable, and provides golf course owners with a better return on investment.

Sustainable golf courses address the top three barriers to golf participation: cost, difficulty, and time. They require less water, fewer chemicals, and less intensive maintenance. Sustainable golf courses cost less to maintain, are less expensive to operate, and theoretically, lower the cost of playing golf. Sustainable golf courses are more fun for most golfers to play because the average golfer often hits his or her golf ball along the ground, somewhat like most golf courses in the United States were played years before real estate developers started building wall-to-wall green vistas to sell real estate. Lastly, sustainable golf courses are more socially responsible in their use of natural resources, in how that greenscape enhances the quality of life and well-being of a community, as well as what can be done beyond what is expected to preserve nature for future generations.

Given the history of golf course development in the US, as well as golf's historical image as a game for the wealthy, it is understandable the general public does not see golf as environmentally and socially responsible. Back in the 1920s, 80 percent of golf courses were private. Today, 28 percent of golf courses are private, and 80 percent of the rounds played are at public courses. Regardless of the facts, the general public's perception is that golf is a rich man's game, and golf courses selfishly and irresponsibly use limited natural resources.

In today's politically charged environmental movement, the golf industry is not viewed in a favorable light. Golf's elitist image along with its gated communities and oases of lavishly maintained green spaces are far from being politically correct and are rejected by those trying to do their part for the planet. While many in the golf industry believe, with some justification, that golf has been unfairly characterized as an environmental villain and social pariah, it doesn't really matter. Public perception, right or wrong, can be the basis for adverse political action and overreaction.

In my doctoral research on sustainable golf development, I interviewed Greg Norman. He spoke extensively on the role sustainable development must play to ensure the future of the game and the economic vitality of the golf industry. Norman, who chairs the Advisory Council of the Golf Course Superintendents Association of America's Environmental Institute for Golf, said his golf course design philosophy focuses on sustainability in the broadest sense of the concept: "When you talk about golf course sustainability, you are talking about more than just environmental sensitivity.

"These are very important considerations, but it would be a mistake to think that is the end-all of the discussion. Golf courses are often the centerpiece of a residential community, and golf courses have both an environmental and an economic impact. To the first point, the environmental impact needs to be minimized, and to the second, the economic impact needs to be maximized. There are no conflicts of interests here. Golf courses are both an environmental and economic asset. Unfortunately, golf just has not done a very good job of telling its side of the story."

Norman's message should be heard and heeded. Few are listening because most do not know there is a problem. Industry insiders know the number of golfers and golf rounds are down, and golfers may have noticed some golf course closings in their areas or that there are fewer club members or that their dues have increased, but few make the connection to the change in the nature and type of golf courses built (or renovated) in the 1990s and the higher cost of playing golf. In the final analysis, this question must be answered: Can an industry be sustainable if the delivery of its products and services (golf courses) are not sustainable?

Greg Norman and I in his office in Jupiter, Florida, in 1999. Norman chairs the Advisory Council of the Golf Course Superintendents Association of America's Environmental Institute for Golf and is an advocate of sustainable golf course development. *Author's collection.*

In today's business environment, it makes dollars and sense for the golf industry to foster the development of sustainable golf courses. About thirty years ago, the golf industry was in a similar situation. As it did in 1986, when the NGF founded the first Golf Summit, the golf industry needs a new strategic vision to foster the growth of the game and the industry.

21

MEANWHILE

My career in the golf business did not end with the sale of the Ben Hogan Company or when I eventually got fired by the new owner with four years left on my contract. However, the brief time I was unemployed seemed like an eternity. My colleagues in the Young Presidents' Organization (YPO) professional business club advised me to move cautiously and wait for the right opportunity, but I was used to going to work every day. The idea of not having somewhere to go was disconcerting and clouded my judgment. I did what my friends told me not to do. I jumped at the first opportunity, and it was a doozy.

Just by happenstance, I received a call from Carl Paul, who along with his wife and younger brother, Frank, owned Golfsmith, the king of the golf components business. They were becoming one of the largest marketers of golf equipment through their golf stores and catalogues. The elder Paul has this humble, good-ole-boy persona down to a science, but don't let that fool you. He is smart, very smart. There is an old saying in golf: when someone hits a golf ball a long way off the tee but really doesn't appear to be a long hitter (based upon his swing or stature), he is called "sneaky long." Well, Paul is sneaky smart.

The Pauls wanted to cash in on Wall Street's interest in golf and strike while the iron was hot. When I came on board at Golfsmith, I was enamored with the notion of an IPO and had dollar signs in my eyes. I hoped and expected to be the point man on the transaction. Everything went well during the first few months at Golfsmith. However, while the Pauls were very accommodating people, I had some trouble adjusting to their somewhat unique corporate culture. I knew I could help them with their business and improve the design and look of their components. Also, I had a whole filing cabinet of ideas and inventions I thought I could develop via Golfsmith.

What I soon learned was the Pauls knew exactly what they were doing. They really weren't concerned about the look of their products and had their

BEN HOGAN   P.O. Box 11276   Ft. Worth, Texas 76110

November 19, 1992

To Whom It May Concern:

    I started the Ben Hogan Company some 40 years ago
and have had the privilege of working with some wonderful people. Their dedication and desire to improve has
resulted in our producing the finest golf equipment in
the world. Among all of these people there is one individual who now deserves special recognition. He is
David Hueber, formerly the President and CEO of the
Ben Hogan Company.

    David has a rather unique combination of skills;
intelligence and creativity, drive and discipline,
sensitivity and mental toughness. He successfully lead
the Ben Hogan Company through some very trying times.
The previous owner, Cosmo World, had some ambitious
plans which were thwarted by serious financial difficulties in Japan. The new owner, AMF, has announced
its plans to relocate the company to Richmond, Virginia,
and that they will be managing the company themselves.

    David is now available and I believe that any
organization in golf would do well to have him lead
them or have him on their management team. I recommend
him because he has the character, integrity, personality,
and skills to be successful. He performed well here at
Hogan and I know he will achieve the results you desire.

                         Sincerely

                         Ben Hogan

While I never used it, I am very proud of this letter of recommendation that Ben Hogan wrote after the Hogan Company was sold. *Author's collection.*

suppliers in the Far East do the R&D and design work. Their business model was to emulate and then direct-market the most popular golf club models. They were not interested in creating and marketing something new on their own. Interestingly, they were doing a variation of what Goodwin wanted me to do at the Ben Hogan Company. Golfsmith's business model was to copy the popular club designs and harvest the demand that the leading golf equipment companies had already created.

Taking a bit of initiative, I made a preliminary deal for Golfsmith to license a line of PGA-brand components and to make a PGA line of custom-fitted clubs. The idea was that the PGA club pros could assemble and sell golf clubs like my dad had done in the 1930s, or they could have Golfsmith assemble the golf clubs to their specifications. It was a good idea, which I thought might give the club pros an edge in selling golf equipment and enable them to profitably get back into the golf equipment business. I discussed the idea with then PGA CEO Jim Awtrey. He liked it, so I ordered a set of custom clubs for him to try and sent him a proposal via FedEx to confirm the general deal we had discussed. A couple of days later, I received a rebuff from one of the Pauls' chief lieutenants saying they never used FedEx or gave away a set of golf clubs. I tried to explain the merits of the deal and offered to pay the costs for both the shipping and the clubs, but I was rebuffed again with the explanation that this just wasn't the way they did business.

I knew this directive came directly from Carl Paul, since his desk was next to mine, and he certainly overheard my conversation with Awtrey in the "fish bowl," which was the nickname given to the arrangement of the senior executives' desks in an open, newsroom-style work area. Paul didn't want to tell me himself. It was his way of having me blend into their corporate culture. They were doing just fine before I came and would do just fine after I left, if it came to that. So the PGA deal went away.

Later, I tried to explain the power they wielded in their publishing and direct marketing. Each month, they sent out 2.4 million catalogs, which was larger than *Golf Digest* and *Golf* magazine's combined circulation at that time. They also published their own bimonthly trade magazine, the *Clubmaker*, and annually sent out about 350,000 two-inch-thick catalogs to their customer base. I encouraged them to sell advertising space to offset the publishing costs and perhaps even make a profit.

I told Paul their list had great merchandizing and marketing power, and they could add a "comp" list of industry insiders and have a trade magazine with a circulation of 180,000-plus, which would make it the biggest trade book in golf—larger than *Golf Shop Operations* or weekly publications such as *Golfweek* and *Golf World*. They were sitting on a pile of gold in the publishing business that could be an even bigger pile if they chose to enter the fray. The IPO could be the key to the vault, but would the Pauls be willing to unlock the door?

The answer was no. One day, the Golfsmith CFO pulled a chair up in front of Carl Paul's desk. When I had first seen the office layout, I viewed it as a variation of the Japanese style for an executive business office. That didn't bother me then, but it did later as I learned this was how Paul kept his fingers in the pie and managed every aspect of the business. He always knew what was happening from beginning to end. Who could argue with him? He made the company what it is.

My desk was situated between the Paul brothers' desks, so when the Golfsmith CFO sat down in front of Carl Paul, I could not help but hear what he had to say. He told Paul that if they became a public company, they could not operate as they had in the past. Shareholders would always be looking over their shoulders and scrutinizing every decision. They could not do some things as they had in the past because strategic decisions would not be theirs to make without guidance and approval from a board. The accounting for their business would be vastly different, and they might have to change a few things operating as a public company. Personally, I think the CFO was terrified of the accounting requirements for a public company, and he probably gave the Pauls some good advice on a number of matters.

After the CFO left, Carl Paul turned to his brother and said, "You heard what he said, Frank. What do you think?"

Frank said, "I don't know, Carl. . . . What do you think? It sounds like coming to work won't be the same if we go public."

Carl Paul said, "Do you like coming to work every day?"

"Yes, I look forward to coming in every day, and I don't know what I would do if I didn't come in to work; maybe I'd play a little more golf."

While this conversation was going on between the two Golfsmith principals, I felt like I was watching a tennis match between two players who didn't like the rules of the new business game and weren't sure that they wanted to play. I watched the ball as it was hit from Carl to his brother Frank and back to Carl as the volley continued.

"Frank, do you get to play enough golf?"

"Yeah, I get to play all the golf that I care to play. To be honest with you, I enjoy work as much as playing golf."

About this time, Carl Paul delivered the overhead slam and the decisive shot when he said, "Okay. Let's not do it and just keep having fun."

With the IPO no longer in the offing, there was no reason for me to stay at Golfsmith. It was time to move on. In November of 1993, I was at bat once again, this time as part owner and CEO of Accuform Golf, a small Canadian firm that made high-quality golf clubs and bunker rakes. Later, I was recruited by a headhunter to work for Raymond Floyd as president of the Raymond Floyd Group. This foray was the third time I did not heed the advice of my friends in the YPO. I took the money and went from one job to the next. I deluded myself, thinking these were all consulting-type engagements, but in the course of eighteen months I managed to swing three times, striking out each time. Unfortunately for me, some people were still interested in what I was doing after my higher-profile positions at Hogan and Pebble Beach. *Golfweek* magazine published a feature story on my travails in the golf industry just prior to the Orlando PGA Show in January of 1995. They had a United States map with my picture and arrows showing where I had been. They interviewed everyone for whom I had worked. No one said anything nasty; most of it was highly complimentary, but I looked silly.

22

THE AMERICAN SAMURAI'S SECOND LIFE

Fortunately for me, the Japanese came back into my life in March of 1995. Isutani, the principal of Cosmo World, had recovered from his financial woes well enough to consider some new ventures (in addition to his ownership of some forty-plus golf courses and resorts). Notably, Isutani was a major player in the $480 billion Japanese pachinko business, where he made the software for the credit card systems integral to the play of that game. He had about an 80 percent share of that business and also had an interest in one of the major companies that made the hardware for the gaming machines.

Our first US ventures involved importing grasses from the United States for use on Japanese golf courses and getting into the air-purification businesses. In Japan, the 18,000 pachinko parlors were filled with smoke, and Isutani had an air purification system that did an amazing job. I assisted in the development and quickly found myself involved in a variety of other ventures. Most of these assignments were related to the golf business. I oversaw his golf-related interests outside of Japan, which involved developing a golf course in Los Angeles.

The golf course project was very complicated because it was located within the city of Los Angeles where it is difficult to get *any* new development project approved. It was a project that had been previously rejected on many political fronts, ranging from the Gabrielino-Tongva Tribe, who claimed to own the land, to environmentalists wanting to protect nonendangered plants and animals, to the nearby equestrian community homeowners who thought they might lose a place to ride their horses, to the Santa Monica Mountains Conservancy, which kept making offers to buy the property with governmental funds they did not have.

The second go-round on this golf course took almost five years and about

$5 million before we finally obtained the necessary permits to build. At one point it was necessary to sue the city of Los Angeles for $215 million in order to force the city council to fairly consider our conditional-use-permit application. Eventually, we prevailed, but it was a time-consuming and expensive process. Fortunately or unfortunately, depending upon your point of view, the golf course had to be built because so much money had been invested. The project should have been a *Harvard Business Review* case study on how not to do something, but describing it in any depth now would lead to the writing of another book.

Isutani pointed out to me on one occasion in Japan that I was an unlucky person, and I needed to have better luck if I was to become a millionaire as he said I would. At that moment, I could not help but remember the last time I had been to Las Vegas with Isutani. Actually, that particular trip started in Los Angeles, where I arranged limousines for Isutani and his entourage at the LAX terminal. As I waited for Isutani with a Japanese associate, Satoru Suzuki, I saw soldiers coming out of the customs area, escorting Isutani and some other distinguished-looking Japanese gentleman with their baggage in tow. Suzuki started bowing repeatedly; I managed a quick, short bow—reflecting my special *gaijin* status, which translated means foreigner in the same pejorative sense the Spanish call us gringos.

I was about to learn one of Isutani's guests was a gentleman by the name of Mr. Sugayama, who was the equivalent of the Speaker of the House in the Japanese Diet. We were headed to San Diego and then to Las Vegas. The first stop would be La Costa, where we would play golf and hang out in the spa. Then it was off to Las Vegas, where I would learn Isutani was a major player in the world of Japanese politics. In Japan, unlike the United States, they do not discourage an alliance between business and politics. Their notion is what is good for business is good for Japan, and therefore is good politics. Isutani often entertained clients in Las Vegas, and it was not unusual for him to wire transfer about $250,000 to a casino for gambling money to entertain his guests. Typically, the casinos would comp a few suites and rooms for Isutani and his guests due to his high-roller status.

It never failed, though, that at the conclusion of a visit to a casino, we would get into some discussion with the hotel management because Isutani might not have drawn down far enough on his account. Usually, he did not go into the wire transfer advance more than $50,000 or so. And more often than not, he had more than $250,000 in his account when we were ready to leave. Each time this occurred, we would explain that Isutani did provide adequate stakes for his guests to gamble, and that they could check with the casino staff to see if they were gambling.

Unfortunately for the casino, Isutani always seemed to win. His guests lost money, but less than what he won. It was amazing. He seemed to win at every game. Not every night, but over time he always made more than he spent.

Sometimes the hotels then wanted to charge us for the rooms. I remember the MGM Grand hotel and casino once being particularly miffed, and we simply said that was fine, charge us what you want for the rooms, but we would not be coming back. They relented, and the rooms were comped.

One day, while we were waiting to see a stage show, Isutani decided he wanted to play roulette. He handed me $500 in chips out of his pocket and kept $500 for himself. No one wins at roulette, but he did. I watched as he turned that $500 into $3000 in less than fifteen minutes. As for me, I quickly lost $300 and put the remaining $200 in my pocket while he wasn't looking.

I never enjoyed gambling because I did not enjoy the prospect of losing money in games of chance, even if the money was given to me. Perhaps Isutani was testing me, but I knew the odds were on the side of the house, and over time, I would not keep what was in my pocket. Perhaps I was too much of what the Japanese call "a salary man," meaning I was too conservative and not a risk taker. Gambling just doesn't make much sense to me. I don't like the odds. I don't buy lottery tickets because the fifteen-million-to-one odds aren't worth the buck a ticket costs.

One evening we were at the Mirage casino. I had been as visible as I could with Isutani and tried to minimize losing the money he had given me. Once Isutani was out of sight, however, I went elsewhere only to find Isutani in the back of the casino playing blackjack at the $300-minimum table. He was playing two hands, and had about $15,000 or $20,000 in chips in front of him. I watched him play for a while. The waitress had just brought him another Perrier, and he gave her two $25 chips. She came around about every five minutes with refills, and Isutani eventually had to go to the bathroom to pee. He looked at me and said to me in Japanese, "Hueber-san, play for me; I will be back."

About ten to fifteen minutes later, Isutani returned. He looked at his pile of chips, which was not as big as it had been when he left. (I estimate I had lost about $4,000 to $5,000.) He shook his head and smiled. I looked at Isutani and said in English, "You really had a run of bad luck while you were gone."

Isutani smiled and then laughed at my comment. He sat down, put his hand in the middle of the remaining chips on the table, and shoved half over to the place just next to him. He then said in Japanese, "Sit down, Hueber-san, and do as I do." I was about to get a lesson in how to play blackjack. I did everything he did. I bet two hands, just as he did. When it was a question of whether to stay or take another card, I would look to Isutani, and he would give me a nod with the blink of his eye. I started out okay. Eventually, one of the pit managers came around and asked me my name so he could rate me (maybe I'll get a free room next time, I thought).

Then, my luck changed inexplicably—almost as soon as the manager took my name and started rating me. I was following Isutani's advice down to a tee. He kept winning. His pile of chips was almost back to the level of his pre-bathroom break. Meanwhile, my pile was dwindling down to a few thousand dollars or so. Isutani looked at me, shook his head, and with a wry smile he said, "Hueber-san, you are not very lucky. This would be a good time for you to stop and go to bed."

I pushed my remaining chips over to his pile and said, "Isutani-san, I am sorry that I did not play very well."

He replied, *"Mondai nai,"* which means "no problem" in Japanese. I then went to my room at the Mirage and went to bed.

I once asked Isutani why he was so successful. He told me the most important ingredient of success was luck. He was not referring to success in gambling; he meant a winning attitude, when intuition, preparation, and opportunity all come together at the right time.

Isutani is the Donald Trump of Japan but without the panache and desire for personal publicity. He mingles among the business elite and political movers and shakers in Japan, but is content to keep a lower profile. Through my association with Isutani, I've drunk with Japan's Minister of Finance and played golf with the president of NTT (Japan's AT&T) and the CEO of Toshiba, all of whom happened to be Isutani's personal friends. Unfortunately, Isutani will be more remembered for losing $350 million on the sale of Pebble Beach than as the visionary and risk taker he truly was. It is very unusual for Japan, a society that encourages conformism, to produce such a nonconformist.

One afternoon we were sitting in the Las Vegas office of Bill Westerman, the CEO of Riviera Holdings Corporation. They had just published their quarterly financial reports, and Isutani was browsing through them. He was impressed with the company's performance. Isutani turned to one of his lieutenants, Satoru Suzuki, and said something to him in Japanese. Suzuki then asked Westerman if Isutani could buy some of the junk bonds, since it seemed like a good investment, given the company's performance.

Westerman then said, "That depends. . . . How much does he want to buy?"

The two Japanese conferred again, and Suzuki replied, "Mr. Isutani would like to buy all of them."

The deal never happened because Isutani would have been required to go through licensure to make such a substantial investment. However, it does illustrate how Isutani thinks. From his standpoint, his cost of capital was much lower than the yield on the bonds. It simply made business dollars and sense.

Pebble Beach
Isutani (Cosmo World) sold the Pebble Beach Company for $500 million to the Lone Cypress Company, a Japanese joint venture of the Taiheiyo Club and Sumitomo Credit Service Company. Considering his costs associated with the original acquisition, Isutani lost about $350 million on the transaction. It took nearly twelve years, but Isutani finally made it out from under the $350 million yoke of the Pebble Beach sale. He was forced to sell a number

of business interests, including the Ben Hogan Company and more recently the Four Seasons Hualālai on the Big Island of Hawaii. (Michael Dell, founder, chairman, and CEO of Dell Computer Corporation, is the new owner of Hualālai.) Hualālai actually rivaled Pebble Beach in terms of the total amount invested. It is one of the finest resorts in the world, and I will dearly miss going there two or three times a year as Cosmo World's ownership representative to participate in the Executive Committee (partnership) Board meetings.

The new owner of Pebble Beach, Lone Cypress, held the company for about seven years and invested an estimated $120 million into improvements for properties that included four golf courses (Pebble Beach, Spyglass, Spanish Bay, and Del Monte); two hotels (the Inn at Spanish Bay and the Lodge at Pebble Beach); the new boutique inn, Casa Palmero, with a full-service spa; and the scenic 17-Mile Drive. In August of 1999, Lone Cypress sold Pebble Beach for $820 million to a high-profile American investor group that included such luminaries as Arnold Palmer, Clint Eastwood, Peter Ueberroth, and Richard Ferris (chairman of the PGA Tour Policy Board and former CEO of United Airlines) as principal investors, contributing some $400 million. Bank of America loaned nearly a half billion for the deal.

It is interesting that they raised a good portion of the money by selling shares to an undisclosed number of investors at $2 million each, which is not too far from the original concept I proposed to Isutani. My approach would have been more broad brush, because I did not then have the same array of friends and prospective investors on my Rolodex as Peter Ueberroth, Richard Ferris, and their group.

Pebble Beach is now back in American hands, and it is likely it will stay there, because, as Peter Ueberroth surmised, the limited partners all have an appreciation and understanding of the intrinsic value of the property gleaned from actually playing golf and staying there. "The other thing is the financial ability to take this investment and sink it somewhere in their estate for the next generation," Ueberroth said. "Father to son or daughter, the units will be passed on; thus, the core of owners will exist in perpetuity."

A noteworthy change since I was there almost ten years earlier was the increase in the greens fee at Pebble Beach from $200 to $425 for hotel guests and $225 to $450 for those not staying at the Inn or the Lodge. Considering that Isutani paid less for Pebble Beach than the new owners, it is quite evident the new owners really do have a better understanding and appreciation of the intrinsic value of Pebble Beach.

The bulk of Isutani's assets remained in golf course properties in Japan, as well as in his interests in the pachinko industry. He also has substantial interests in a few golf equipment companies and opened a new Nicklaus Design golf course in Los Angeles called Angeles National Golf Club.

Now that Isutani is well past age seventy, he is at that point in life when he is consolidating interests. He is one of those people who will never retire,

Minoru Isutani (far left), me (center), and Minoru's brother, Shigeru Isutani (far right) before a round a golf at Lakelands Golf Club in Merrimac on Australia's Gold Coast. *Author's collection.*

however. He is active in Japanese politics and wields considerable political influence behind the scenes. One of his most treasured items in his Tokyo office is a picture of himself and President Reagan, which is a reminder of better times for him and the Japanese when he owned the Ben Hogan Company and Pebble Beach.

I was involved in the development and disposition of a number of golf courses ranging from a $250 million project in Australia named Hope Island, to the nearly $1 billion investment in the Four Seasons Hualālai, to golf projects in Western Europe such as Paris International. These projects took me all over the world. In 1999 and 2000, I made seven trips to Australia, sometimes staying for a month or two. I traveled to Hawaii and Japan at least three or four

Teeing off on that first hole at Lakelands, I am pretty sure I nailed that shot straight down the middle, but then again, maybe I didn't. *Author's collection.*

times a year for more than ten years. I was in LA at least a week each month, with an occasional trip to Western Europe—lots of frequent-flyer miles and too much jet lag.

Isutani's interests in a few golf companies included two graphite-shaft businesses, Graphite Design and United Sports Technologies (UST), both of which are now public companies on the Japanese stock exchange. UST is a subsidiary of Mamiya-OP Ltd., which once owned Fin-Nor, a saltwater fishing tackle company. I eventually learned a little about that business as a company director and discovered it is even more challenging than the golf-equipment business.

23

THE BACK NINE

In November of 1999, Isutani funded the development of Imagine Golf Company, which introduced the first patented, hybrid woods that I invented called the Middleclubs. These clubs replaced the long and middle irons and eventually created the new $150 million hybrid club product category. We introduced the product with an infomercial featuring famed former Redskins Super Bowl quarterback and sports commentator Joe Theismann and my former high school golf adversary, five-time PGA Tour winner and ESPN golf commentator Bill Kratzert.

This direct-marketing approach did well, but the infomercial only ran for three months because it was necessary to divert funding from advertising in order to take care of some critical expenses related to the development of Angeles National Golf Club. When the funds became available again sometime later, it was too late. I thought we had lost our sales momentum, and my Japanese partners lost their appetite for both print and television infomercial advertising.

***

My forays into the golf equipment business have had mixed results. By the time I finally received the utility patent for the Middleclub in April of 2004, a former employee had teamed up with a Canadian investor and Peter Kessler, formerly of Golf Channel fame, to knock off the idea with a product called the Perfect Club. I was wrong about losing sales momentum on my clubs, because the infomercial about my copied invention was very successful. They made a lot of money. I was also wrong in thinking that my patent-pending status provided the protection I needed to pursue litigation. What I learned from this experience is that it is important to challenge any patent infringement while the patent is pending. At the time, I was having problems with the patent examiner and didn't want those challenges aired. And as it turned

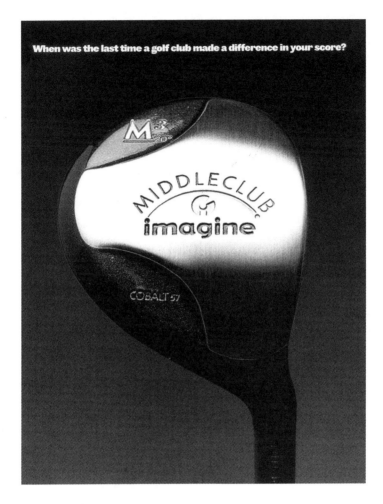

The print advertisement for the patented hybrid woods, the Middleclubs, appeared in *Golf Digest*, *Golf*, *Golfweek*, and *Golfworld*, as well as the *Wall Street Journal*. The television infomercials featuring Joe Theismann and Bill Kratzert ran on the Golf Channel and in select markets after PGA Tour telecasts. They may be viewed at www.mindseyegolf.com. *Courtesty of Mind's Eye Golf Company.*

out, my claims in the patent application were too narrowly defined. Someone could create a club or clubs with specifications just outside those specified for the Middleclub. They could vary the loft and weight of the clubhead or change the length of the club in order to avoid violating the patent.

With respect to the Perfect Club, they made those minor changes to circumvent the patent issues. And since my former employee knew all of my suppliers and because they had no development costs, they were able to quickly turn a profit. I could have pursued litigation for "misappropriation of business values," but by the time I figured this out, they were winding down the business. If I sued and prevailed, there wouldn't be much left to get—maybe some old clubs in inventory, but not worth the effort.

Tom Stites (Hogan's former director of R&D when I was running the company) later started his own business venture, Impact Golf Technologies. He did the engineering and patent work for the Middleclub. When I presented the idea to Nike, he was part of the formal business proposal. Later, Stites became the head of R&D for Nike. They liked the Middleclub so well after we presented it to them in 1999 that they introduced their version, called the Nike CPR, in 2003. Once again, I could have pursued litigation with Nike. Bob Wood, the general manager of Nike Golf, invited me to sue them if I believed that one visit to Nike headquarters in Beaverton, Oregon, and disclosure of my idea warranted it.

At this point, there were other companies also selling hybrids, so the prospect of litigation with Nike was too risky and costly. It didn't make sense to pursue this or any other litigation. The satisfaction I enjoy is not measured in financial terms. Every time I see a pro on television chipping from the edge of the green, or hitting a hybrid instead of a long iron, I feel vindicated. Even more, I feel a great sense of satisfaction in knowing I helped many golfers play better and enjoy the game. Over the past few years, I have accumulated twelve patents and have a few more pending. That is the fun part of the golf business, but the business lesson I learned had to be relearned again and again. Building a better mousetrap will not result in the world beating a path to your door, and marketing that mousetrap will prove to be a bigger challenge.

Unfortunately, what I did not realize at the time was that the Japanese did not like using infomercials to develop a golf company. In Japan, only junky products are marketed in this fashion, which is the way it used to be in the United States. Only sometime later did I learn this was the reason they decided not to fund the marketing of a putter company they had previously asked me to develop.

The putter concept was revolutionary in that it addressed every golfer's misalignment of the putterface at address because of the golfer's eye dominance. At the time, I was told they wanted to pursue a revolutionary golf-shaft concept instead. Instead of saying no directly, the Japanese always offer an alternative. After working with the Japanese for so many years, it should not have taken me so long to understand this.

I continue to do what I enjoy. For twenty years, my wife and I have owned and operated a business, Sabertooth Golf Company, which sells a patented line of bunker rakes to golf courses across the country.

In 2005, I acquired my Japanese partners' interest in Imagine Golf and

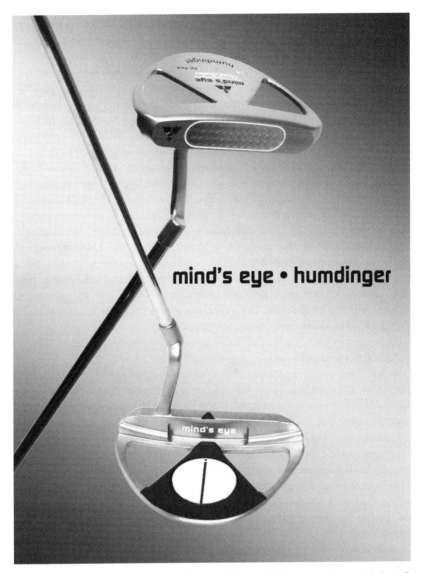

The patented Mind's Eye line of putters feature a line angled about one degree to help golfers compensate for their eye dominance when lining up putts. Right-handed golfers who are right-eye dominant aim their putters to the right, while those who are left-eye dominant aim to the left. Five models were developed (plus three left-handed versions), all named after highways in California. Visit www.mindseyegolf.com for more information. *Courtesy of Mind's Eye Golf Company.*

started a new company to market a line of golf clubs under the brand Mind's Eye. This time, I had the patents in hand before I went forward with the marketing. In September of 2005, I received a utility patent for the line of putters which compensate for a person's eye dominance. Next, I had hoped to remarket the Middleclubs as Mind's Eye hybrids with an alignment feature and follow this with fairway woods, drivers, and wedges. I wanted to be in the loose-club business just like TaylorMade founder Gary Adams. Unfortunately, I was unable to secure the funding to launch that enterprise. Golf is no longer the darling of Wall Street, and investors are very cautious about startups.

The golf equipment business continues to change and evolve. It now looks like the day will someday come when online purchases of golf equipment could eclipse off-course sales (like Dick's and Golf Galaxy). The business is changing. No one really knows what's in the offing. My guess is off-course stores will be fully integrated with online operations. It might be something like an Apple store, where customers who want to see and touch the products can take a closer look. And, if the price is close to the online price, customers may be willing to pay a slight premium for the convenience and satisfaction of an immediate purchase. But, as it is with any large purchase, price often dictates the buying decision. The successful companies that recognize these changes today will be the leading companies tomorrow.

Catching My Second Wind

Cosmo World paid me well, and I still have some partnership interests with them, but since leaving them, I am doing more on my own. I was Isutani's point man, but by the summer of 2007, I realized it was time to move on. Much of what I was doing related to the disposition or consolidation of his assets outside of Japan.

I knew I didn't want to retire; I enjoyed what I did too much to quit. I had friends, both younger and older, who had retired. Some seemed to handle it well; others seemed lost. They began to atrophy intellectually, emotionally, and physically. Knowing how lost I might also be, I decided I needed to do something else. At this point in life, I didn't want to play golf every day. There's nothing wrong in retiring and playing golf, especially if you didn't get to play as much as you wanted when you were working full time. But that wasn't me. I played as often as I wanted, and I knew if all I was doing was playing golf, it wouldn't be long before I defined myself in terms of my golf score.

Everyone gets a second chance if they work for it. In my case, I feel like a runner in the middle of a race who has caught his second wind. I decided to go back to school and earn a doctorate. What I wanted to do was teach, write, and do some consulting work. I really wasn't concerned about how much money I might earn. I wanted to be the type of teacher that I most admired and appreciated in both undergraduate and graduate school—the professors who shared both their personal and professional experiences in their teaching. They were all good storytellers but with a purpose. That's what I wanted to do.

Though I didn't know how to go about it, I knew where I wanted to go: Clemson University, a top-twenty public university and one of the most beautiful campuses in the country. I had to take the GMAT and GRE tests a couple of times. It was difficult, and my skills in advanced mathematics had deteriorated. I would later learn I had ADD (attention deficit disorder). The prescribed medication really helped, and I was able to survive the required doctoral statistics courses and SAS (Statistical Analysis System) programming classes needed for my dissertation research.

Earning my doctorate at Clemson University was a wonderful and rewarding experience. You have probably heard the expression, "the journey is the destination," which was very much the case for me. It was much harder than I expected it would be, but I have a tendency to underestimate challenges. I lectured in the business school on strategic planning, entrepreneurship, sports marketing, and real estate and resort development. Eventually, I became a good teacher, but it was a steep learning curve.

In August of 2012, I received my PhD from Clemson University. My dissertation focused on sustainable golf course development and management. No one ever wants to hear about someone's doctoral research, but the subject matter was relevant both to my lifelong interest in golf and to my new academic and professional quest. The gist of my dissertation, "The Changing Face of the Game and Golf's Built Environment," is that golf courses built or renovated in the United States during the 1990s boom period were more costly, longer, more difficult, and take longer to play than golf courses built during the other two golf course booms in the 1920s and 1960s. This research proves there has been a paradigm shift in golf's built environment and also offers some insight as to what the golf industry needs to do in order to grow the game (foster sustainable golf course development and management).

Regrets and Lessons Learned

If I had it all to do over again, I would do many things differently, but I still would have left the secure environment of the PGA Tour to rejuvenate and resurrect the National Golf Foundation back in 1984; it needed to be done in order to get the golf industry back on track. What was accomplished at the PGA Tour and the NGF led to Beman's recommendation of me for the Hogan Company job. It was the chance of a lifetime to run a prominent golf equipment company and to work with the legendary Ben Hogan. It also introduced me to the Japanese and Pebble Beach, which was another extraordinary professional opportunity.

Every business has its ups and downs, and while I would like to take credit for the ups, I must also take some responsibility for the downs. I do have some regrets in that regard. There are no good guys or bad guys in business. No one ever deliberately messes things up. When things go badly, there are many villains and many to blame. When things go well, everyone is a hero, and everyone wants to take the credit. The rise and fall of the Ben Hogan Company has many unsung heroes and many maligned villains. Sometimes they are the same people.

For my part, I should have held my ground with both Isutani and Goodwin. I should have resisted lending the $3 million in Hogan Company funds to Cosmo World for option rights on property at Hualālai. This one decision led to a series of draconian management decisions that accelerated financial problems at the Ben Hogan Company. The Hogan Company probably would have been sold anyway, but the company's circumstances might have been different.

The continuing challenges of accommodating the wishes of Cosmo World's ownership under such financial duress were formidable, and I take responsibility for the accommodations that were greatly detrimental to the Hogan Company's financial well-being. The cultural divide between the Americans and the Japanese was often irreconcilable. We could not operate our business in the United States as they needed it to be operated in Japan.

Isutani viewed the Ben Hogan Company as one piece in a much larger puzzle. I kept trying to morph my piece to fit into the Japanese picture, but I just couldn't seem to make it fit. Isutani was creating a consortium of related international golf interests that he hoped would fit together and have some synergism. The problem was that the pieces only fit together in Isutani's mind. We spoke different languages in more ways than can be deciphered culturally.

Isutani made mistakes as well. We are all ethnocentric to some extent. What works in the United States certainly ought to work in Japan and vice versa, right? I am convinced cultural differences could have been mitigated to some extent, with some time and money. However, in the end, we had neither. The Japanese are honorable people. Their culture is wonderful, but they seem to see us as an inferior breed, irreparably tainted by our mix of cultures, races, and ethnicities.

When these two cultures come together, it is like oil and water; we can occupy the same space or vessel, but neither seems to mix very well with the other. The answer is not to force the blending of the two cultures; rather, it is to let the two coexist, recognizing the differences of each. We did not have enough time at the Hogan Company. I honestly believe that if the financial situation and circumstances had been different, Isutani would have made the needed adjustments to allow the Ben Hogan Company to be successful on both sides of the Pacific.

With respect to Goodwin, I have already said about as much as I need to say. Goodwin is a player in the business world. And, like any player, you win some, and you lose some. By his own admission, he lost quite a bit while he owned the Ben Hogan Company. It was a costly lesson. Sometimes, when someone has enjoyed great success in one area, they think they are infallible and can do no wrong. It is quite evident, with respect to the Hogan Company, that business skills in one field are not necessarily transferable to another. He had already made up his mind on what was right and wrong about the Hogan Company and what needed to be done. Fortunately, he was able to take that financial blow and not go down for the count.

It turns out that he is a very generous person. When he later sold AMF Bowling, he gifted a substantial amount of the profit to many of his long-term associates and employees. Goodwin made a $13 million dollar grant to the Darden School of Business at the University of Virginia and made significant contributions to Virginia Tech, as well as to many charities. He purchased the Kiawah Island Golf Resort, where the Ryder Cup and the PGA Championship were played, and later purchased the (Hilton Head) Sea Pines Resort where the PGA Tour Heritage Classic, now the Verizon Heritage, is played at the Harbour Town Golf Links.

***

From the age of fourteen I've never had a time when I didn't have a job. Once I was out of the shadows and on my own, I jumped at the first opportunity. Like most men, my self-image was tied too closely to my work. I felt I had to do something and could not let a month go by without having a job, something to do. I should have been more patient and judicious. It was not money that motivated me. I had enough money. I just did not know how to bide my time. The work I have done since Hogan and Pebble Beach has been interesting and rewarding, but hustling for consulting work and job hopping didn't help my career prospects as a golf-company chief executive. Luckily, the Japanese came back into my life. If they had not, I would have probably continued to pursue entrepreneurial interests.

I will continue inventing products, which, along with writing, is almost as fun for me as playing golf. Perhaps I will find a golf company willing to license some revolutionary golf products like a driver with a shaft enabling average golfers (not the pros) to hit the ball ten to fifteen yards farther than they are able to now. Failing that, I may continue my quest to develop a golf equipment company.

Unfortunately, after numerous overtures to the CEOs of Callaway to acquire the Ben Hogan Company, I missed out on licensing that brand. They sold the Ben Hogan brand to Perry Ellis International, an apparel company. Perry Ellis then licensed the brand for golf equipment sales to a group headed by Terry Koehler, who was once director of marketing for the Hogan Company when Bill Goodwin owned it. Koehler is an excellent club designer and has done a great job in bringing back the Ben Hogan Company

If I want to continue working in the game and business that I love, it's now time for me to take advantage of that experience to create my own opportunities. I have a few irons I am stoking in the fire; something good will happen.

My friend Kay Slayden, whom I greatly admire and for whom I worked at the PGA Tour, retired twice from being the CEO of two major corporations. He seemed to be handling his second retirement well, so I asked him how he was doing. Slayden's response was his usual insightful and colorful quip. He said, "It's okay. The older I get, the better my golf game used to be. But, then again, every time I play, I remember those glory days less . . . and my golf game doesn't reflect how good I used to be. Also, I seem to be spending an inordinate amount of time at ACE Hardware."

I owe a great deal of whatever success I have had to Deane Beman, Ben Hogan, and Minoru Isutani. They all believed in me; they inspired and encouraged me by their examples and provided great opportunities. What I have learned from those experiences is that in the end, you create your own opportunities.

HOGAN'S SECRET

Hogan told me the Secret on three occasions, and it was different each time. The first time was one summer evening in 1990 when I was out at Shady Oaks hitting balls on the range. I was a struggling scratch player, but I enjoyed practicing. My continuing golf malady was that I hit the golf ball too high. It is a result of my tendency to keep my weight on the right side during the swing, which adds loft to the clubface as my wrists supinate at impact. I developed this swing motion overcompensating for a low hook I learned to hit as a high schooler while working at the Golf-O-Mat indoor golf facility. And because I grew up in the Nicklaus era, I also emulated his golf swing.

As I was hitting balls on the practice range, I looked over and noticed Hogan walking briskly toward me. He did not look happy. My first thoughts were: *Oh boy, I am really in for it now. I don't know what I did, but I do not like the body language I am seeing.* I stopped swinging as Hogan walked the last thirty yards or so over to me. I turned to face him and asked, "Is everything okay, Mr. Hogan?"

And he responded, "No, it is not. I was watching you, and I just couldn't stand it any longer. Are you chopping wood or trying to hit a golf ball?" By this time, I could tell Hogan had already enjoyed a drink or two, but I was relieved to know his displeasure was not with my job but with my golf swing. He looked me straight in the eye and then asked me, "What are you working on? What are you trying to accomplish?"

"I am working on what I am always trying to fix. I hit the ball too high and can't control the trajectory."

"So why are you practicing your faults?"

"I guess that I just don't know how to fix it."

Hogan then cleared his throat—it may have been an expression of his dismay—and said, "I'll tell you what you need to fix, but you are going to have to figure out how to do it. But before I tell you, you must not tell anyone what I told you."

"Okay."

"First of all, you are hitting balls in a left-to-right wind. Never do that. Hitting into the wind is best," said Hogan. "A right-to-left wind is okay, but a left-to-right wind will wreck your swing. When I practiced, I avoided the wind when I could; when I couldn't, I never hit balls in a left-to-right wind."

"Will that fix my problem?"

"No, not at all," Hogan said. "But the wind will make it worse. If you are going to practice, you need a plan. You need to know what you are trying to accomplish. Don't mindlessly hit balls like a robot."

Hogan then had me address the ball and told me to make a backswing and to stop my swing at the top. As I did so, he said, "Look here, you are out of balance at the top of your swing, and the left-to-right wind only makes it worse. At the top of your swing, your weight is on your toes. You lean into the ball on your downswing and then pull away. Your swing is too upright and steep for your body type, but that will fix itself automatically if you maintain your balance at the top of your swing, round out your shoulder turn, and flatten your swing plane.

"Now, if you want to control your trajectory and hit it lower, you need to decrease the loft of the club as you impact the ball. Decreasing the loft of the club as you impact the ball is the Secret, but you are going to need to figure out what you and only you need to do on your way back to the ball in order to be in that position to strike the ball. Do you understand?"

"Yes," I said, and thanked him. But I really didn't understand the avalanche of advice I had just been given.

***

Sometime later, in the early winter of 1990, Hogan said he wanted Herbert Warren Wind, the legendary sports journalist, to write the long-promised book, a sequel to *Ben Hogan's Five Lessons: The Modern Fundamentals of Golf*. But every time I tried to follow up on this notion, Hogan hedged and said he really was not ready just yet. *Five Lessons* is a classic and still ranks as one of the all-time best-selling golf instructional books. Mr. Wind was retired, and Hogan didn't feel he could improve upon *Five Lessons*, so this idea of writing a book languished as something he would like to do—someday.

Then, in the spring of 1991, Hogan told me he was ready to reveal the Secret to the world of golf, but he had changed his mind about a book and wanted to reveal the Secret in a magazine article instead. When I went into Hogan's office for our regular coffee visit on that morning, he asked me which golf magazine had the biggest circulation. I told him *Golf Digest* had the largest circulation, somewhere in the neighborhood of 1.5 million readers. He said he would reveal the Secret once and for all. I said, "That's great! What do you want me to do?"

Ignoring my response, he proclaimed, "I am going to call the story 'The Keys to the Vault' because that is just what it will mean to those who understand the Secret and apply the principles. It will be as if someone gave them the keys to the bank vault."

I left his office, walked across the shared common area between our offices, and called Jerry Tarde, *Golf Digest*'s editor-in-chief. I related what Hogan had just told me. I do not know who was more excited. *Golf Digest* would have the biggest scoop and cover story of the past fifty years, a blockbuster they could legitimately title "Ben Hogan Reveals his Secret: The Keys to the Vault." I was equally excited because this would be an extraordinary promotional opportunity. We were a hot company at the time with the top-selling Hogan Edge irons. We were the title sponsors of the thirty-event Ben Hogan Tour, which was professional golf's version of triple-A ball (later it would become the Nike, the Buy.Com, the Nationwide, and now the Web.com Tour). The Hogan Company also had the premier professional tour staff in golf with all-time-leading PGA Tour money winner Tom Kite, as well as Davis Love III, Lanny Wadkins, David Frost, Steve Pate, Doug Tewell, Chip Beck, Don January, Tom Byrum, Mark Brooks, etc., all playing for the company namesake, the legendary Ben Hogan. So in my mind, this article had the potential of catapulting the Ben Hogan Company into the top echelon of golf equipment companies.

Tarde and I worked out the details of the deal. It would be a major cover story, requiring one or two issues, depending upon the extent of material from Hogan. The Ben Hogan Company would buy three full-page ads, and get at least two more for no charge. Tarde intended to write the article himself. I invited him to be my guest at the Shady Oaks Country Club member-guest event; Tarde would work on the story during that time.

About a month before the member-guest at Shady Oaks, I was once again in Hogan's office having a cup of coffee. I could tell something was on Hogan's mind. He seemed distracted and distant from our conversation. Then, he finally asked me, "What are we getting from *Golf Digest* for the story?"

I enthusiastically said it would be a cover story, possibly taking two issues to tell, which would really be great for our business!

He then said abruptly, "What are they paying us?"

Based upon the tone of his question, I knew better than to say more than the facts, so I simply said, "Other than the great promotion for the company, we are getting a couple of free pages of advertising."

"How much is a page of advertising in *Golf Digest*?"

"About seventy-five thousand," I replied.

Hogan then said, "Okay, then you can have them send me a check for $150,000. After all, it's *my* Secret." *Life* magazine had paid him $10,000 for the Secret in 1954, so in current dollars, that probably was not out of line. Still, I tried to get him to reconsider and even considered having the Ben Hogan Company pay the fee if *Golf Digest* wouldn't pony up. I then called Tarde and explained the situation.

After he overcame the initial shock of Hogan's fee requirement, he respectfully declined, stating that would nearly exhaust his entire editorial budget for the year. I knew Hogan would not want us to pay the fee out of our company coffers, so the "Keys to the Vault" were never given to the golf world.

***

The second time Hogan told me the Secret was in October of 1991, a few months after the canceled deal with *Golf Digest*. I was once again having a cup of coffee with him in his office. We were talking about a variety of things. I remember mentioning to him that his signature on a piece of white paper was then worth about $600.

He looked at me in utter amazement and said, "Six hundred dollars . . . did you say six hundred?" I nodded and he continued. "Well," he said, and cleared his throat, "Well . . . I'll tell you what, David. Let's quit selling golf clubs,"—laughing—"and go into the autograph business."

From there we spoke about the company business. He was not happy with our apparel line because at the time it was not as high a quality as it should have been. Anyway, Hogan was still in a pretty good mood and said something to me that he never said to me before or after that day. He asked me about my golf game. He wondered if I was able to do what he told me that evening on the practice range at Shady Oaks. After overcoming my initial shock, I had to admit that I had not had much success, although I did try my best to do it when I had a chance to practice.

"Mr. Hogan," I said, "I have done everything I could to keep the ball down [hit it lower and control the ball flight trajectory]. I have tried to decrease the loft of the club at impact, like you said, but I don't seem to know how to do it. I've tried to hit low wedges—just to get the feeling. Sometimes it works, but often I just hit it higher."

Hogan looked at me with some chagrin and genuine disappointment. After an uncomfortable moment of silence and contemplation, he finally said, "David, you are a good enough player, you really should have been able to figure it out by now—you need to dig it out of the dirt yourself. I told you everything that you needed to know. I would prefer not to explain it in my way of understanding it, because you need to understand it in yours.

"Now, stand up," he ordered. "Take this club." He handed me a seven iron from a prototype set leaning against the wall, "and show me where you are at the top of the swing." I took off my suit jacket, moved to the right of his desk where there was a little more room and no furniture, gripped the club, and assumed my position at the top of my swing. He looked at me, then took my hands gripping the club and pushed them lower saying, "Remember, I told you that your swing was too upright for your build, and it is easier to tuck in that elbow"—he pushed my flying right elbow down with his hand—"if your swing isn't so damn upright. Now, stick your butt out a little more and get into a more athletic position. Now from here, how do you start your downswing?"

I looked up to him. He was now facing me, and I responded by trying to remember what he said in his book, *Five Lessons*, as I said, "What I am trying to do is start my downswing with a forward movement and the unwinding of my hips toward the target."

Hogan then said, "That's almost right, but you arch your back instead of turning your hips. The golf swing is more like the steering wheel of a car. It goes around a center. If you do it right, you can swing the club as hard as you want. However, you need to be in better balance at the top of your swing, and I want you to cup your wrist more at top. Your left wrist is too flat. You can't get from the top to the bottom of your swing if your hands aren't in the proper position at the top.

"Most importantly, you must keep that right leg bent as you turn on your backswing, and set the club at top. This will keep you from sliding too much. Now, this is the most important part for you:" He now moved to my side with one hand on my right hip and the other on my right elbow. "The hips initiate the *slightly* lateral move of the downswing. See how that move puts your club and arms on plane?

"The turning of the hips is the pivotal element in the chain reaction. Starting them first and moving them correctly puts the downswing in the proper sequence. The key to making this all work for you is to turn your hips and shoulders as much as you can while being braced against your right knee. From this position, you can now clear your left side as you drive and rotate the right hip as fast as you can—the arms and hands will follow, catch up, and the club will accelerate ahead. You can't stop it. You can swing as hard as you want and you won't hit the ball so high if you do it right.

"Now remember this, even before you are at the top of your swing, you need to understand that the swing never stops; it may slow as you change directions, but there is no pause. You pause at the top, which is okay, but it is hard to time and to be consistent. Your hips then unwind before you reach the top of your swing, before the backswing is finished. Once again, be sure to keep your right knee pointed at the ball, and then push and pivot from that right knee. It will release and uncoil the power you have wound up. If you do this, you will be in the right position to hit the ball as hard as you want. Your clubface will be in the proper position at impact. You won't hit it too high, and you will be able to better control your trajectory."

At this point, I was pretty sure I had just been given the Holy Grail, so I said, "Thank you, Mr. Hogan. I will work on it."

***

The third and last time that Hogan told me the Secret was in the grillroom at Shady Oaks in November of 1992. We were commiserating on the plight of the Ben Hogan Company. The vodka was clear, and so was his explanation.

This is the rest of what he said: "David, the Secret is inside you. You just need to figure it out for yourself. There are certain principles that everyone must apply if they want to hit the golf ball properly, but ultimately you have to learn how to make it work for you. You gotta dig it out of the dirt for yourself, and then it's yours forever."

After he said that, I remembered that he had told Faldo something similar just a couple of weeks earlier.

***

A couple of years later, in January 1994, I ran into Jody Vasquez, an old friend from Fort Worth, at the PGA Show in Orlando. He was with Faldo when Faldo and his manager visited Hogan on that cold November day in 1992. We had gone our separate ways after the sale of the Ben Hogan Company, and I had moved back to Ponte Vedra Beach, Florida. We decided to play a round of golf before the PGA Show began, and we reminisced about Hogan. We both had been told the Secret by Mr. Hogan, and both of us had been sworn to secrecy, or our status as "Hoganites" would be forever revoked. Still, we both talked about the Secret without really admitting it to each other.

Later, Vasquez wrote a book titled *Afternoons with Mr. Hogan*, which described his experiences as a teenager shagging balls for Hogan. In that book, he related a detailed analysis of the Secret as told to him by Hogan when he was retrieving balls—a job that wasn't very difficult because Hogan rarely hit a wayward shot. As told to a seventeen-year-old, Hogan's revelation of his Secret was probably a little less technical than what Vasquez had learned over time and then revealed some thirty-five years later; however, his description closely mirrored what I understood the Secret to be when I was in Hogan's office back in October of 1991. Vasquez's technical description of the Secret was the clearest, most intuitive version I have ever read. After reading it, I actually better understood what Hogan was trying to tell me in his office.

The gist of what Vasquez had to say was that the Secret is the correct functioning of the right leg, with emphasis on maintaining the angle of the right knee on the back and forward swings. Combined with a slight cupping of the left wrist, it produces optimum balance and control, and allows you to apply as much speed and power as you wish. Vasquez was able to say it more succinctly than I could. In his book, he went into some detail and explained what I believe are the technical principles of the Secret. Vasquez's understanding reflects his own experimentation over the years and how he learned the principles.

Golf Digest published an article on the Secret in its March 1994 issue called "Ben Hogan's Secret." The author, Guy Yocom, identified the key swing changes that Hogan made, which were based primarily upon the 1955 *Life* magazine article, "Ben Hogan Tells His Secret," as well as on Hogan's 1957 book, *Five Lessons*. Yocom described Hogan's Secret as "a play in three acts." The three steps were as follows:

"Step 1: Weaken left hand grip" by putting left thumb on top of the grip, which correspondingly moves the right hand into a more passive position;

"Step 2: Fan the clubface open" by pronating the hands and forearms on the backswing so far that it is difficult to close the clubface on the downswing; and,

"Step 3: Cup left wrist at the top." Hogan's flat wrist angle at the top of the backswing fostered a lower shot trajectory and avoided the dreaded hook. With the cupped wrist position at the top of swing, it enabled Hogan to better control the trajectory of the ball, to hit it higher and to fade the ball.

Yocom then said that in executing these three swing cues, Hogan was able to get rid of the hook because he could supinate his wrists and keep his hands ahead of the golf ball at impact. In doing so, Hogan decreased the effective loft of the club and kept the clubface square through impact. The end result was conceptually similar to what Hogan had told me when he first told me to decrease the loft of the clubface at impact—what I needed to do in order to hit the ball lower. I just didn't know how to do it. How does one get from the cupped-wrist position at the top of the backswing to the supinated wrist position at impact? Perhaps someone with Hogan's talent and swing could do it, but this idea was still conceptually illusive and without any practical application for most mortals.

Notably, Yocom quoted Hogan in the article as saying, "I never called it a Secret. The magazine people called it that for the article. It was a modification I made in my swing, that's all, and it worked like a charm." Still, with the publication of Yocom's article, there was once again renewed speculation about what the Secret really was. Current and former PGA Tour players were quoted in the media. Claude Harmon was once quoted after the Secret was revealed in 1954 as saying, "The left hip leads," which seemed to be a succinct and accurate technical description. Sam Snead always doubted there ever was a Secret. He was suspicious of Hogan's ploys and groused something along the lines of anyone can claim to know a secret, especially if he won't tell anyone what it is.

Leading golf magazines and famous teachers weighed in. However, I believe that the one person who probably understood Hogan better than anyone else and said it best was Ken Venturi—one of Hogan's most devoted disciples (down to the detail of wearing the Hogan-style cap). Venturi simply said, "the Secret is somewhere between your ears."

Al Barkow, a noted golf writer and a good player in his own right, shared

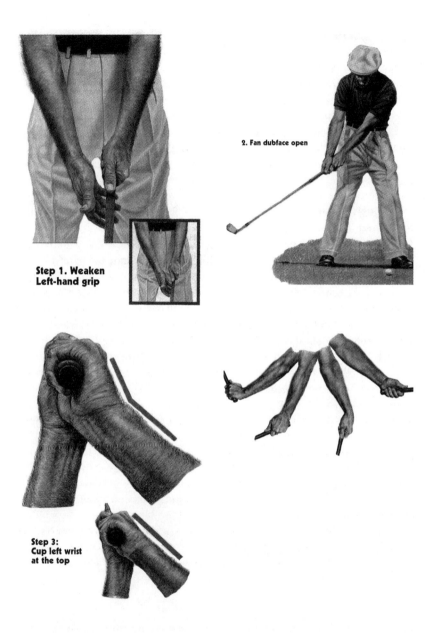

Step 1. Weaken Left-hand grip

2. Fan dubface open

Step 3: Cup left wrist at the top

The steps of "Ben Hogan's Secret," as published in *Golf Digest* magazine. The artwork is by Paul Lipp. *Copyright* Golf Digest *1994, reprinted with permission.*

what he said Hogan told him was the Secret in a 2009 issue of his newsletter. Barkow had been asked by the PGA Tour to interview Ben Hogan, Commissioner Beman, and me (when I was the Hogan Company president) for some video footage to promote the Ben Hogan Tour. The location, Shady Oaks Country Club, was a comfortable setting for Hogan.

After the interviews, Barkow said he had lunch with Hogan at the club and took advantage of that opportunity to ask him what the Secret was, and Hogan said he would tell him later.

Barkow described it as follows: "Some time passes, lunch is over, and Hogan and I are walking down the hallway at his hangout club, Shady Oaks. I still hadn't gotten the Secret and asked him when it was coming. At that he steered me through the swinging doors of the kitchen, saying he didn't want anyone else to hear. Fine.

"'Take your stance,' he commanded. I did. 'Now turn your head to the right,' he said. I did. I waited for the next phase. It wasn't coming. I asked if that was it; he said yes, and I said it was a gimmick. He said it wasn't. The lesson was over. Hogan had given me a piece of swing business that went back to Bobby Jones, at least. Some secret."[1]

Later in that same newsletter, Barkow shared another very interesting piece of information given to him by PGA Tour professional Loren Roberts. Reportedly, it was a copy of a thirteen-page, handwritten letter by Hogan to Pat Mahoney in 1948. Mahoney was the head professional at Pasatiempo Golf Club (near San Jose, California). This was at a time when Hogan's game was peaking, perhaps a year or so before the accident.

In Hogan's letter, he described how to swing a driver: "The most important part of a good golf swing is to take the club back correctly so as to keep the head in one place. This can be accomplished in only one correct way, by moving the left knee in toward the right knee while moving the left shoulder in a slight, downward arc . . . It feels like the hips are moving to the right, but this is not so. Sagging the left side keeps the hips in one position and permits them to make a true concentric turn." Barkow likened Hogan's description of the concentric golf swing as similar to the Stack & Tilt method, which advocates moving the left shoulder in a slight downward arc and not transferring any weight to the right side. Was this the Secret before there was a Secret?

***

I honestly believe the Secret evolved with its telling over time. And over time, it took on mystical proportions. In fact, we were all told the Secret if we just took the time to look for it.

In December 2012, I was having a cup of coffee with former PGA Tour Commissioner Deane Beman at the TPC, like the ones I used to have with Hogan so many years before. The subject of Hogan's Secret came up when I told Beman I was going to start playing again after teaching and working on my PhD at Clemson University. Getting back into the swing of golf was more difficult than I had expected. I asked Beman for some swing tips. I noted that Hogan had told me the Secret a few times, and that it was different each time.

Beman bristled at my suggestion and said, "Ben Hogan never conjured up anything that he did not thoroughly believe. He had too much integrity to do otherwise. He told you what he thought you could understand. It was up to you to translate it into terms that you could comprehend and apply. In actuality, I really don't think that Hogan understood his Secret in terms that most golfers could interpret and do. I know exactly what Hogan's Secret was."

Beman was never one to mince words, so I bit on the bait and said, "Well then, what was Hogan's Secret?"

After setting the hook, Beman jerked the rod and said, "Hogan's Secret was all about the setup, shoulder turn, and the sequence. Stand up, and setup like you are about to hit the ball."

Fondly remembering my similar sessions with Hogan, I stood up, assumed my stance, and addressed the ball.

"You need to address the ball with your shoulders open, and your hips and stance square to the target line," Beman said. "Your right foot should be square and not open."

"Hogan's stance was square," I interjected, "but really slightly closed because his left toe was open—the alignment line formed from the back of his heels was closed."

"David, Hogan never came over the top like you. Squaring the right foot is one of the keys in the sequence that makes Hogan's Secret work . . . Let me finish, so that you can understand. It's simple. Since your shoulders are open, and your hips and stance are square, the swing starts with the turning of the shoulders. Turn or rotate the shoulders as much as you can. Because your right foot is square, you can maintain the angle of your right knee and brace against the right leg, which will prevent you from turning your knee outward and sliding or swaying as you have always done. Now, as you get to the top of your swing, you start the downswing with a slight slide and turning of the hips. The shoulders will follow. The club automatically drops into the slot. The elbow tucks in. The club unwinds and catches up by the time you impact the ball. Now, this is the important part: The hands still lead through impact. The clubface is square to the intended target line. Hogan squared the clubface longer than any golfer ever, which explains why he could control the shot trajectory and hit it exactly where he intended. With the hips cleared, Hogan finished the golf swing with the club following down the line."

Beman's explanation was an epiphany for me; he had connected the dots that Hogan had described before. The Secret wasn't just a single element of the swing or a position I needed to attain at various points in the golf swing. It was a sequence of moves, based upon having a solid foundation (stance and address) and an understanding of principles that make the swing flow naturally around a center point.

***

Still, I sensed there was something more that I needed to know. A few months later, in April 2013, I was out West doing some consulting work, and on my return flight, I came across a book at the airport PGA Tour Shop, *The Complete Hogan*, by famed golf instructor Jim McLean. This book has still photos of Hogan's swing sequence from several angles. McLean makes insightful and illuminating frame-by-frame analyses of what he proclaims was "golf's greatest swing." In the first chapter of the book, McLean identifies fifteen critical points that constitute "The Many Secrets of Hogan's Swing." Interestingly, not all of these points are the actual physical movements in the golf swing, and much of what he has to say transcends the speculative analyses from an array of pundits and other firsthand accounts, including my own.

McLean speaks of Hogan's personality and natural physical gifts, ranging from his focus and single-minded determination to his strength and flexibility, as being the foundation for building golf's greatest swing. He went as far as to say in points fourteen and fifteen that Hogan's ethic, preparation to play, and competitive demeanor—even the way he dressed—exuded confidence and intimidated the competition. In today's talk, McLean might be saying that Hogan was the first professional athlete to "walk the talk."

Hogan was a student of the game and a graduate of the school of hard knocks. He took nothing for granted and learned by trial and error, which was what he had told Faldo in his office so many years ago: "If you dig it out of the dirt yourself, it's yours forever." Why it was difficult for Hogan to explain his Secret is understandable, because learning how to play your best golf is more than just learning how to swing the golf club.

Still, McLean's fifteen tenets for the many secrets of Hogan's swing is perhaps the most astute analysis, as it is through the lens of someone who has studied, played, and taught the game. McLean clearly understands the laws, principles, and preferences of the golf swing, especially Hogan's. McLean spoke with Hogan's contemporaries for insights only those who knew him could reveal, and put the pieces of the Hogan puzzle together in a way that we can see and understand. Hogan learned what he could from watching his competitors, but most of what became golf's greatest swing was an exercise in finding out what worked for him. It was a never-ending journey of self-discovery.

Hogan honed each step in the swing so that it flowed fluidly and seemed effortless, like water out of a pitcher. There was no pause at any point in the swing sequence because each movement flowed into the next. This is the problem confronting McLean in his frame-by-frame analysis, but he does a pretty good job in explaining how one movement enables the next and why it worked for Hogan. McLean noted Hogan's setup and address were precisely choreographed. He first put the clubhead behind the ball; next, he stepped in with his right foot and put his left foot down before setting his right foot in place. It was like a dance step, and the choreography of the full swing never varied from the driver to a wedge shot.

The fluid motion continued in preparing to swing the golf club, starting with the waggle. McLean said Hogan learned how to release preswing tension by copying Johnny Revolta's waggle, which was a mini-swing rehearsal for the full swing to follow.

The next movement in the flow was the beginning of the swing, known as the takeaway. McLean noted this important motion is overlooked by most. The golf swing begins with a slight move toward the target, and then there is recoil away that enables the golfer to begin the backswing in smooth, one-piece motion—with the hands, arms, shoulders, and club all moving together. The synchronization of the backswing components is especially important under pressure.

At this point in the golf swing are some technical adjustments Hogan devised to help him deal with issues that were unique to his swing. He had problems hooking the ball. What he did to eliminate the hook was to weaken his left-hand grip by moving his left thumb more on top of the club, which enabled him to open the clubface during his backswing. At the top of his backswing, there was a slight cupping of the wrist that enabled Hogan to absolutely prevent closing the clubface on the downswing, thereby eliminating any chance of a hook. Hogan could swing as hard as he wanted.

For 99 percent of the readers, the analysis at this point in the swing has no personal relevance or application, but what is happening while this is going on is important. McLean describes it poetically, saying that "The downswing begins before the backswing ends." There is no pause at the top of the swing. The transition from the backswing to the downswing is in one smooth and uninterrupted motion. McLean explains how difficult this move is for most everyone "because there is no top of the backswing. While the club was still going back, Hogan leaned his body forward" slightly toward the target and uncoiled his left hip as fast as possible. McLean added, "It gives the feel of the left arm pulling, but there is no conscious pulling of the left arm and no effort required to produce a tremendous amount of club lag, meaning that the club is trailing behind the leaning and pivoting motion of the body." Yet make no mistake about it: the club is trailing the body, and as Hogan always stated, this meant that he could never hit "over the top." To me this two-way move is perhaps Hogan's biggest secret of all.

McLean described what Yocom tried to explain in his 1994 *Golf Digest* article as the supination of the left wrist through impact. It is what Hogan had told me the first time he explained the Secret to me in terms that he thought I could understand and apply: "Decrease the loft of the clubface as you hit the ball." McLean noted that Harmon called this action hitting "into the bow," which enables the golfer to hit the ball farther and to better control the trajectory of the golf ball.

From this moment on, most of the movements in the golf swing flow from the inertia of the previous movements. McLean describes Hogan's swing as being "so powerful and coordinated that it looked like he was about to run down the fairway. It was explosive, forceful, and committed." He went on to say that another secret taught to him by Ken Venturi was the extension after impact of Hogan's right arm, which he then straightened out to the target and follow-through. This sounded a lot like Beman describing how Hogan's clubface was square to the intended target line (longer than any golfer ever) and explains why he could control the shot trajectory and hit it exactly where he intended.

When he wanted, Hogan was swinging as hard as he could, but he made the golf swing look easy. All of this occurred in one continuous motion that finished the swing in perfect balance. McLean's analyses of Hogan's swing put the pieces of the puzzle of Hogan's Secret into a picture I could see and understand. Back when I was CEO of the Ben Hogan Company, I had the opportunity to watch Hogan hit balls but only from a respectful distance. I can vividly remember the fluidness and seemingly effortless flow of his swing. It was a motion and an uninterrupted movement that had the power, grace, and command of a ballet leap from Baryshnikov. Even in his late seventies, Hogan could still enjoy the art of great shotmaking. It was beautiful to behold.

***

Recently, a friend who was helping me edit this book sent me a video of Hogan swinging a golf club. Based upon the golf equipment he was using and his youthful, slim physique, it appears the film was taken probably sometime in the early or mid-1930s. No source for this grainy, 8 millimeter film was available. My friend described the video as "the Sacred Tapes." This is probably one of the first films of Hogan's swing ever recorded. I searched the Web, and could not find anything like it.

This vintage film clearly reveals something very interesting from the rear vantage point, as if you were standing just behind Hogan and watching him swing down the target line. It is quite evident that at the top of his backswing, Hogan has a closed clubface and lays the club off on the downswing. These swing characteristics flattened his swing plane and explain why he hit the ball so low and and tended to hook the ball in his early years as a professional golfer. This footage is too short and grainy to use in any detailed, technical swing analysis, but it shows what Hogan's swing was like before he learned the Secret.

I have later film footage of Hogan from the same vantage point as the earlier vintage film. It is evident that Hogan has the same swing tendencies as in the earlier film, but they are less pronounced. I do not know the exact date of the later film, but it appears to be post-WWII and illustrates the changes Hogan made to improve his golf swing.

What Hogan learned would become his Secret (a series of swing cues that enabled him to keep his clubface square and not closed at the top of his backswing and enabled him on his downswing to powerfully supinate, square, and release his clubface at impact without worry about the unwanted hook). This is what I learned from Hogan, his books, and what others have said and written; however, I knew I needed someone with the experience and expertise to take a look. So I asked Craig Hanson, an Australian PGA professional and a highly regarded golf instructor, to make a video combining the two films to provide an analysis of Hogan's swing before and after he learned the Secret.[2]

Hanson noted that in the earlier vintage video Hogan's swing was much longer, which gave him more time for his arms to catch up to the hips. It's easy to see that his body is outracing his arms, compared to later in his career. In those early years, Hogan had a stronger grip, which led to a more closed clubface position and a different wrist alignment at the top. This explains why he had problems hitting low and hooking shots.

In side-by-side video analysis, Hanson noted it was still evident in the "before" video that Hogan laid the club off at the top of the swing, which is often prevalent in swings that have a closed face compared to swings where the face is neutral or weaker. Otherwise, it's harder to match up the arms and the body on the way down. It's harder to get the correct or perfect sequence where everything collects at the bottom, and it's more difficult to repeat.

In the "after" video, Hanson stated Hogan was able to fix this problem by weakening his grip and by cupping the wrist slightly at the top in the newer swing. These seemingly small changes in his grip and wrist angles enabled Hogan to completely eliminate the problem with the unwanted hook, as well as to fade the golf ball and better control the trajectory of his shots.

In conclusion, Hanson's video analysis confirms what Hogan *said* his Secret was, as well as what so many other experts also have said. The change in Hogan's grip and his wrist position at the top of his swing was the Secret to his golf swing. The nuance here is, this is what worked for Hogan, given his swing tendencies and talent. These swing cues enabled Hogan to become the best ball-striker of all time. Controlling the trajectory of the golf ball is critical in controlling the distance of a golf shot, which in turn enabled Hogan to better manage his game. Hogan always said that course management was the key component of his success; this was self-evident because if he had not learned how to manage his game with the same precision that he managed his golf swing, Hogan would not have become the legendary player he clearly became.

What Hogan had told me the first time—about decreasing the loft of the club as I hit the ball—was the Secret, but only in part. I didn't understand how to do it any more than Guy Yocom understood it in his 1994 *Golf Digest* article, because we all interpret Hogan's Secret in terms we can understand and apply. I am not sure that Hogan really understood how he was able to get from the cupped wrist position at the top of his backswing to the supinated and strong wrist position at impact, because it was natural for him to do so. This might explain why it wasn't described in the *Life* magazine article or in his book. It was natural for Hogan "to lay the club off" and to close the clubface. The cupping of the wrist prevented him from doing so, and he learned how to fade and to better control his shot trajectory.

What Hogan told me the second time about turning the shoulders and bracing my turn against the right leg and then unwinding the hips was an application of the same concept. Vasquez described it in his book, and Harmon's version was in the same vein—that "the left hip leads." Or, for that matter, what Barkow revealed Hogan had written about the pivot: "Feeling like the hips are moving to the right, but this is not so. Sagging the left side keeps the hips in one position and permits them to make a true concentric turn." For me, the pieces of the puzzle were coming together, and I could finally see the picture Hogan had described but in terms I could understand. Beman explained the Secret in clearer terms, as did McLean in his book.

The bottom line is that the Secret for Hogan was what he told us; he was unequivocal. However, the Secret for Hogan, given his capabilities and swing tendencies, was very different than the Secret for a golfer who comes over the top and slices the ball. Or for example, let's test the Hogan theory for Dustin Johnson, a gifted and talented PGA Tour player, who in 2015 was in the top ten in the Official World Golf Ranking. Johnson's wrist position at the top of his backswing is angled in the opposite position from what Hogan had done. His wrists are bowed at the top of his backswing; his clubface is closed. However, Johnson is an extraordinary athlete and has figured out what works for him.

The point here is that Hogan applied what he learned over the years and shared it with his trusted confidants in terms that he believed they could understand, learn, and apply. That is why so many of his friends had a different understanding regarding what the Secret was. Just as there is not a miracle pill for losing weight, there is no miracle, secret solution to the golf swing or how to play the game. The Secret is not a matter of executing specific swing cues because they will vary to some degree for most golfers. Rather, the Secret is a sequence that involves doing the right thing at the right time, and this is done within the context of understanding one's tendencies, strengths, and weaknesses and how to best manage one's own game.

Hogan enjoyed all the speculation on what the Secret might be. It provided some competitive advantage when he was playing. It created a mystique that he perpetuated by making everyone promise not to tell what he had told them. He teased us with the notion of secrecy, which caused further speculation.

It is this sojourn to understanding that is the Secret. The cliché is true:

the journey is the destination. It is a study of the game and the development of one's own swing that comes with the understanding of key principles that apply to every golfer. The Secret is complex in its explanation, simple once it is understood, and universal in its application. The Secret is found in the pursuit of personal excellence. It really cannot be taught, but it can be learned.

Hogan wasn't telling us anything philosophical. His purview and pursuit of excellence was in becoming a better golfer—the best that he could become. In his words, "My goal was to improve my game every day." He never had a bad day playing golf, just as long as he learned something that made him a better player.

Hogan was simple and complex; he was confident and humble. He was driven, sincere, and unpretentious and focused upon being the best golfer and golf clubmaker he could be. Under any circumstances, the revelation of the Secret would be anticlimactic and perhaps disappointing to devotees who expected a burning bush revelation they could etch onto stone tablets like the Ten Commandments.

Hogan kept his Secret, in part, because there probably was no single secret that could be universally understood and applied. He shared his Secret publicly via publications and privately with friends. He wasn't revealing anything as grand as the meaning of life. He was talking about his Secret to the golf swing as it might be applied to your game within your physical and mental capabilities. He defined himself by what he did and worked very hard at it— nothing more, nothing less.

The endgame of golf for Ben Hogan was becoming the best he could be, improving his game, earning a living; and in the process, he inspired us to improve and to make a difference in our brief time on this earth. In the end, the Secret will never be fully known; however, never revealing the Secret in its entirety was probably an appropriate epitaph for a man who got a great deal of mileage out of marketing his own mystique. The world of golf is more interesting and better for it.

> *For when the One Great Scorer comes*
> *To mark against your name,*
> *He writes—not that you won or lost—*
> *But how you played the game.*

— GRANTLAND RICE[3]

NOTES

Chapter 1
[1]World Golf Hall of Fame golfer, Nick Faldo, was knighted by Queen Elizabeth on November 10, 2009, the second golfer to receive the honor.

Chapter 3
[1]Peter Barbour, coauthor with Jacqueline Hogan Towery and Robert Towery, *The Brothers Hogan: A Fort Worth History*, published by TCU Press, Fort Worth, Texas, 2014.

Chapter 6
[1]Source: Allan Solheim, Karsten Solheim's second-eldest son and cofounder of Ping with his dad and two brothers, Lou and John.

Chapter 10
[1]A 1990 PGA Tour promotional video produced by PGA Tour Entertainment featured the Ben Hogan Company and its title sponsorship of the Ben Hogan Tour. This video may be viewed at www.mindseyegolf.com.

Chapter 11
[1]In 1988, *Inside Golf* a nationally syndicated cable TV program, featured the NGF and one of the television ads produced by PGA Tour Entertainment promoting the need for more golf courses. The PGA Tour also aired these ads as PSAs on its golf telecasts in 1988 and 1989. The program may be viewed at www.mindseyegolf.com.

Chapter 12
[1]The raw footage of this October 22, 1990, interview may be found at www.mindseyegolf.com. It is a rare and candid look at one of the game's most private personalities. I am sitting off-camera to the right of Jim Kelly offering some topics for further discussion. The video was produced by PGA Tour Entertainment for the Ben Hogan Company.

Chapter 13
[1]A 1990 PGA Tour promotional video featured the Ben Hogan Company and its title sponsorship of the Ben Hogan Tour. This video may be viewed at www.mindseyegolf.com and is provided under license by PGA Tour Entertainment, copyright 2016 PGA Tour Inc., all rights reserved. More information about the Ben Hogan Company may be found at www.benhogangolf.com.

Chapter 14

[1]These groundbreaking ads appeared in a 1992 video produced by PGA Tour Entertainment that showcased the career of Ben Hogan, the founding of the Ben Hogan Company and its sponsorship of the Ben Hogan Tour. "No one makes clubs like we do," was the most effective advertising campaign produced by the Ben Hogan Company. The video and ads may be viewed at www.mindseyegolf.com and are provided under license by PGA Tour Entertainment copyright 2016 PGA Tour Inc., all rights reserved. More information about the Ben Hogan Company may be found at www.benhogangolf.com.

Chapter 16

[1]In Japan, there was a formal commodities-type exchange dedicated to the buying and selling of golf memberships, whereby investors speculated on their growth in market value.

Epilogue

[1]*The Barkow Quarterly*, a webzine, issue #1: Winter 2009
[2]Craig Hanson specializes in video swing analyses of many of the great players and offers video analysis and instruction to average golfers. His take on Hogan's swing changes may be found at www.mindseyegolf.com or www.CraigHansonGolf.com.
[3]From the poem, *Alumnus Football*, by Grantland Rice, an American sportswriter (1880-1954).